MEDIEVAL IRISH PILGRIMS TO SANTIAGO DE COMPOSTELA

Bay of Biscay and environs on 1550 map of Europe. Sebastian Munster.

Medieval Irish Pilgrims to Santiago de Compostela

BERNADETTE CUNNINGHAM

FOUR COURTS PRESS

Set in 10.5 pt on 12.5 pt Ehrhardt MT for
FOUR COURTS PRESS LTD
7 Malpas Street, Dublin 8, Ireland
www.fourcourtspress.ie
and in North America for
FOUR COURTS PRESS
c/o IPG, 814 N Franklin St, Chicago, IL 60622

A catalogue record for this title is available
from the British Library.

ISBN 978-1-84682-729-7

Printed in England,
by TJ International Ltd, Padstow, Cornwall.

Contents

Illustrations

Abbreviations

A.Clon	Denis Murphy (ed.), *Annals of Clonmacnoise from the earliest period to A.D. 1408, translated into English by Conell Mageoghagan, A.D. 1627* (Dublin, 1896)
A.Conn	A.M. Freeman (ed.), *Annála Connacht: the annals of Connacht, AD 1224–1544* (Dublin, 1944)
AD	Anno Domini
Add.	additional
AFM	John O'Donovan (ed.), *Annála Ríoghachta Éireann: annals of the kingdom of Ireland, by the Four Masters, from the earliest period to the year 1616* (7 vols, 2nd ed., Dublin, 1856)
A.Inisfallen	Seán Mac Airt (ed.), *Annals of Inisfallen (MS Rawlinson B 503)* (Dublin, 1951)
A.LCé	W.M. Hennessy (ed.), *The Annals of Loch Cé: a chronicle of Irish affairs from AD 1014 to AD 1590* (2 vols, London, 1871)
A.Lecan	John O'Donovan (ed.), 'The annals of Ireland from the year 1443 to 1468 translated from the Irish by Dudley Firbisse, or as he is more usually called, Duald Mac Firbis, for Sir James Ware in the year 1666' in *Miscellany of the Irish Archaeological Society*, 1 (Dublin, 1846), pp 198–302
AU	W.M. Hennessy & B. MacCarthy (eds), *Annála Uladh: Annals of Ulster from the earliest times to the year 1541* (4 vols, Dublin, 1887–1901)
BL	British Library, London
Cal. Carew MSS	*Calendar of the Carew manuscripts preserved in the archiepiscopal library at Lambeth* (6 vols, London, 1867–73)
Cal. doc. Ire.	*Calendar of documents relating to Ireland* [1171–1307] (5 vols, London, 1875–86)
Cal. papal letters	*Calendar of entries in the papal registers relating to Britain and Ireland: papal letters*, ed. W.H. Bliss, et al. (14 vols, London, 1893–1960; Dublin, 1978–)
Cal. papal petitions	*Calendar of entries in the papal registers relating to Britain and Ireland: petitions to the pope*, vol. 1, 1342–1419 (London, 1896)
Cal. patent rolls	*Calendar of the patent rolls preserved in the Public Record Office* (London, 1906–)

Cal. S.P. Ire.	*Calendar of the state papers relating to Ireland* (24 vols, London, 1860–1911)
Cal. S.P. Spain	*Calendar of letters, despatches and state papers relating to the negotiations between England and Spain, preserved in the archives at Simancás and elsewhere* (London, 1862–)
Cat. Ire. MSS in BL	S.H. O'Grady & Robin Flower, *Catalogue of Irish manuscripts in the British Library* [formerly *British Museum*] (3 vols, London, 1926–53)
Cat. Ire. MSS in RIA	T.F. O'Rahilly, Kathleen Mulchrone, et al., *Catalogue of Irish manuscripts in the Royal Irish Academy*, 1–28 (Dublin, 1926–70)
CSJ	Confraternity of St James (London)
DIB	James McGuire & James Quinn (eds), *Dictionary of Irish biography* (9 vols, Cambridge, 2009) (dib.cambridge.org)
EETS	Early English Text Society
Fairs & markets rep.	*Report of the commissioners appointed to inquire into the state of the fairs and markets in Ireland*, House of Commons, 1852–3 [1674], xli.
IMC	Irish Manuscripts Commission
ITS	Irish Texts Society
JCHAS	*Journal of the Cork Historical and Archaeological Society*
JGAHS	*Journal of the Galway Archaeological and Historical Society*
JKAS	*Journal of the County Kildare Archaeological Society*
JLAHS	*County Louth Archaeological and Historical Society Journal*
JRSAI	*Journal of the Royal Society of Antiquaries of Ireland*
MS	manuscript
NHI	*A new history of Ireland* (9 vols, Oxford, 1976–2005)
NMS	National Monuments Service
OS	Ordnance Survey
Proc. RIA	*Proceedings of the Royal Irish Academy*
Rep. Nov.	*Reportorium Novum: Dublin Diocesan Historical Record*
RIA	Royal Irish Academy
s.a.	*sub anno*
TCD	Trinity College, Dublin
TNA	The National Archives (Kew)
trans.	translation/translator
UCD	University College, Dublin
UCD-OFM	UCD Archives, Franciscan manuscripts
ZCP	*Zeitschrift für celtische Philologie*

Preface

In medieval times, as now, every individual pilgrim had their own motivations and their own understanding of the pilgrimage to Santiago de Compostela. It was personal to them, part of their own journey of life. There was no single path, no fixed route, no rigidly prescribed way of engaging with the phenomenon that was and is the pilgrimage to Santiago, its spirituality or its history. No two pilgrim stories were the same. Yet, those who walk the Camino de Santiago in the twenty-first century become very conscious of the shared experience of walking in the footprints of others from earlier times. For the more than 5,000 people annually from Ireland who have walked at least 100 km of a pilgrim route to Santiago in recent years, the question inevitably arises – did Irish people travel to Santiago in medieval times? If so, who were they? Why did they go? How did they get there? Why Santiago? This book explores the answers to these questions.

Writing the book has itself been a journey, made easier by following in the footsteps of other historians. I am particularly indebted to the many scholars whose editions, catalogues and calendars of medieval and early modern texts have made it possible to identify and retrieve stories of medieval Irish pilgrims from the archival sources that survive. I am grateful to the custodians of research collections I have used, principally the library of Trinity College, Dublin, the National Library of Ireland, Dublin City Libraries, Maynooth University Library, NUI Galway Library, UCD Library and the library of the Royal Irish Academy. I have also drawn on the specialist collection of secondary literature at the library of the Confraternity of St James in London, and the unrivalled collections of the British Library at St Pancras. The interdisciplinary scholarly pursuits of the Group for the Study of Irish Historic Settlement have been my informal university for the past quarter century, shaping my approach to the study of the past. Individuals who have provided additional information include Victor Buckley, Howard B. Clarke, Miriam Clyne, Peter Harbison, Jim Higgins, Con Manning, Liz Mullins, Colmán Ó Clabaigh, Tim O'Neill, Dagmar Ó Riain Raedel, Pádraig Ó Riain, Roger Stalley and Paul Walsh. I am particularly grateful to Matthew Stout for drawing the maps. Members of the Camino Society of Ireland have provided the stimulus to undertake this research, led by Turlough O'Donnell's enthusiasm for Camino history. My interest in the history of the Camino de Santiago originated with the six memorable summers when my sister, Mary Cunningham, and I walked a variety of routes on the Way of St James in four countries (France, Spain, Switzerland and Portugal), and I thank her for her wonderful companionship and support. Last but not least, my husband Raymond Gillespie didn't walk to Santiago but has accompanied me on every step of the journey of this book, seeking out the yellow arrows when the path through the sources seemed obscure.

Quotations in the Irish language follow the form of the published editions cited. Where published translations into English are available these have been used, making amendments only where existing translations are misleading. Extracts from sources in other languages are given in English translation only. Personal names of Gaelic origin are given in Irish in the text unless the person is better known under an English form of the name. Names of families and individuals of Anglo-Norman origin are given in English throughout. Names of Irish saints follow the style in Pádraig Ó Riain, *A dictionary of Irish saints* (Dublin, 2011). Place-names are given in the anglicized form.

Introduction: the modern pilgrimage

In this place there was a record kept of the names of them that had been
pilgrims of old, and a history of all the famous acts that they had done.
—John Bunyan, *The Pilgrim's progress*, part 2 (London, 1684)

The plaza in front of the twelfth-century cathedral of Santiago de Compostela was
a building site in the winter of 1953. There were very few pilgrims present, but local
workmen were busy completing the conversion of the sixteenth-century pilgrim
hostel on the north side of the plaza into a state-owned luxury hotel. The work was
part of extensive preparations undertaken in anticipation of an increase in pilgrim
visitors to Santiago in 1954. In that year, the feast of St James (25 July) would fall
on a Sunday, making it a jubilee year, one that would coincide with the celebration of a special Marian Year. Over the previous fifteen years in Catholic Spain,
under the dictatorship of Galicia native General Francisco Franco (1892–1975),
the medieval pilgrimage route leading to Santiago de Compostela had seen a surge
in popularity. The roots of this transformation can be traced even further back. In
1879 the relics believed to be those of St James and his two disciples, reputedly
lost in the sixteenth century, were re-discovered in the cathedral in Santiago – just
in time for the 1880 jubilee – and this prompted a revival of the local pilgrimage.

Through the first half of the twentieth century, the increasingly popular pilgrimages to Santiago resembled those at Lourdes and other major shrines, with
most pilgrims arriving by train or bus. While this element of the Santiago pilgrimage continues to the present time, the international reputation of the Santiago de
Compostela pilgrimage is now shaped by the journey – usually by walking – to the
cathedral, rather than the final destination. From about 1954 there was a deliberate
policy of promoting the Camino Francés walking route across northern Spain from
Roncesvalles rather than concentrating on the cathedral and its shrine of St James.[1]
In 1965, special certificates began to be issued for the first time in the modern era
to pilgrims who had walked at least 300 km, theoretically entitling them to claim
some free meals and lodging on arrival in Santiago.[2] The introduction of new minimum distances in 1993 – 100 km on foot or 200 km by bicycle – for those seeking
to qualify for a Compostela certificate on arrival in Santiago, coincided with further expansion of a more organized pilgrim experience.

Since then, the growth of environmental and heritage tourism alongside the
business of pilgrimage has seen the route attract interest as a cultural-activity
holiday as well as a spiritual undertaking. The numbers walking or cycling to
Santiago have risen steadily in the late twentieth and early twenty-first centuries.

---

1 Sasha Pack, 'Revival of the pilgrimage to Santiago de Compostela: the politics of religious, national
and European patrimony, 1879–1988', *Journal of Modern History*, 82:2 (2010), 335–67, at 363.   **2** Ibid.

High-profile pilgrims, known from cinema or television, have further popularized the route. Word of mouth, the proliferation of guidebooks, the involvement of national societies that promote the pilgrimage, cheap air travel and state-funded tourism promotion have all combined to make the pilgrimage better known and more accessible to people from many parts of the world, including Ireland. Nurtured in a political environment of European integration, and with a growing emphasis on multiculturalism and environmental spirituality, at a time of declining Sunday attendance at formal Christian liturgies, the pilgrimage has probably changed more in the past 40 years than in the previous 800 years since it first began to draw international pilgrims to Galicia's shores.

The first Irish person in modern times to write at length about his pilgrimage to Santiago was Walter Starkie, professor of Spanish at Trinity College, Dublin, who completed his fourth journey there in 1954. Starkie was exceptionally well travelled. An accomplished musician and a scholar immersed in Spanish literature and culture, he knew Spain intimately. His interest in music, literature and the history of art and architecture dominate his account of his 1954 pilgrimage, which he claimed to have undertaken as a retirement project, when his perspective on life was changing and he was in search of 'healing solitude'.[3] He had begun at Arles in southern France that year. His pilgrimage involved a combination of bus journeys, lifts from friends and acquaintances, and some walking. He also recalled having used a mule, in true medieval fashion, in the vicinity of Foncebadón on an earlier pilgrimage.[4] He received a scallop shell from the cathedral's pilgrim office to mark his achievement in the Marian Year. In that same year, 1954, Spanish youth groups who had walked from Burgos, Barcelona or Madrid swelled the crowd,[5] but the idea that most pilgrims to Santiago would walk there had not yet taken hold. Yet, over the years, Starkie had met a walker who had done the pilgrimage to fulfil a vow – fasting and barefoot – as can still happen now on Croagh Patrick. He complained of the 'pilgrimages without tears' that had been created for the multitudes of people who arrived in Santiago on package tours in 1954, with only a few arriving on foot. Even the walker he thought, were 'more gregarious in spirit and more robot-like' than in his younger days.[6] He summed up his pilgrimage philosophy by quoting French essayist Michel de Montaigne (1553–92): 'The greatest thing in the world is to know how to belong to ourselves.'[7]

More recently, other Irish pilgrims have recorded their experiences of the pilgrim routes in book form. David Gibson's account of his 1998 pilgrimage from St Jean Pied-de-Port and Frainc Mac Bradaigh's description of his walk from Le Puy-en-Velay to Pamplona in 2002 were each written by experienced participants in the discipline of religious retreats. Gibson had sought a break from the daily business of administration in his religious order and understood that 'the human quest for

---

3 Walter Starkie, *The road to Santiago: pilgrims of St James* (London, 1957), p. 83.   4 Starkie, *Road to Santiago*, p. 285.   5 Ibid., pp 315–16.   6 Ibid., p. 323.
7 Ibid., p. 84.

meaning is acted out in physical movement where the outward journey of walking allows the journey inward to begin'.[8] He found that the walk allowed him become 'more aware of the great gift that God's presence is during my journey through life'.[9] Frainc Mac Brádaigh, SJ, had devoted much time to working with people suffering drug addiction and he needed a break. His walk was undertaken as part of a sabbatical year, in which he wished just to be himself, and to have some time free from onerous, depressing responsibilities. Along the way, he contemplated ways to make the world a fairer place, and pondered whether people can reform and change their lives, an indication, perhaps, that pilgrims do not really leave their concerns behind when they embark on the Santiago pilgrimage.[10] Like Mac Brádaigh, the life experience of retired Australian diplomat Tony Kevin, who walked from Granada to Santiago in 2006, had left him looking for ways to achieve 'a decent and caring human society'. The pilgrimage restored his 'hope in the possibilities for the fullness of life', and made him appreciate 'the rich joys of ordinary family life and domesticity'.[11]

Mícheál de Barra fulfilled a long-held ambition in 2004 when he walked the Camino Francés. Finding the rhythm of walking to be like a mantra, the journey was more rewarding than the destination. Delighted with his achievement, he nonetheless wondered what St James would make of the whole business of the shrine erected in his name and felt that many visitors to the cathedral seemed more interested in the spectacle of the *botafumeiro* incense burner than the Eucharistic celebration. For de Barra, the sense of peace and finding himself was achieved amid the beauty of the natural world at Finisterre on the Atlantic coast rather than in Santiago itself.[12] His disappointment with the pilgrimage experience was shared by Austrian René Freund who walked from Le Puy-en-Velay to Santiago in 1998, and recorded his observations on 'Europe's first road of culture' in a daily diary. For him, arriving in Santiago was an anti-climax: 'It is a little like going to the cinema when too many people have already told you about a fantastic film. When you finally watch it you feel like you already know it and are necessarily disappointed.'[13]

Father and daughter Peter and Natasha Murtagh from Dublin walked the Camino Francés to bond with each other on a long walk and to write a book. Armed with a laptop and camera to record the journey, and a gregarious nature, Peter experienced the Camino as 'a place and a state of mind, where you meet people from all corners of the world and we look out for each other'.[14] Natasha concluded that the experience had made her less materialistic, while Georgio, whom they met along the way, observed that the Camino was a call to return to traditional values of self-reliance.[15] Belfast based Brendan McManus, SJ, who had suffered great personal

8 David Gibson, *Walking in my shadow: a pilgrim walk to Santiago de Compostela* (Dublin, 2002), p. 1. 9 Ibid., pp 178–9. 10 Frainc Mac Brádaigh, *Conair na Fraince go Santiago: Le Puy-en-Velay go Pamplona na Spáinne* (Dublin, 2014). 11 Tony Kevin, *Walking the Camino: a modern pilgrimage to Santiago* (London, 2008), pp 291, 295. 12 Mícheál de Barra, *An bothar go Santiago* (Dublin, 2007), p. 294. 13 René Freund, *The road to Santiago: walking the Way of St James* (London, 2016), pp 4–5, 124. 14 Natasha & Peter Murtagh, *Buen Camino! A father-daughter journey from Croagh Patrick to Santiago de Compostela* (Dublin, 2011), p. 37. 15 Ibid., pp 116, 195.

tragedy, succeeded in using the Camino del Norte and Camino Primitivo in 2011 as a way through his grief, aided by his practice of Jesuit spirituality. For him, arriving in Santiago was 'a bit of an anti-climax'; the remote Atlantic setting of Finisterre proved a more personal and appropriate place to let go of his burden and experience a new sense of hope at the end of his pilgrimage.[16] Writer Liam Ó Muirthile made his third pilgrimage from St Jean Pied-de-Port in 2015, well aware that it had developed into a form of international mass tourism.[17] While observing that many of those on the Camino have rejected the formal rituals of the Christian churches, he noted that the modern-day Camino has its own rituals and its own disciplines – put on your pack and walk, day after day, rain or shine. He concluded that many of the young pilgrims he encountered were in search of a pre-Enlightenment form of humanism, based on harmony between the person and the planet.[18] John Brierley, writing a practical guidebook and 'mystical manual' rather than a memoir, reminded his readers that 'as we set out towards the fabled city of Santiago we need to be mindful ... that the true temple is not a structure at all'. He encouraged pilgrims to explore the 'landscape temple' that is the Camino so as to experience the pilgrimage on a spiritual level.[19]

As these writers indicate, the meaning of pilgrimage for Irish and other pilgrims in modern times can be very varied. After a less-than-inspiring evening in Roncesvalles, Frainc Mac Brádaigh refrained from debating the spiritual significance of the pilgrimage with a Frenchwoman who claimed to be an authority on the topic. What could the Irish know of the spirituality of the pilgrimage, he thought, when so few of them had ever walked the route, and then only in the very recent past?[20] Little has been written about them, but pilgrims from Ireland did go to Santiago in medieval times, though not in the same numbers or by the same routes as the French or other continental Europeans. There is an Irish story that differs is some respects from the French one, while sharing a common heritage.

This historical study draws on documentary and archaeological evidence from Irish, English and European sources to explore the phenomenon of the medieval pilgrimage from Ireland to Santiago. It discusses themes ranging from medieval religious belief in the efficacy of pilgrimages and indulgences to the dissemination of information and the practicalities of travel on the Atlantic fringe of Europe in the pre-modern age. Pilgrims from Ireland, both from a native Irish and an Anglo-Irish cultural background, were indeed part of the Santiago de Compostela phenomenon in the Middle Ages. This was particularly so during the boom years of the fifteenth century, when improved transport networks and increased wealth, combined with a desire to gain indulgences for the good of their souls, allowed the Irish to join believers from throughout the Western world at one of the world's best-known Christian pilgrimage destinations.

16 Brendan McManus, *Redemption road: grieving on the Camino* (Dublin, 2014). 17 Liam Ó Muirthile, *Oilithreach pinn* ([Dublin], 2017), p. 6. 18 Ibid., pp 228–9. 19 John Brierley, *A pilgrim's guide to the Camino de Santiago. St Jean – Roncesvalles – Santiago: a practical and mystical manual for the modern day pilgrim* (Forres, 2003; reprint 2017), p. 37. 20 Mac Brádaigh, *Conair na Fraince go Santiago*, p. 147.

Motives for medieval pilgrimage

We should not underestimate the magnitude of the undertaking entered into by those from Ireland who went on pilgrimage to Santiago in the centuries after 1200. It involved leaving family and property unprotected for a prolonged period, expending a considerable sum on travel and enduring personal hardship in lands where the language and lifestyle were unfamiliar. Moreover, those from Ireland were not alone on the Santiago road. Pilgrims from all over Europe were to be found making their way not only to Santiago but also to other international pilgrimage destinations such as Jerusalem and Rome, as well as the many regional and local shrines that dotted the landscape of Europe. By the standards of the Middle Ages, pilgrimage was neither a random nor, despite what Reformation critics would say, an irrational act. To attempt to enter into the world of the medieval Irish pilgrims who journeyed to Santiago, their experience needs to be placed within contemporary understandings of the divine economy of salvation, and the real spiritual and personal benefits on offer to devout pilgrims.

Pilgrimages can be defined as 'journeys to holy places undertaken from motives of devotion in order to obtain supernatural help or as acts of penance or thanksgiving'.[1] They were and are a universal feature of Western Christianity and of other major world religions.[2] Medieval pilgrimage operated at many social and religious levels to meet the varied expectations and needs of pilgrims. The purpose of the pilgrim quest varied, ranging from the search for a cure for an ailment to the desire to express devotion to a cult, or to make reparation for sin. It was a way in which people could seek an encounter with the divine, and often involved the shrine of a saint.[3] There was usually a communal element, so that pilgrimage was a social leveller, but at the core of each pilgrimage was 'the journey by the individual to the sacred place in pursuit of some individual personal goal'.[4] For many people, a journey to a purely local pilgrimage site, often one associated with an obscure but locally important saint, was enough to meet their needs. For others, a visit to a shrine of regional or national importance was desirable, and these drew pilgrims

---

1 Here I have used the definition of 'pilgrimage' given in F.L. Cross & E.A. Livingstone (eds), *The Oxford dictionary of the Christian church* (3rd edn, Oxford, 1997), p. 1288.   2 For an overview of Jewish, Buddhist, Muslim and Hindu pilgrimage traditions, see Mircea Eliade (ed.), *The encyclopedia of religion* (16 vols, New York, 1987), xi, pp 327–54.   3 See generally, Robert Bartlett, *Why can the dead do such great things? Saints and worshippers from the martyrs to the Reformation* (London, 2013).   4 Crispin Branfoot, 'Pilgrimage in South Asia: crossing boundaries of space and faith' in R. Barnes & C. Branfoot (eds), *Pilgrimage: the sacred journey* (Oxford, 2006), pp 45–79, at p. 62.

from a wider area. Santiago de Compostela belonged to a third tier, a great international shrine that developed into one of the most renowned Christian pilgrimage destinations in the world.

The legend associated with Santiago de Compostela involved a story that St James, one of Christ's twelve Apostles, had preached in Spain. The Apostle later returned to Jerusalem and was martyred for his faith in AD 44 at the hands of Herod Agrippa. A story was told that after his death his decapitated body was transported in a stone boat back to Galicia, where it was brought ashore at Padrón, formerly known as the port of Iria. When the story arose is not clear but it was certainly in circulation by the seventh century. Then in the early ninth century, so the legend says, a hermit named Pelayo was drawn by a light and celestial music to the location where St James was buried, and the shrine was established.[5] The story was written down in the twelfth-century work known as the *Codex Calixtinus*, a compilation misleadingly attributed to Pope Calixtus II (1121–4) that recounted the origins of the medieval pilgrimage to Santiago, giving it ecclesiastical authority and spreading its fame, with stories of the shrine even reaching Ireland at the edge of the known world.[6] The authenticity of the story has long been doubted, but that has not undermined its appeal to pilgrims. James was a well-known Apostle, aspects of whose life and career were known from the Christian Gospels and the Acts of the Apostles. Biblical sources presented St James as one of the favourite disciples of Jesus. As a result of this, St James was regarded as an effective intercessor in the heavenly court on behalf of those who prayed to him or went on pilgrimage to his shrine in Galicia.

From the twelfth century, Santiago de Compostela emerged to rival Rome and Jerusalem in popularity and status, particularly for pilgrims from northwest Europe. In Galicia during the early twelfth century, an entrepreneurial local bishop, Diego Gelmírez, secured papal recognition for the Santiago pilgrimage from Pope Calixtus II.[7] Santiago had been evolving as a pilgrimage destination for some time, and the building of the Romanesque cathedral had begun in 1075, designed to integrate with the surrounding streetscape, with seven doors providing easy access for pilgrims.[8] Gelmírez also worked to keep the main French and

---

5 Javier Dominquez Garcia, 'St James and Santiago de Compostela' in L.J. Taylor, et al. (eds), *Encyclopedia of medieval pilgrimage* (Leiden, 2010), pp 707–11.   6 The earliest parchment manuscript is preserved in the archives of Santiago cathedral, and is dated to *c.*1138–*c.*1173. For details of this and other early manuscript copies, see Alison Stones, et al. (eds), *The pilgrim's guide to Santiago de Compostela: critical edition, i: the manuscripts* (London, 1998), pp 51–195. Copies of the *Codex Calixtinus* manuscript do not appear to have circulated widely, but the stories it contained were transmitted by other writers.   7 R.A. Fletcher, *St James's catapult: the life and times of Diego Gelmírez of Santiago de Compostela* (Oxford, 1984); Xunta de Galicia (ed.), *Compostela and Europe: the story of Diego Gelmírez* (Milan, 2010).   8 Manuel Castiñeiras, 'Didacus Gelmirius, patron of the arts: Compostela's long journey: from the periphery to the center of Romanesque art' in Xunta de Galicia (ed.), *Compostela and Europe*, pp 32–97, at 49–55; John Williams, 'The basilica in Compostela and the way of pilgrimage' in Xunta de Galicia (ed.), *Compostela and Europe*, pp 110–21.

Italian route to Santiago through northern Spain open and by the end of the twelfth century, the Camino Francés route from the Pyrenees to Santiago was reputedly 'the busiest trunk road in Christendom'.[9] The promotion of the pilgrimage there has been described as 'the most successful commercial enterprise of the Middle Ages', drawing a steady stream of international pilgrims to northwest Spain.[10]

For those in Western Europe seeking a pilgrimage destination, those places associated with the early Christian church were most desirable. Jerusalem was clearly the premier destination but for Christians living in Ireland the long journey to Jerusalem was never an easy undertaking, even though a predominantly overland route from Western Europe was considered viable from the end of the tenth century.[11] Some Irish certainly attempted this route. They included Colman, an Irish pilgrim who was killed at Stockerau, 20 km north-west of Vienna, in 1053 on his way to Jerusalem. As a stranger in central Europe, he had aroused suspicion and was killed by a mob.[12] At Stockerau he was still a very long way from Jerusalem and there were many stories of other Continental pilgrims failing to complete the long journey through the Balkans.[13]

For pilgrims from Western Europe planning to go to Jerusalem, the choice was between a walk of some 5,000 km, taking up to six months, or about six weeks on board ships in unpredictable weather, with a variety of companions.[14] From the late thirteenth century, a sea journey from Venice through the Adriatic Sea and the eastern Mediterranean to the Holy Land became the norm, being regarded as a safer option than an overland route, though still a challenging one.[15] Returning to the north Atlantic from the Mediterranean was particularly problematic because of the strong currents in the straits of Gibraltar, and thus Jerusalem pilgrims opted for an overland route within Western Europe. Ports such as Marseilles, Genoa, and Venice saw a regular trickle of pilgrim traffic. The ship taken by an English pilgrim, Felix Fabri, from Venice to Jaffa in 1483 counted among its passengers 'Latin priests, Scavonians, Italians ... Franks, Germans, Englishmen, Irishmen, Hungarians, Scots, Dacians, Bohemians, and Spaniards', who celebrated by singing a *Te Deum* when they eventually sighted the mountains of Israel.[16]

9 Jonathan Sumption, *Pilgrimage: an image of medieval religion* (London, 1975), p. 116. 10 Alison Stones, 'Medieval pilgrimage writing and its manuscript sources' in Taylor, et al. (eds), *Encyclopedia of medieval pilgrimage*, p. 399. 11 Sumption, *Pilgrimage*, p. 115; Matthew Gabriele, *An empire of memory: the legend of Charlemagne, the Franks and Jerusalem before the First Crusade* (Oxford, 2011), pp 86–91. 12 Sumption, *Pilgrimage*, pp 182–3, citing 'Passio S. Cholomanni' in *Monumenta Germaniae Historicae: Scriptores*, iv, 675. See also Dagmar Ó Riain-Raedel, 'Ireland and Austria in the Middle Ages: the role of the Irish monks in Austria' in P. Leifer & E. Sagarra (eds), *Austro-Irish links through the centuries* (Vienna, 2003), pp 11–40, at pp 27–32. 13 Sumption, *Pilgrimage*, pp 183–4. 14 Ibid., pp 182–3. 15 J. Wilkinson, *Jerusalem pilgrimage*, Hakluyt Society, 2nd ser., 167 (London, 1988), p. 94; Sumption, *Pilgrimage*, pp 184–92. 16 H.F.M. Prescott, *Jerusalem journey: pilgrimage to the Holy Land in the fifteenth century* (London, 1954), p. 101.

Difficulties of access for pilgrims were compounded by other problems. Exposure to diseases against which people had no immunity was one of several possible causes of death while on an overseas pilgrimage. The scarcity of clean water and fresh food were other challenging aspects of a long sea journey, and adverse weather conditions must have delayed or ended many a voyage.[17] Travelling through regions of desolate terrain without adequate supplies of food and water could be fatal. Andrew Borde's nine Scottish and English pilgrim companions, who travelled overland from Orléans to Compostela in the 1530s, all died on the way home 'by eatynge of frutes and drinkynge of water' from local streams in northern Spain, something he had warned them not to do.[18] Alongside these natural hazards, wealthy foreign pilgrims on overland sections of their pilgrimage, and even on board ship, were targets for thieves. Carrying the money needed for the journey, and for offerings at the shrine, made pilgrims vulnerable to theft. The First Lateran Council (1123) deemed it necessary to impose a punishment of excommunication on those who stole from pilgrims, suggesting that the risks were causing concern.[19] Elite women pilgrims would have travelled with a suitable entourage of male protectors as well as maids,[20] and their male counterparts probably took similar care not to travel alone, and to travel in the company of trusted people who knew the way. The cost of the journey from Scotland to Rome in 1456 has been calculated at £66 stg, equivalent to the annual income of a prosperous knight.[21] The cost of an overland journey to Santiago might have been slightly lower. For the few people from Western Europe who could afford to contemplate overseas travel in medieval times, the journeys to Rome or to Santiago de Compostela were more feasible than to Jerusalem.

The difficulties and expense of travel to centres of international pilgrimage, with their prestigious saints, encouraged the promotion of regional pilgrimage centres, many of which localized the universal story of salvation through the acquisition of relics of Christ's life and Passion. Examples include the shrine of the Holy House erected in the eleventh century at Walsingham in East Anglia,[22] or the

---

17 Sumption, *Pilgrimage*, p. 185.   18 Andrew Borde, *The fyrst boke of the introduction of knowledge*, ed. F.J. Furnivall, EETS extra ser. (London, 1870), pp 205–6, cited in David Ditchburn, '"Saints at the door don't make miracles"? The contrasting fortunes of Scottish pilgrimage, *c*.1450–1550' in J. Goodare & A.A. MacDonald (eds), *Sixteenth-century Scotland: essays in honour of Michael Lynch* (Leiden, 2008), pp 69–98, at pp 88–9.   19 Constance Mary Storrs, *Jacobean pilgrims from England to St James of Compostela from the early twelfth to the late fifteenth century* ([Santiago de Compostela], 1994), p. 77.   20 Diana Webb, 'Freedom of movement? Women travellers in the Middle Ages' in C. Meek & C. Lawless (eds), *Pawns or players? Studies on medieval and early modern women* (Dublin, 2003), pp 75–89; Leigh Ann Craig, '"Stronger than men and braver than knights": women and the pilgrimages to Jerusalem and Rome in the later Middle Ages', *Journal of Medieval History*, 29:3 (2003), 153–75.   21 See Ditchburn, '"Saints at the door don't make miracles"?', pp 69–98. (£66 stg was equivalent to £200 Scots).   22 Gary Waller, *Walsingham and the English imagination* (Farnham, 2011). For a modern Irish pilgrim walking to Walsingham, see Frainc Mac Brádaigh, *Cá bhfuil Walsingham? 'The fumbles of our funny God'* (Dublin, 2010).

similar shrine at Loreto in the Italian peninsula, for those who could not embark on an extended pilgrimage to Jerusalem.[23] Relics of the Holy Cross or of Christ's blood were equally attractive.[24]

There were shrines that appealed to regional or national loyalties, at which powerful protectors in the court of Heaven could be invoked. Adventurous people from Ireland might embark on a journey to the shrine of the murdered archbishop Thomas Becket (d. 1170) at Canterbury, which attracted a huge pilgrim trade from the late twelfth century. Especially popular were the jubilee years there – every fiftieth year beginning in 1220 on the fiftieth anniversary of the martyrdom. Income from the shrine at Canterbury increased significantly in jubilee years, but so too did expenditure on hospitality for pilgrims.[25] Souvenir pilgrim badges from that shrine have been found in excavations at Dublin and Waterford, indicating that it attracted pilgrims from Ireland.[26] It is possible that a stone replica of that shrine was made for the abbey of St Thomas in Dublin, and in the seventeenth century James Ware claimed that St Catherine's chapel, attached to the abbey of St Thomas, had contained the vestments worn by St Thomas the Martyr when he was killed.[27] Other prominent regional shrines that might have attracted pilgrims from Ireland included St Davids in south-west Wales, which was reflected in a well-established cult of St David in Ireland, and St Andrews in south-east Scotland, which had many parallels with Santiago as an apostolic pilgrimage destination but never attained the same level of popularity among the Irish.[28]

23 Victor Turner & Edith Turner, *Image and pilgrimage in Christian culture* (New York, 1978), pp 185–7; on the longevity of the shrine at Walsingham, see Sumption, *Pilgrimage*, pp 278–9. For a pilgrimage to the Loreto shrine by the Irish earls en route to Rome in 1608, see Nollaig Ó Muraíle (ed.), *Turas na dtaoiseach nUltach as Éirinn: from Ráth Maoláin to Rome* (Rome, 2007), pp 180–257; Mícheál Mac Craith, 'Tadhg Ó Cianáin agus Loreto', *Bliainiris*, 11 (2016), 78–128; www.santuarioloreto.it, accessed 3 Mar. 2018. **24** Charles Freeman, *Holy bones, holy dust: how relics shaped the history of medieval Europe* (New Haven, 2011), pp 186–96. **25** Eveleigh Woodruff, 'The financial aspects of the cult of St Thomas of Canterbury', *Archaeologia Cantiana*, 44 (1932), 13–32. **26** Colmán Ó Clabaigh & Michael Staunton, 'Thomas Becket and Ireland' in E. Mullins & D. Scully (eds), *Listen, O Isles, unto me: studies in medieval word and image in honour of Jennifer O'Reilly* (Cork, 2011), pp 87–101, at p. 96. Louise Nugent, 'Medieval pilgrim's tokens and other souvenirs in Ireland: a review of the archaeological and historical evidence' in J. Higgins, A. Conneely & M. Gibbons (eds), *Irish maritime heritage: proceedings of the 3rd Galway International Heritage Conference, 2013* (Galway, 2013), pp 37–8. For the ubiquitous nature of souvenir metal badges in medieval Europe, in secular contexts as well as in association with pilgrimages, see A.M. Koldeweij, 'Lifting the veil on pilgrim badges' in J. Stopford (ed.), *Pilgrimage explored* (York, 1999), pp 11–88. **27** Paul Duffy & Tadhg O'Keeffe, 'A stone shrine for a relic of St Thomas Becket in Dublin?', *Archaeology Ireland*, 31:4 (2017), 18–22; Robert Ware's notes on Dublin churches, BL, Add. MS 4813, fol. 41 (NLI, microfilm P 17). **28** Mona Rees & Terry John, *Pilgrimage: a Welsh perspective* (Llandysul, 2002), pp 171–85; for St David's cult in Ireland, see Bernadette Cunningham & Raymond Gillespie, 'The cult of St David in Ireland before 1700' in J.R. Guy & W.G. Neely (eds), *Contrasts and comparisons: studies in Irish and Welsh church history* (Llandysul, 1999), pp 27–42; Peter Yeoman, *Pilgrimage in medieval Scotland* (London, 1999), pp 53–74; Ian Campbell, 'Planning for pilgrims: St Andrews as the second Rome', *Innes Review*, 64:1 (2013), 1–22.

Within Ireland, there were also sites of regional significance. St Patrick's Purgatory at Lough Derg was an unconventional pilgrimage site since it focussed on the experience of Hell and Purgatory rather than devotion to a saint. However, it attracted a steady stream of medieval foreign pilgrims, who documented their experiences.[29] Evidence also survives of three foreign pilgrims – two French priests from Lyon and their servant – who visited both Lough Derg and Croagh Patrick, and who received a certificate of their pilgrimage from Archbishop Octavian of Armagh in 1485.[30] Like any major pilgrimage destination, Lough Derg required an infrastructure of pilgrim hospitality, and religious houses in that neighbourhood at Lisgoole, Devenish, Cleenish, Rossolly and Derrybrusk all catered to the needs of pilgrims there in the fifteenth century.[31]

In addition to Lough Derg there were other Irish pilgrimage sites that were nationally or internationally known. Croagh Patrick in Mayo, Clonmacnoise in Offaly, Monaincha and Holy Cross in Tipperary, Mount Brandon in Kerry and Glendalough in Wicklow all drew pilgrims from far and near, and their popularity continued for centuries. In 1543, Heneas MacNichaill, from the diocese of Armagh, was given a particularly onerous penance for having killed his own son. He was required to go on pilgrimage to fifteen of the most significant pilgrimage destinations in Ireland, including remote places such as the Skelligs and Aran, as well as more usual places such as Cashel and Croagh Patrick. He eventually returned to Armagh with proof or certificates that he had visited all of the shrines and he was then granted absolution.[32]

Early pilgrim roads have been traced approaching many of these pilgrimage locations.[33] In some instances medieval devotional markers may also be found. For example, the carved stone at Clonfinlagh, Co. Offaly, probably marked a stage on the pilgrim route to Clonmacnoise,[34] while it has been suggested that the high cross at Carndonagh, Co. Donegal, with its depiction of three pilgrims at the foot of the shaft, beneath the feet of Christ, may have been connected to a local *turas* or pilgrimage associated with St Colum Cille on the Inishowen peninsula.[35] In a late fifteenth-century context in Co. Meath, the wayside crosses at Keenoge and in

29 Peter Harbison, *Pilgrimage in Ireland: the monuments and the people* (London, 1991), pp 51–75, 111–33; Michael Haren & Yolande de Pontfarcy (eds), *The medieval pilgrimage to St Patrick's Purgatory, Lough Derg and the European tradition* (Clogher, 1988); Hiram Morgan, *Ireland 1518: Archduke Ferdinand's visit to Kinsale and the Dürer connection* (Cork, 2015), pp 89–94.   30 Shane Leslie, *Saint Patrick's Purgatory: a record from history and literature* (London, 1932), p. 61.   31 Helen Lanigan Wood, 'Ecclesiastical sites in County Fermanagh from the early Christian period until the end of the medieval period' in C. Foley & R. McHugh, *An archaeological survey of County Fermanagh, vol. 1, pt 2: the early Christian and medieval periods* (Newtownards, 2014), pp 637–65.   32 Aubrey Gwynn, *The medieval province of Armagh* (Dundalk, 1946), pp 268–9.   33 Harbison, *Pilgrimage in Ireland*, pp 69, 71, 111, 139–46; Geraldine Carville, *The heritage of Holy Cross* (Belfast, 1973), p. 101.   34 Elizabeth Shee-Twohig, 'Context and chronology of the carved stone at Clonfinlough, County Offaly', *JRSAI*, 132 (2002), 99–113. Comparisons with Galicia are noted by Shee-Twohig.   35 Tessa Garton, 'The influence of pilgrimage on artistic traditions in medieval Ireland' in M. Cormack (ed.), *Saints and their cults in the Atlantic world* (Columbia, SC, 2007), pp 174–201, at p. 174.

Dunsany churchyard that include images of St James of Compostela among other saints might have been familiar to pilgrims from that region.[36]

At the lower end of the Irish pilgrimage hierarchy were local devotions centred on holy wells or other local landscape features, associated with local saints, which attracted the laity on patronal feast days and at other times.[37] The pall of sanctity was spread unevenly across the landscape and at some places, sanctified by the action of a saint, the veil between Heaven and earth was thought to be thin and the power of the saint was magnified. It was to such places that most pilgrimages led. The motivations of pilgrims when visiting such therapeutic landscapes varied, but a search for cure from illness or an opportunity for special prayers for assistance in some aspect of life were important considerations. Friar John Clyn recorded large numbers at St Mullins in Co. Carlow in 1348, observing that 'some came from feelings of devotion, others (the majority) from the fear of the plague that then prevailed beyond measure'.[38] The ecclesiastical buildings on that site included a chapel of St James.[39] Visits to local wells were ritual events, outside of official liturgical structures, in which children as well as adults participated.[40] The rituals at holy wells varied from place to place (and have adapted greatly over time), but would generally have involved recitation of familiar prayers, ritual movement in the vicinity of the well, drinking water from the source and making an offering. Within the local Irish pilgrimage tradition corporeal relics did not play a large part. Few pilgrimage sites in Ireland had relics of their saints and the normal focus was on the place associated with the saint in the landscape. In this tradition, the journey and the landscape setting were more important than the encounter with the remains of the saint.

MOTIVES

Those who travelled to Jerusalem or Santiago also probably visited regional or local pilgrimage sites at other times, and their motives in making the journey varied little between their destinations. Each pilgrimage to an international, regional or local cult site was, as theologians and others insisted, a rational act, and so it should be possible to describe the reasons why pilgrims undertook the task. Pilgrimage drew together many of the disparate aspects of devotion to saints, such as the veneration of relics and images and even the hope for miracles. However, pilgrimage, especially local pilgrimage, was so much a part of the fabric of society and religious

36 Heather A. King, 'Late medieval crosses in County Meath, *c.*1470–1635', *Proc. RIA*, 84C (1984), 79–115, at 98–9; Roger Stalley, 'Maritime pilgrimage from Ireland and its artistic repercussions' in Vicente Almazán (ed.), *Actas del II Congreso Internacional de Estudios Jacobeos* [Ferrol 1996]: *rutas Atlánticas de peregrinación a Santiago de Compostela* (2 parts [Santiago de Compostela, 1999]), i, pp 255–75. 37 Patrick Logan, *The holy wells of Ireland* (Gerrards Cross, 1980). 38 Bernadette Williams (ed.), *Annals of Ireland by Friar John Clyn* (Dublin, 2007), p. 246. 39 Anna Brindley & Annaba Kilfeather, *Archaeological inventory of County Carlow* (Dublin, 1993), no. 603. 40 Logan, *The holy wells of Ireland*, pp 21–34.

practice that pilgrims usually did not think it worthwhile to leave a record of their journeys or motivations. While some pilgrim accounts of the journey to Santiago have survived from England, France and elsewhere, no personal accounts survive from any medieval Irish pilgrims. At best we can discern general rather than specific motives of such pilgrims. Those who went on pilgrimage to local, regional or international centres had overlapping expectations. Most obviously, the journey was usually to a place where the pilgrim could encounter the saint through his or her relics. Thus, Santiago de Compostela's attraction as a pilgrim destination was as the site of the relics of St James, with their ability to channel the power of the Apostle to meet specific needs.

While relics were not a normal part of Irish pilgrimage sites, they were the norm within the medieval Christian worldview, and visits to shrines containing relics of particular saints offered the opportunity to experience the power of a saint. Across Europe, relic collections at pilgrimage centres were common, but in Ireland less so.[41] Among the exceptions to this were the Augustinian canons at Christ Church cathedral in Dublin, who were deeply involved in the pilgrimage business in the fifteenth century and possessed a wide range of relics. The cathedral was home to the *baculus Ihesu*, the staff of Christ reputedly given to St Patrick by an angel. They also had a thorn from the crown of thorns and a miraculous speaking crucifix. They claimed to have relics of saints Patrick, Brigid and Laurence, bones of saints Peter and Andrew, and relics of Thomas Becket, St Oswald, St Audoen and St Edmund, among others.[42] St Foy (Faith) of Conques was also among those represented, Conques being one of the major shrines in southern France on the main French pilgrimage route from Le Puy-en-Velay to Santiago.[43] In 1497 both the Irish parliament and the corporation of Dublin promised that pilgrims would not be 'vexed, troubled or arrested' while in Dublin to visit the relics at Christ Church, indicating that the pilgrimage business was valued in the city.[44] Monetary offerings at shrines were an important source of income for such institutions; Irish pilgrims departing from Dublin in pursuit of indulgences at overseas shrines had to swear not to take more gold than needed for the journey, suggesting that the financial aspect of the pilgrimage was of concern to the civil authorities.[45]

Relics allowed people to reach out and touch holiness when they longed for remedies for physical ailments or spiritual difficulties. For this reason, there was an emotional and devotional attraction to the place recognized as the burial place of a

41 A.R. Bell & R.S. Dale, 'The medieval pilgrimage business', *Enterprise and Society*, 12:3 (2011), 601–27.   42 For a list of the more important pre-Reformation relics in Christ Church cathedral, see Raymond Refaussé with Colm Lennon (eds), *The registers of Christ Church cathedral, Dublin* (Dublin, 1998), pp 39–40.   43 Raghnall Ó Floinn, 'The late-medieval relics of Holy Trinity church, Dublin' in J. Bradley, A.J. Fletcher & A. Simms (eds), *Dublin in the medieval world: studies in honour of Howard B. Clarke* (Dublin, 2009), pp 369–89, at p. 384.   44 Raymond Gillespie, 'The coming of reform, 1500–58' in K. Milne (ed.), *Christ Church cathedral, Dublin: a history* (Dublin, 2000), pp 151–73, at pp 157–8; J.T. Gilbert, *Calendar of ancient records of Dublin*, i (1889), p. 383.   45 G. Hartwell Jones, 'Celtic Britain and the pilgrim movement', *Y Cymmrodor*, 23 (1912), 77; 570n.

particular saint, or associated with the saint in another tangible way. Belief in the power of relics, and the benefits that might be sought by visiting the burial place of a saint, drove people from all sections of society to participate in pilgrimage. The challenges of the journey added an extra dimension to the spiritual experience. As a martyred Apostle, the relics of James the Great were particularly valued, and many were drawn to the holy place where those relics could be venerated.

In the case of extended pilgrimages to distant places, the practical realities of the long journey, in circumstances where the pilgrim was far from their home, reliant on the kindness of strangers, created an altered perspective on social and moral values. Some, familiar with Bible stories, were conscious of the idea of life as a journey, and of Christians as 'strangers and pilgrims on the earth' (Hebrews 11:13) whose ultimate citizenship was in Heaven (Philippians 3:20), and may have viewed their pilgrimage in that context.[46] In the Western Christian tradition, pilgrims following the advice of the Book of Revelation 21:27 took steps to cleanse themselves of their sins before setting out. Pilgrims were also expected to choose the path of poverty, giving away their possessions. That injunction, too, allowed people to view their lives from a new standpoint, whether or not they translated that into personal reformation. For some, it had echoes of entering a monastery, and the pilgrim cloak that came to be associated with extended pilgrimages could be seen as imitating the monastic habit. The ritual blessing of the pilgrim staff and scrip (wallet) in a liturgical setting, widely performed in the fifteenth century prior to setting out on a long pilgrimage, may have enhanced this sense of a new spiritual departure.[47] Pilgrims going overseas might make a will before setting out. David Lombard, 'captain of his nation', living at Blarney Castle, Co. Cork, made his will in 1479 on the eve of his departure for Santiago, in a jubilee year. There are earlier examples of wills being made by pilgrims from Ireland planning to go to Jerusalem.[48] Given the dangers and difficulties of international pilgrimage, this was a practical measure but it also emphasized the sense of removal from the existing world, and the death of the old self. It separated out the major pilgrimages, which required such preparation, from the regional and local ones that did not.

In analysing major pilgrimages, Edith Turner has argued that the experience can be understood as having the classic three-stage form of a rite of passage: '(1) separation (the start of the journey), (2) the liminal stage (the journey itself, the sojourn at the shrine, and the encounter with the sacred), and (3) reaggregation (the homecoming)'. In this anthropological interpretation, the central pilgrimage element (in modern times) would be 'marked by an awareness of temporary release from social ties and by a strong sense of *communitas* ('community, fellowship'), as well as by a preference for simplicity of dress and behaviour, by a sense of ordeal,

46 Cross & Livingstone (eds), *Oxford dictionary of the Christian church*, 'pilgrimages', p. 1288.   47 See below, pp 35–6.   48 For a transcript of Lombard's will, see John Ainsworth, National Library of Ireland: Reports on private collections, no. 46: Lombard MSS. For the wills of pilgrims to Jerusalem, see J.T. Gilbert (ed.), *Chartularies of St Mary's abbey, Dublin* (2 vols, London, 1884–6), i, pp 237, 435.

and by reflection on the basic meaning of one's religion'.[49] Local pilgrimage, where pilgrims were well known to each other, may not have succeeded in overcoming well-established local bonds of hierarchy and neighbourhood. Eamon Duffy has suggested that local pilgrimages were part of a familiar social reality, and that local pilgrims were 'consolidating, not dissolving, their social and religious world'.[50]

Whether local or international, the journey to reach a holy destination tended to be an informal, unstructured aspect of the venture, allowing the pilgrim to approach the sacred in a way that was free from the restrictions of liturgical convention. The movement away from home that was inherent in the act of pilgrimage gave people a sense of participating in a spiritual experience not under routine clerical control. Paradoxically, while journeying towards a specific place, deemed a location of special sanctity, the pilgrim could discover the divine in the everyday experiences of their lives. Despite the sense of spiritual freedom that the journey encouraged, efforts were made to ensure that the pilgrimage phenomenon in Western Europe was subject to ecclesiastical control. In the ninth century, Pope Nicholas (858–67) and Pope Stephen V (885–91) allowed pilgrimages to be substituted for ecclesiastical penances and criminal or civil penalties, and this use of pilgrimages as an extension of the sacrament of Penance persisted in many areas, including Ireland.[51]

For the devout, the journey to the holy place, through its challenges and hardships, was also an imitation of the Passion of Christ. The *imitatio Christi* was a major element of late medieval Christian piety and devotion, and a significant aspect of the practice of pilgrimage.[52] Drawing on this genre of late medieval spiritual devotion, a particular collection of meditations on the life and sufferings of Christ known as the *Meditationes vitae Christi* was translated into Irish in the mid-fifteenth century. The translation was the work of Tomás Gruama Ó Bruacháin, working at Killala in north Connacht. His translation survives in numerous manuscript copies, including some from the late fifteenth century.[53] Its popularity is an indicator of the late medieval Irish preoccupation with intense personal devotion

49 Edith Turner, 'Pilgrimage: an overview' in M. Eliade (ed.), *The encyclopedia of religion*, vol. 11 (New York, 1987), p. 328. For the Turners' classic interpretation, see Victor Turner & Edith Turner, *Image and pilgrimage in Christian culture* (New York, 1978).   50 Eamon Duffy, 'The dynamics of pilgrimage in late medieval England' in C. Morris & P. Roberts (eds), *Pilgrimage: the English experience from Becket to Bunyan* (Cambridge, 2002), pp 164–77 at p. 177.   51 For the Irish evidence, see Ludwig Bieler (ed.), *The Irish penitentials* (Dublin, 1963); T.M. Charles-Edwards, 'The social background to Irish *peregrinatio*', *Celtica*, 11 (1976), 43–59; for wider context, see Sumption, *Pilgrimage*, pp 98–113; Diana Webb, *Pilgrims and pilgrimage in the medieval West* (London, 1999), pp 52–63.   52 A.H. Bridero, *Christendom and Christianity in the middle Ages* (Grand Rapids, MI, 1994), p. 99.   53 Cainneach Ó Maonaigh (ed.), *Smaointe beatha Chríost .i. innsint Ghaelge a chuir Tomás Gruamdha Ó Bruacháin (fl. c.1450) ar an* Meditationes vitae Christi (Dublin, 1944). The manuscript on which Canice Mooney based his edition is RIA, MS 23 B 3, a vellum manuscript dated to 1461, the work of Diarmuid Ó Conuill. For other manifestations of this devotional tradition in Ireland, see Colmán Ó Clabaigh, *The friars in Ireland: 1224–1540* (Dublin, 2012), pp 191–3.

centred on the sufferings of Christ, and an accompanying sense of obligation to imitate that suffering.

The portrayal of the Passion and death of Christ in both literature and art in the later Middle Ages became more graphic. This is perhaps best exemplified in the woodcuts of German artist and engraver Albrecht Dürer, used in early Continental printings of prayerbooks and missals from the 1490s.[54] A wide range of Passion metaphors persisted in Irish religious literature and there was a strong devotion to the cult of the five wounds.[55] Embarking on an extended pilgrimage was one way of journeying on a path of suffering in emulation of the life of Christ.

While pilgrimage was a positive spiritual experience inviting personal reflection and reformation, it also had a darker side. Fear of eternal punishment for sins committed in life troubled many late medieval Christians. The doctrine of Purgatory emerged to cater for the needs of those who sought purification from their sins.[56] It recognized that there was a middle ground between the saints and the damned, and gave hope of salvation to those who had lived less-than-perfect lives. Time spent in Purgatory was understood as a period of purification after death. The concept allowed for the possibility that those who died as Christian believers but as sinners might still be able to achieve purification before the Last Judgment.[57] The requirement for annual reception of the sacrament of Penance and of the Eucharist in their own parish was introduced for all Christians at the Fourth Lateran Council in 1215, a gathering attended by many Irish bishops. There emerged a greater interest in the proper confession of sin as preparation for a good death, and this became a popular theme in preachers' handbooks.[58] Preachers may have been advocating repentance while on earth, but a sense of dreaded anticipation of the virtually unavoidable, though temporary, horrors of Purgatory persisted.[59] The idea emerged that remission of the penance still due after confession could be gained through indulgences, often earned through pilgrimage, and that indulgences could be obtained either on behalf of the penitent or on behalf of those who had already died.

54 Willi Kurth (ed.), *The complete woodcuts of Albrecht Dürer* (New York, 1927; reprint 1963). **55** Salvador Ryan, '"Reaping a rich harvest of humanity": images of redemption in Irish bardic religious poetry' in B. Leahy & S. O'Connell (eds), *Having life in His name* (Dublin, 2011), pp 239–51; Salvador Ryan, 'Reign of blood: devotion to the wounds of Christ in late medieval Ireland' in J. Augusteijn & M.A. Lyons (eds), *Irish history: a research yearbook* (Dublin, 2002), pp 137–49. **56** Diarmaid MacCulloch, *A history of Christianity* (London, 2009), p. 369; G.R. Edwards, 'Purgatory: "birth" or evolution?', *Journal of Ecclesiastical History*, 36 (1985), 634–46. **57** Cross & Livingstone, *Oxford dictionary of the Christian church*, pp 1349–50; Vincent Kerns, 'The traditional doctrine of Purgatory', *Irish Ecclesiastical Record*, 80 (1953), 326–42. **58** Salvador Ryan & Anthony Shanahan, 'How to communicate Lateran IV in 13th-century Ireland: lessons from the *Liber Exemplorum* (*c.*1275)', *Religions*, 9:75 (2018), 1–14, at 8–10. **59** Eamon Duffy, *The stripping of the altars: traditional religion in England, 1400–1580* (New Haven, 1992), ch. 10: 'The pains of Purgatory'; Salvador Ryan, 'Fixing the eschatological scales: judgement of the soul in late medieval and early modern Irish tradition' in P. Clarke & T. Clayton (eds), *The church, the afterlife and the fate of the soul*, Studies in Church History, 45 (Woodbridge, 2009), pp 184–95.

Franciscan preachers at work in the thirteenth century emphasized the value of the indulgences granted to those who listened to their sermons.[60] Among the moral tales preserved in a preacher's handbook compiled by a Franciscan friar from Warwickshire who spent his career preaching in Ireland was the story of a man who having gained many indulgences sold them to the owner of a house in which he was lodging, a man whose son had just died. That night, the dead son appeared to them saying the indulgences had rescued him from the torments he was suffering and he was now going to Heaven. The seller of the indulgences then realized their value and thought he should attempt to get them back for his own benefit, but the householder refused and the son benefited. The moral was emphasized: 'therefore, the living should not despise indulgences, whose benefits the dead deserve to receive in this remarkable fashion'.[61]

The institutional church, seeking to maintain control over shrines that had emerged as popular centres of devotion, particularly through the cult of relics, sanctioned special indulgences at selected shrines. At Santiago the devout pilgrim could earn valuable indulgences if certain standard conditions were met. These conditions included formal engagement with the sacraments through confession of sins and participation in the Eucharist. The ecclesiastical approval of, and the generous indulgences attached to, the shrine of St James in Galicia, when coupled with belief in the pains of Purgatory and Hell, motivated people to travel there as part of their personal path towards redemption.

A very clear idea was formed that those who made a major pilgrimage in their lifetimes as an act of repentance, as part of their quest for salvation, could earn time off Purgatory for themselves or for the souls of others.[62] Gradually, there emerged a hierarchy of pilgrimage destinations in the Western Christian tradition, as indicated by the level of indulgence sanctioned by the church. By this measure a visit to Santiago was on a par with both Rome and Jerusalem in terms of approved indulgences.[63] William Wey, an English pilgrim at Santiago de Compostela in 1456, recorded in detail the indulgences that could be gained there:

> Whoever has come on pilgrimage to the church of St James, son of Zebedee, at any time, has one-third of all his sins remitted. If he should die on his way there, while there or during his return, provided he repents of his sins, they are all remitted to him.
>
> Moreover, all who go on any Sunday in the procession of the church of St James, have, for each procession and ministration of the sacrament, 40

60 See F.J. Cotter, *The Friars Minor in Ireland, from their arrival to 1400*, ed. R.A. McKelvie (New York, 1994), p. 78, on the granting of indulgences to those who heard Franciscan sermons. 61 David Jones (ed.), *Friars' tales: thirteenth-century* exempla *from the British Isles* (Manchester, 2011), pp 126–7. 62 Luigi Tomasi, '"Homo viator": from pilgrimage to religious tourism via the journey' in W.H. Swatos Jnr & L. Tomasi (eds), *From medieval pilgrimage to religious tourism* (Westport, CT, 2002), pp 1–24, at pp 4–5. 63 Laurie Dennett, *The origins of holy years and the Compostela*, CSJ Occasional Paper 7 (London, 2004), pp 3, 6–7.

days of indulgence, and similarly throughout the whole week. If it is a feast day they have 300 days in addition to the aforesaid indulgence of a third of all their sins. Moreover, on the eve of St James's day and on the day itself and the feast of the dedication of his church, all who have gone there on pilgrimage have 600 days, both on the eve and on the day itself, in addition to the aforementioned indulgence of a third part of all their sins.

Likewise, all who hear Mass said by an archbishop, bishop or cardinal at the altar of St James have 200 days indulgence for each Mass, in addition to the aforesaid indulgences. All these privileges, listed above, have been granted and confirmed, in the manner described, to St James's pilgrims, who have confessed and are truly penitent, by Bulls issued by the Holy Fathers of the Apostolic See.[64]

The precise origin of some of these Santiago indulgences is obscure, and they were modified over time, but it is evident that they mattered to pilgrims such as William Wey in 1456.[65] Indulgences were also, of course, of benefit to the shrines authorized to dispense them, as pilgrims gave significant offerings in return.

Jubilee years at Santiago, when the feast of St James fell on a Sunday, gave pilgrims the added incentive of acquiring the enhanced indulgences that could be gained in those years. It is sometimes claimed that the award of a plenary indulgence to pilgrims who visited Santiago in a jubilee year was first sanctioned by Pope Calixtus II in 1122, and was confirmed by Pope Alexander II in the bull *Regis Aeterni* in 1179, but the authenticity of the source on which this is based has rightly been questioned.[66] The surviving version of the papal bull contains anachronisms that are inconsistent with a twelfth-century date, not least its mention of equivalent jubilee indulgences at Rome, which were not initiated until 1300.[67] Whatever its precise origin, the idea of a jubilee year in Santiago was certainly one that attracted international attention by the late fourteenth century, possibly enhanced by the fear of untimely death in the wake of the Black Death in Europe after 1348.

Studies by Constance Storrs and Wendy Childs have each shown in respect of medieval Britain that pilgrim traffic to Santiago was at its most significant in jubilee years, which occur in a cyclical pattern of every six, five, six and eleven years.[68] The first year in which the impact of a Santiago jubilee can be measured by numbers of pilgrims travelling by sea from Britain is 1395.[69] Among those licensed to carry pilgrims in that year was a ship called *Jelyan*, with Richard Skelby as master,

64 'An account of the pilgrimage made by Master William Wey', translated from Latin in Francis Davey, *William Wey: an English pilgrim to Compostella in 1456* (London, 2000), pp 33–5.   65 Dennett, *The origins of holy years*, p. 7.   66 Fletcher, *St James's catapult*, p. 199; Dennett, *The origins of holy years*, pp 5–7.   67 Ibid., p. 6.   68 Storrs, *Jacobean pilgrims from England*; Wendy Childs, 'English ships and the pilgrim route to Santiago' in Almazán (ed.), *Actas del II Congreso Internacional de Estudios Jacobeos*, i, pp 79–91, at pp 82–3.   69 Storrs, *Jacobean pilgrims from England*, appendix 2: 'Enrolled ships' licences, 1235–1484', pp 174–5.

which routinely sailed between Ireland and England, and was permitted to carry 60 pilgrims to Santiago.[70] In the first half of the fifteenth century, 1428, 1434 and 1445 were particularly busy years for ship owners operating out of the ports on the south coast of England. At least 2,300 pilgrims were licensed by the English king in 1434, permitting them to go to Santiago on pilgrimage, while in 1445 some 1,700 pilgrims obtained similar licences.[71] In the second half of that century, the jubilee years 1451, 1456, 1462, 1473 and 1484 also showed an increase in pilgrimage traffic by sea from southern English ports, with almost no ships being licensed to carry pilgrims outside those years.[72] The more scant Irish evidence points to a similar trend in favour of making the pilgrimage in a jubilee year.[73] Even now, the number of pilgrims to Santiago de Compostela is much higher in jubilee years than at other times, and the eve of the feast of St James is still regarded as the most desirable time to arrive at the cathedral.[74]

For every pilgrim who made the journey to Santiago, there were others who would have liked to have done so but could not. Some had made a formal vow to go on pilgrimage, usually at a time of crisis in their lives, and subsequently had to live with the burden of being unable to fulfil their vow. In 1320, while serving as justiciar of Ireland, Edmund Butler, 1st earl of Carrick (father of James, 1st earl of Ormond), vowed to go on pilgrimage to Santiago, but it is unclear whether he completed the journey. He certainly passed through Dublin and planned to travel through England to Santiago, which was then the normal route. However, he submitted a request to the archbishop of Dublin that he and his wife and son be absolved of their vow. They explained that they were unable to complete the pilgrimage because of wars between the English and the Irish that necessitated his presence in Ireland as justiciar.[75] The archbishop of Dublin was mandated to absolve them of their vow on condition that the expenses of the journey to Santiago were calculated and an equivalent amount paid to the Holy Land subsidy.[76] Edmund Butler died in London in September 1321, and was brought home to Gowran, Co. Kilkenny, for burial on St Martin's Eve.[77]

Elizabeth de Burgh, widow of the major Ulster landowner John de Burgh, earl of Ulster, had vowed in her husband's lifetime to go on pilgrimage to both Santiago and the Holy Land but was unable to do as she had promised. She petitioned the

---

70 *Cal. patent rolls, 1391–1396*, p. 568.   71 Luis Vazquez de Parga, et al., *Las Peregrinaciones a Santiago de Compostela* (3 vols, Madrid 1948; reprint Pamplona, 1992), i, pp 92, 94. The numbers of licensed pilgrims were calculated from the documents printed in Thomas Rymer, *Foedera, convenciones, literae ...* (1704).   72 Vazquez de Parga, et al., *Las Peregrinaciones*, i, pp 92, 94.   73 See appendix 1.   74 Jubilee years in the first half of the twenty-first century are 2004, 2010, 2021, 2027, 2032, 2038 and 2049.   75 *Cal. papal letters, ii, 1305–42*, p. 196.   76 *Cal. papal letters, ii, 1305–42*, p. 196; some sources indicate that Edmund Butler did go to Santiago, and died in England on his return. See J.T. Gilbert (ed.), *Account of facsimiles of national manuscripts of Ireland* (London, 1884), p. 104.   77 Williams (ed.), *The annals of Ireland by Friar John Clyn*, pp 77–8, 218; A.V. Hogg, 'The collegiate church of St Mary, Gowran, County Kilkenny, and its monuments', *JRSAI*, 40:4 (1910), 340–5.

pope in 1343 to be released from her vow, because she was now 40 years old and unable to undertake the pilgrimage.[78] She was absolved from her vow on the condition
that she undertake other works of piety. Elizabeth's mother-in-law, Matilda, wife of
William de Burgh, made a similar petition in the same year, and was absolved on
stringent conditions.[79] That both women, then widows, had intended to go on pilgrimage in the same year suggests that an extended family group may have planned
to travel together from England. When Matilda petitioned the pope at Avignon to
be absolved of her vow to go to Santiago, her request was granted on condition
that she found a chapel in England in honour of St James, or make a contribution
towards the campaign against the Turks equivalent to the expense of her journey, or
give 200 florins to the papal nuncio in England for the expedition against the Turks.
Her two servants, Petronilla and Agnes, were likewise absolved of their vows, on
condition that they each pay 20 florins to the fund for the war against the Turks.[80]

Vows to go on overseas pilgrimage to Santiago, Rome or Jerusalem were taken
very seriously by the papacy, and permission was rarely granted to allow such vows
to be commuted to almsgiving.[81] In 1351, Richard FitzRalph, archbishop of Armagh,
applied to have the faculty to allow people to choose confessors to give them plenary absolution at the hour of their death. The faculty was granted to him for 100
persons. He also applied to have the faculty to commute the vows of those who had
sworn to visit Rome, Santiago or the Holy Land, and this was granted to him for
20 persons, suggesting that the papacy guarded this right and used it sparingly.[82]
Various faculties were granted to Irish Franciscans in 1612, including dispensation
from vows, but not vows relating to the pilgrimage to Santiago or the Holy Land.
A similar exemption featured when special faculties were granted to the archbishop
of Dublin.[83] However, given the absence from the papal registers of petitions from
Ireland for the commutation of such vows, it seems likely that unfulfilled vows were
quietly exchanged for 'works of piety' without specific permission.

SCEPTICISM ABOUT PILGRIMAGE

Not all of those who observed the pilgrimage phenomenon believed in the value
of extended journeys to holy places. Christian doubt, after all, has a long pedigree,
traceable back to James's fellow Apostle, Thomas (John 20:24–30). For the cynical,
pilgrimages were simply adventures or holidays, or at worst a means of evading
responsibilities at home, although there were laws to minimize this. Canon law
required that a man or wife had to have their spouse's consent to go on pilgrimage.[84]

---

78 *Cal. papal petitions, i, 1342–1419*, pp 22–3.   79 Ibid., p. 74.   80 Ibid.   81 For an Irish example of such commutation being denied, see N.B. White (ed.), *Irish monastic and episcopal deeds, AD
1200–1600* (Dublin, 1936), p. 108.   82 *Cal. papal petitions, i, 1342–1419*, pp 206, 207.   83 Brendan
Jennings (ed.), 'Miscellaneous documents, i, 1588–1634', *Archivium Hibernicum*, 12 (1946), 70–200,
at 74 and 111.   84 Gillian Kenny, *Anglo-Irish and Gaelic women in Ireland, c.1170–1540* (Dublin,
2007), p. 100.

Similarly, Irish secular law required married pilgrims to obtain the permission of their spouse before embarking on an overseas pilgrimage, and one partner going on pilgrimage was among the accepted legal grounds for temporary separation.[85] Pilgrims could claim exemption from legal obligations, and sometimes, because of that, people may have used pilgrimage as a way of escaping their responsibilities at home in Ireland.[86] Many medieval commentators doubted the efficacy of pilgrimage to far distant shrines. A fourteenth-century English contemplative writer, Walter Hilton (*c.*1343–96), observed in his *Scale of perfection*, 'there is no need to run to Rome or Jerusalem to look for [Jesus] there, but turn your thought into your own soul where he is hidden'.[87] Hilton's work was first printed in English at London in 1494, at the end of a century that had seen a huge increase in overseas pilgrimage traffic from Britain and Ireland. The medieval Irish view of pilgrimage was similarly cautious. According to her Latin Life, the eighth-century Irish female saint Samthann held that there was no need to go on an overseas pilgrimage because the way to the Kingdom of Heaven was an equal distance from every land. She advised her disciples that God was just as near to Ireland as to Rome or other holy places.[88]

Several centuries earlier than Hilton, a quatrain questioning the value of pilgrimage was scribbled in the margin of a manuscript written by an Irish scribe, probably at St Gallen. The poem, written in Old Irish, is found in the margin of the *Codex Boernerianus*, a ninth-century manuscript containing the epistles of St Paul in Greek, with Latin interlining.[89] It voiced the perennial dilemma at the heart of pilgrimage.

> Coming to Rome,
> much labour and little profit.
> The King whom you seek here,
> unless you bring him with you, you will not find him.[90]

> *Téicht do Róim*
> *mór saído becc torbai!*
> *In rí chon-daigi hi foss*
> *Manim-bera latt, ní fogbái.*[91]

85 Fergus Kelly, A *guide to early Irish law* (Dublin, 1988), p. 75. **86** Kathleen Hughes, 'The changing theory and practice of Irish pilgrimage', *Journal of Ecclesiastical History*, 11 (1960), 143–51, at 145–6. **87** Walter Hilton, *Scale of perfection*, book I.49.5, cited in Maggi Dawn, *The accidental pilgrim: new journeys on ancient pathways* (London, 2012), p. 100. **88** Charles Plummer (ed.), *Vitae sanctorum Hiberniae* (London, 1910), ii, p. 260. **89** The manuscript is now Dresden, Sachsische Landesbibliothek, MS Misc. A 145b, and the stanza is found in the lower margin of fol. 23. A digitized version of the manuscript is available on www.slub-dresden.de See also Louis Gougaud, *Gaelic pioneers of Christianity* (London, 1933), pp 33–4; Patrick Sims-Williams, *Irish influence on medieval Welsh literature* (Oxford, 2011), pp 31, 33. **90** This translation is given in K.H. Jackson, *A Celtic miscellany* (London, 1971), p. 148. **91** This transcription of the Irish text is from James Carney, *Medieval Irish lyrics* (Dublin, 1967), p. 80.

A late Life of St Maighneann of Kilmainham (Co. Dublin), preserved in a fifteenth-century Irish manuscript, contains a conversation between Maighneann
and St Mochuda of Rahan on the subject of visiting the Holy Sepulchre in
Jerusalem.[92] Maighneann explained the futility of pilgrimage in circumstances
where the pilgrim was less than fully commited to the task in hand. The saint
advised Mochuda:

> There be three species under which one, when he leaves his country, enters
> on a journey of pilgrimage; and but one cause for which of God he wins the
> heavenly kingdom, all which is as thus: when of his heart and mind and of
> veritable zeal one breaks with the world's vices, then in such wise he attains
> unerringly to God; but when he goes on a pilgrimage indeed, the while his
> mind dwells on his children, on his wife or on his land, and he prefers them
> to God, then is his peregrination in vain, nor saving displacement of body
> and idle toil, has he any profit of the same ... for to have gone abroad out of
> his own natural patrimony is but small gain to any unless thereafter he shall
> have made the pilgrimage efficaciously.

> *Atáit trí hérnaile ar a fácbann nech a dúthchas in uair téid ar turus na hailitri,*
> *ocus atá aenadbhar as a faghann sé in cathair nemda ó Dia ocus is é so sin .i.*
> *in uair scarus nech ó craide ocus ó menmain ocus ó caindúthracht fri duailcib in*
> *tsaegail do geib sé Dia co dírech fó'n cuma sin. Induair téid ar ailitri ocus bios*
> *a menma for a cloinn nó for a mnái nó for a ferann ocus beirios do rogain iat*
> *tar Dia, is dímáineach a ailitre ocus ní fhagann tarba di acht imluad cuirp ocus*
> *saethair dímáin, ár is bec a tarba do neoch éirgi assa atharda dúthchais mina*
> *derna in ai[lithre] dia éis.*[93]

This echoed the Middle Irish Life of Colum Cille, written before the mid-twelfth
century, which was explicit on the requirements of pilgrimage, citing the example
of Abraham:

> It is as if God himself said openly to Abraam: 'From henceforth, while on
> your pilgrimage, shun with body and soul the sins and vices of the land
> where formerly you dwelt in body, since it is the same as staying in the
> fatherland for a person if he follows its customs while on pilgrimage ... For
> it is not by the track of feet nor by physical movement that one draws near
> to God, but by practice of good habits and virtues.'

---

92 British Library, Egerton MS 91, fol. 49, edited in S.H. O'Grady (ed.), *Silva Gadelica* (2 vols,
London, 1892), i, 37–49, at p. 48. See also Pádraig Ó Riain, *A dictionary of Irish saints* (Dublin, 2011),
pp 424–5.   **93** O'Grady (ed.), *Silva Gadelica*, i, p. 48 (Irish text); ii, p. 48 (English translation).
For another story of Mochuda being persuaded by Comhghall not to go on pilgrimage, see Charles
Plummer (ed.), *Bethada náem nÉrenn: Lives of the Irish saints* (2 vols, Oxford, 1922), i, pp 310–11
(Irish text); ii, pp 301–2 (translation).

Amal bid ed at-berad Dia fein co follus re hAbraam: 'Imgaib o churp 7 ó anmain o shund amach it ailithrí, pecdai 7 dualchi in tire in ro atrebais inallana iar curp, uair is inann do deoch 7 no aittrebad ina atharda dia n-inntamlaiged besa a atharda ina ailithri.' ... Uair nocon ó shet choss nó o imluad cuirp chomhfhocsiges nech do Dia acht is tria denam sobés 7 sualach.[94]

Others advocated visiting a local rather than a far distant shrine. The late medieval Irish Life of St Berach records that his pupil Colman Cáel determined to go to Rome. Berach and Ciaran Máel both tried to stop him but

> Colman Cáel said that he would not rest till he should see Rome with his eyes. Berach sained the air, and made the sign of the cross over Colman's eyes; and they three, Berach and Colman Cáel and Ciaran Máel, saw Rome, and praised the Lord in that place, and erected a cross and a mother church there to Berach, and to Ciaran Máel, and to Colman Cáel. And another cross was erected there to Paul and to Peter. And the visiting of those crosses is the same to any one as if he should go an equal distance of the road to Rome.

> *Ocus ro raid Colmán cáol, na hanfadh no co ffaicedh dia suilibh in Roimh. Sénais Berach an táer, 7 dobert airrde na croiche dar roscc Cholmáin caoil, 7 atconncatar a ttríur, Berach, 7 Colman cáol, 7 Ciaran máol, inní Roimh, 7 ro molsatar an Coimde annsin, 7 doronsatar cros 7 annoid annsin do Bherach, 7 do Chiaran máol, 7 do Colman cáol. Ocus doronadh cros ele do Pol 7 do Pettar; 7 an ionann do neoch ionnsaigidh na ccros sin 7 do imeochadh a coimhmeit do shligidh na Romha.*[95]

The Irish Life of St Molaise, written *c*.1500, recorded that he brought home numerous relics from Rome and deposited them in Devenish. They included relics of Peter, Paul, Clement, and the martyrs Laurence and Stephen, along with some soil. The reason Molaise brought them home was that 'unless they went for some weighty reason ... it should not be imperative on the Gael to repair to Rome'.[96] In the same vein, a late medieval Irish Life of St Kevin recorded that he went on pilgrimage to Rome and while there was authorized to establish a pilgrimage to Glendalough in perpetuity. Seven pilgrimages to Glendalough would achieve indulgences and benefits equal to one pilgrimage to Rome.[97]

---

94 Máire Herbert, *Iona, Kells and Derry: the history and hagiography of the monastic* familia *of Columba* (Oxford, 1988), p. 221 (Irish text); p. 250 (translation).   **95** Plummer (ed.), *Bethada náem nÉrenn*, i, p. 42 (Irish text); ii, pp 41–2 (translation).   **96** O'Grady (ed.), *Silva Gadelica*, ii, pp 30–1.   **97** Plummer (ed.), *Bethada náem nÉrenn*, ii, pp 155–6.

ON THE WAY

Despite this scepticism about the value of long-distance pilgrimage, it remained an appealing prospect in the Middle Ages. Those who set out on extended pilgrimage were aware of the physical challenges of the journey. Some may have understood the oft-expressed wisdom that the journey was futile without an internal journey towards greater piety, repentance or spiritual change, but the desire to experience holiness in a tangible way ensured the perennial attractiveness of relics and of places in the landscape that were associated with the cult of saints. The promise of significant indulgences for those who visited high-ranking Christian shrines – and particularly Jerusalem, Rome or Santiago – ensured that many people attempted to reach those destinations. However, this was by no means an easy option.

Armed with information about the selected shrine, the pilgrim was equipped to begin. The journey had to be well planned, and preparations were probably prolonged. One element of the leave-taking involved a liturgical service in which travellers and pilgrims (whatever their destination) received a special blessing. In the diocese of Limerick, Bishop Gilbert listed the blessing of pilgrims among the routine duties of parish priests in the twelfth century.[98] The Order of Service for the blessing of pilgrims, in the form recorded in the Sarum missal, was in use in Ireland in the fourteenth and fifteenth centuries.[99] The pilgrims first confessed their sins, then they prostrated themselves at the altar and three psalms were recited over them. These included Psalm 25, with the lines

> Yahweh, make your ways known to me,
> Teach me your paths.
> Set me in the way of your truth, and teach me,
> For you are the God who saves me.
> ...
> All Yahweh's paths are love and truth
> For those who keep his covenant and his decrees.
> For the sake of your name, Yahweh,
> Forgive my guilt for it is great.
> (Psalm 25:4–5, 10–11)

This was followed by an expression of repentance and appeal for forgiveness in Psalm 51, and then an invocation of God's protection in Psalm 91:

> No disaster can overtake you,
> No plague come near your tent;

---

98 Marie Therese Flanagan, *The transformation of the Irish church in the twelfth century* (Woodbridge, 2010), pp 225–6. 99 See F.E. Warren (ed.), *The Sarum missal in English* (2 vols, London, 1913), ii, pp 166–73, for the Order of Service for pilgrims. See also Daniel Rock, *The church of our fathers as seen in St Osmund's rite for the cathedral at Salisbury* (London, 1903), pp 376–8.

He will put you in his angels' charge
To guard you wherever you go.
They will support you on their hands
In case you hurt your foot against a stone;
You will tread on lion and adder,
Trample on savage lions and dragons.
'I will rescue all who cling to me,
I protect whoever knows my name,
I answer everyone who invokes me,
I am with them when they are in trouble;
I bring them safety and honour.
I give them life, long and full,
And show them how I can save.'
(Psalm 91:10–16)

The prayers of blessing that followed combined the idea of protection in the journey through life and in the physical journey of pilgrimage. Then the pilgrim's scrip and staff were blessed:

that whosoever, for love of thy name, shall desire to wear the same ... and so on his pilgrimage to seek the prayers of the saints, with the accompaniment of humble devotion, may be found worthy, through the protecting defence of thy right hand, to attain unto the joys of everlasting vision, through thee, O Saviour of the world.

The scrip was placed on the pilgrim's neck, with the prayer

In the name of our Lord Jesus Christ receive this scrip, the habit of thy pilgrimage; that after being well chastened thou mayest be found worthy both to reach in safety the thresholds of the saints, whither thou desirest to go; and that when thy journey is finished thou mayest return to us in safety.[100]

Such a service was designed to contain the pilgrimage phenomenon within the ambit of the institutional church while authorizing the departure of the pilgrim and praying for their protection and safe return. It marked the transition of the pilgrim from one lordship context to another, a shift from an earthly patron and protector to a heavenly one for the duration of the pilgrimage, acknowledging that they would inhabit a liminal space for a period of time. Above all, it directed the pilgrim's attention to the ultimate objective of reaching the heavenly kingdom.

Pilgrims to Santiago departing from Ireland began their journey by sea, relying on local and foreign merchants. Trade links with the Continent were an important

---

100 Warren (ed.), *Sarum missal*, ii, pp 166–73.

determinant of the routes available to pilgrims. In the thirteenth and fourteenth centuries, they chose short sea crossings and followed overland routes much of the way, whereas by the fifteenth century a direct sea voyage from Ireland or southern England to the Iberian coast was more common. This significant change, which greatly shortened the time it took to reach Spain, was made possible by improvements in ship design. Prior to the fifteenth century, the average cargo on the ships trading between Ireland and Britain had been less than 20 tons. These were usually 'buoyant but tubby' cogs, small ships with a single mast, routinely used on short voyages prior to the fifteenth century, generally for cargo rather than passengers.[101] These cogs were a regular sight on the Irish Sea and similar boats would have been used to cross the English Channel, with pilgrims following an overland route from there. By 1400, the average ship operating out of Bristol carried 88 tons of cargo and this had increased to 150 tons by 1450. (A ship of 150 tons would have capacity for about 150 pilgrims in addition to the crew.)

By the mid-fifteenth century, when the boom in pilgrimages from Gaelic Ireland occurred, larger three-masted ships known as carracks had been introduced on the north Atlantic, and these were being used in the Bay of Biscay as merchant ships and in warfare. Their ability to undertake the sea crossing from Britain and Ireland direct to Spain facilitated greatly increased pilgrim traffic. The carrack had several decks, and access to the lower decks was through small hatches that could be secured in bad weather. These carracks had a small triangular forecastle and a larger aftercastle used for accommodation. The *Mary* of London, the ship that reputedly transported 400 pilgrims from New Ross in 1473, was probably a large carrack; it was stated to have been 320 tons.[102] The carracks in use in Irish waters were usually foreign-owned, but sometimes had Irish captains.[103] In general, more Irish than Bristol ships were in use for trade across the Irish Sea in the fifteenth century, with larger Bristol-based ships tending to go further afield.[104]

The other design of sailing ship that became popular with merchants in the fifteenth century was the caravel. Developed in Portugal, this was a longer ship, lower in the water. It too had several decks and a multi-storey aftercastle to accommodate passengers. By the second half of the fifteenth century caravels weighing 150–200 tons were being used in trade between Iberia and England, and between Iberia and West Africa. Similar caravels were also used by merchants trading in

101 R.R. Menard, 'Transport costs and long-range trade, 1300–1800: was there a European "transport revolution" in the early modern era?' in J.D. Tracy (ed.), *The political economy of merchant empires* (Cambridge, 1997), pp 228–75.   102 *Cal. patent rolls, 1477–1485*, p. 78; R.B. Tate, *Pilgrimages to St James of Compostella from the British Isles during the Middle Ages*, CSJ Occasional Paper 5 (London, 2003), pp 20–2; see below, pp 113–14.   103 John de Courcy Ireland, 'A survey of early maritime trade and ships' in M. McCaughan & J.C. Appleby (eds), *The Irish Sea: aspects of maritime history* (Belfast, 1989), pp 21–5, at p. 24. A modern replica of a carrack – the *Matthew*, which was used by John Cabot in the 1490s to cross the Atlantic (www.matthew.co.uk) – can be seen in Bristol harbour.   104 E.M. Carus Wilson, 'The overseas trade of Bristol' in E. Power & M.M. Postan (eds), *Studies in English trade in the fifteenth century* (London, 1933), pp 183–246, at pp 193–5.

luxury goods in the eastern Mediterranean. The caravel was regularly used by wine merchants, and because of its speed was also favoured by pirates.[105] The availability of such ships on the Atlantic seaboard from the mid-fifteenth century certainly facilitated the Santiago pilgrimage from northern Europe, including Ireland. The kind of sailing ship that allowed the seafaring adventures of Vasco da Gama from Lisbon to the Indian Ocean in the 1490s, or Christopher Columbus to sail to the Americas, was at the disposal of those venturing on long voyages between northern Europe and the Iberian peninsula. As the route became more popular, sailing directions were drawn up to guide those navigating between Spain and the west coast of England and Ireland in the fifteenth century.[106] Pilgrims using the sea route to Galicia could complete their journey in much less time, and at less expense, than those who took an overland route down through England and France, over the Pyrenees and across northern Spain. Indeed, it was not just pilgrims from Britain and Ireland who favoured the sea route by the fifteenth century. Those living on continental Europe with access to the Hanseatic ports on the North Sea coast often opted for a sea voyage in preference to the slower overland routes.[107]

In the decades before 1453, the wine trade between England and Bordeaux was significant, and Ireland's overseas trade followed a similar pattern involving Bordeaux and other ports on the French Atlantic seaboard.[108] However, after England lost control of Bordeaux in 1453, that trade shifted and the wine trade with France was largely replaced by trade with northern Spain and Portugal.[109] Some direct trade between Ireland and Bordeaux continued in the late fifteenth century, the route being dominated by Breton ships, and Bordeaux continued to be an important hub for international commerce and travel.[110] At no stage, however, would English or Irish merchants trading with north-west Spain have contemplated walking from Bordeaux, and it seems equally unlikely that medieval Irish pilgrims destined for Santiago would normally have done so. Sailing to Bordeaux in the first instance would not have been the preferred option for fifteenth-century pilgrims but those who opted for such a route would surely have sought an onward ship from there, destined for a Galician port such as Ferrol, A Coruña or Vigo.

105 R.W. Unger, *The ship in the medieval economy, 600–1600* (London, 1980), p. 214; Timothy O'Neill, *Merchants and mariners in medieval Ireland* (Dublin, 1987), p. 111; see also 'Gaelic lordships, Anglo-Norman merchants and late medieval mariners, AD 1100–1500' in Aidan O'Sullivan & Colin Breen, *Maritime Ireland* (Stroud, 2007), pp 159–98. 106 Wendy Childs, 'The perils, or otherwise, of maritime pilgrimage to Santiago de Compostela in the fifteenth century' in Stopford (ed.), *Pilgrimage explored*, pp 123–43, at pp 141–2. 107 Almazán (ed.), *Actas del II Congreso Internacional de Estudios Jacobeos*, i. 108 A.F. O'Brien, 'Commercial relations between Aquitaine and Ireland, *c*.1000 to *c*.1500' in Jean-Michel Picard (ed.), *Aquitaine and Ireland in the Middle Ages* (Dublin, 1995), pp 31–80. 109 Childs, 'The perils, or otherwise, of maritime pilgrimage', pp 136–9. 110 Jacques Bernard, 'The maritime intercourse between Bordeaux and Ireland, *c*.1450–*c*.1520', *Irish Economic and Social History*, 7 (1980), 7–21.

1.2 Caravel from Claes Visscher engraving.

The account of his journey to Santiago in 1456 given by an English cleric, William Wey, gives us a sense of what it was like to sail directly to Galicia on pilgrimage. William left his home in Eton (west of London) on 27 March 1456, arriving at Plymouth on 30 April, having completed a distance of about 300 km overland. Averaging less than 10 km a day, he must have sojourned at various religious houses along the way, though he says nothing of his route. There were many other ports on the south coast of England that would have been closer to his home; he must have heard that Plymouth would be the best option for a direct sailing to A Coruña. The ship he found at Plymouth finally sailed on 17 May. They went in convoy with five other ships, which was normal practice on long voyages. The other ships had originated at Bristol, Lymington, Portsmouth and Weymouth as well as Plymouth. The ship carrying William Wey reached A Coruña at noon on 21 May after barely five days at sea. William wasted no time there, because he arrived in Santiago on the eve of the feast of the Holy Trinity, which fell on 23 May in 1456. A mere day and a half had taken him from A Coruña to Santiago, a journey that must have been done on horseback.[111]

111 Davey, *William Wey: an English pilgrim*, pp 21–3.

1.3 Carrack from contemporary Flemish engraving.

The rise in popularity of the pilgrimage from Ireland at this time mirrored the expansion in the English pilgrimage to Santiago. The availability of larger ships, capable of long voyages along the Atlantic coast of Europe, made the journey between the British Isles and Galicia a potentially profitable one for ship owners in jubilee years when significant numbers of pilgrims were keen to travel. It has been suggested that this might be regarded as the first age of the overseas package

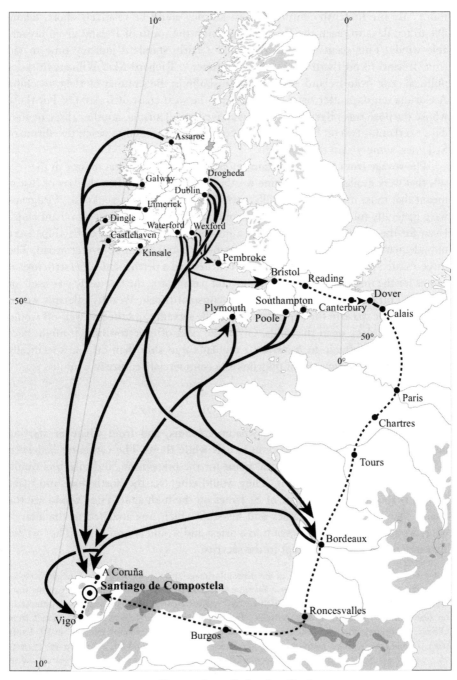

1.4 Routes from Ireland to Spain.

tour.[112] By the fifteenth century the sea journey could be relatively short, taking five to ten days to reach the Iberian coast from the south of Ireland given favourable winds. This seems to have remained a fairly standard journey time to sail from Ireland to northern Spain in the summer.[113] Richard Mac William Burke, a political exile from Ireland, sailed from Inisbofin in the summer of 1603, reaching A Coruña ten days after his departure from the west coast of Ireland.[114] For those whose purpose was pilgrimage, having arrived at A Coruña, another three or four days overland – two on horseback – was all that was needed to reach the shrine of St James, some 75 km to the south.

The voyage from Ireland to Spain can never have been a pleasant one in the vessels that were available. Even in fine weather the Atlantic swell on the Bay of Biscay meant that most unseasoned travellers would have suffered seasickness.[115] Pilgrims were generally tolerated rather than encouraged by the captains of merchant ships. Even for the wealthy it was probably a miserable expedition since the ships were not adequately fitted-out for passenger transport, and could be overcrowded. The three-masted ships used by the fifteenth century had a permanent superstructure of cabins for the master and the most important passengers; the forecastle was used for defence – pirates and enemy ships were a constant threat. Wealthy pilgrims would have opted for space in the superstructure while servants and the less well-off would have slept on deck or in the holds. Given the risks of overcrowding, it might have been more comfortable to travel on a regular cargo ship than on one specifically opting to carry large groups of pilgrims as a commercial venture in a jubilee year.[116]

AT THE SHRINE OF ST JAMES

Pilgrims arriving in Santiago, by whatever means, and from whatever starting point, would have shared in certain rituals while there. The cathedral had been designed and built to serve as focal point for the pilgrimage, and pilgrims would have been naturally drawn to it. They would enter via the north door and make their way to the wooden shrine of St James on the high altar. They would see the chains that had bound St James and his staff which was attached to the altar.[117] They would make their confession to a priest and would attend Mass. They would also seek to view the relics kept in the sacristy.

112 Childs, 'The perils, or otherwise, of maritime pilgrimage', pp 133–5.　113 Don Sinclair, personal communication, May 2017. The *Jeannie Johnston* sailing ship took six days to reach A Coruña from Dingle in May 2007; this was followed by three days' walking. See Pádraig Ó Fiannachta, 'Oilithireacht ón Daingean go Santiago de Compostella', *Irisleabhar Mha Nuad* (2007), 167–90.　114 Ciaran O'Scea, 'Irish emigration to Castille in the opening years of the seventeenth century' in P.J. Duffy (ed.), *To and from Ireland: planned migration schemes, c.1600–2000* (Dublin, 2004), pp 17–37, at p. 26.　115 Roger Stalley, 'Sailing to Santiago: medieval pilgrimage to Santiago de Compostela and its artistic influence in Ireland' in J. Bradley (ed.), *Settlement and society in medieval Ireland: studies presented to F.X. Martin* (Kilkenny, 1988), pp 397–430, at pp 402–3.　116 Childs, 'The perils, or otherwise, of maritime pilgrimage', pp 136–7.　117 Anthony Goodman, *Margery Kempe and her world* (London, 2002), p. 158.

The rituals to be followed during pilgrim visits to the shrine had been laid down in the cathedral statutes at the end of the thirteenth century. Jonathan Sumption has explained that

> After the morning Mass, the sacristan and another priest stood behind the shrine with rods in their hands and with these they would tap each pilgrim on the back or on the arms and legs. A third priest, wearing a surplice, invited them to make an offering, addressing each pilgrim in his own language. Pilgrims were then asked whether their offering was for St James, i.e. for alms for general purposes, in which case it was placed on the altar; or whether it was for the building fund, when it was placed on a side-table. This ceremony marked the moment at which the pilgrim 'received' his indulgence. Only cash or jewellery was accepted.[118]

The pilgrims would regard these monetary offerings as an intrinsic part of their prayers of intercession for whatever benefit they sought through their pilgrimage.[119] After the formalities had been completed some might take time to admire the sculptures in the Portico of Glory, and to pray in some of the many chapels within the cathedral. On leaving the cathedral, they would then be able to purchase souvenirs, including scallop shells, as evidence of their achievement. For those who had felt obliged to fulfil a vow by completing the pilgrimage, there was a sense of relief. Those motivated by curiosity and a sense of adventure might have enjoyed the sights at their destination, much as modern tourists do. In the longer term, most would have profited from the experience of seeing their lives from an altered perspective.

Few pilgrims would have remained in Santiago for much longer than was necessary to complete the prescribed rituals and obtain the indulgences they sought. In a jubilee year, there would have been pressure on accommodation, and they could rely on the hospitality provided by religious houses, innkeepers or local residents for just a short time. Pilgrims would certainly have rejoiced at reaching their intended destination and achieving the indulgences they had longed for as part of their personal quest for salvation. After a few days of rest and rejoicing, the long journey home still beckoned.

---

118 Sumption, *Pilgrimage*, p. 160.   119 For comparable pilgrim rituals at Canterbury, see Ben Nilson, 'The medieval experience at the shrine' in Stopford (ed.), *Pilgrimage explored*, pp 95–122.

2

Santiago de Compostela in context: the overseas pilgrimage tradition from Ireland

In the twelfth century Santiago de Compostela emerged as a pilgrimage destination that was an alternative to the older major Christian pilgrimages to Jerusalem and Rome. It would not have developed outside that wider pilgrimage context, and some insight into Irish participation in medieval pilgrimages to Jerusalem and Rome is important for an understanding of the devotional and cultural worlds of Irish pilgrims to Santiago. Late-medieval Irish enthusiasm for pilgrimage to Santiago de Compostela was not a new development but an expression of a deep-rooted understanding in Ireland of the value of the pilgrim experience, and the motives of those travelling to Santiago were much the same as those who went to Jerusalem or Rome.

PEREGRINATIO

The biblical idea of pilgrimage as voluntary exile in obedience to God was a familiar one in the early Christian world, not least in Ireland. Partly under Irish influence, a form of 'itinerant devotion' had developed within Western Christendom by the seventh century.[1] Stories of the lives of Irish saints who had gone into permanent exile in the early medieval period were common in late medieval Irish sources, and were probably used to illustrate homilies.[2] Christian *peregrinatio* in the early medieval Irish context involved the renunciation of the world, as the person became an 'exile of God' (*deorad Dé*).[3] The separation of the holy man from society allowed him take on a role as communicator of divine authority.[4] Among the first and best known such *peregrini* was St Columbanus (d. 615), who went on perpetual pilgrimage to Western Europe, establishing foundations at Luxeuil and elsewhere in Gaul before eventually settling at Bobbio, where an influential monastic house was established.[5]

Irish monks on the Continent provided some of the essential infrastructure that supported pilgrimage by establishing hostels at various key locations in the eighth century, including St-Omer, Péronne, Honau and St Gallen. Two of these

---

1 Tomasi, '"Homo viator"', p. 4.   2 Michael Maher, '*Peregrinatio pro Christo*: pilgrimage in the Irish tradition', *Milltown Studies*, 43 (1999), 5–39.   3 T.M. Charles-Edwards, 'The social background to Irish *peregrinatio*', *Celtica*, 11 (1976), 43–59, at 53.   4 Charles-Edwards, 'Social background', 58.   5 Aidan Breen, 'Columbanus' in *DIB*; Westley Follett, *Céli Dé in Ireland: monasatic writing and identity in the early Middle Ages* (Woodbridge, 2006), pp 46–9.

developed into major monastic sites, although their pilgrim hostels ceased to function in the ninth or tenth centuries, as attitudes towards pilgrimage changed.[6] In
the ninth century, Fintan (d. 878), an Irish pilgrim and hermit, went to Rome on
pilgrimage, visiting the monastery of St Martin of Tours in Gaul before continuing through Switzerland and Lombardy. On the return journey he remained in
Rheinau (Switzerland), first as a Benedictine monk and later as a hermit.[7] His
personal transformation from wandering pilgrim to monk and finally to hermit
reflected a change in attitudes to pilgrimage in ninth-century Europe where stability in a monastic setting was favoured over perpetual pilgrimage. The wandering
Irish monks or bishops of earlier centuries no longer found encouragement, but
extended overseas pilgrimage from Ireland continued in a different form in later
centuries to a range of destinations that eventually came to include Santiago.[8]

    Through stories of Irish saints such as Columbanus at Bobbio, or Colum Cille
at Iona, the idea of going on an extended pilgrimage continued to be part of the
tradition of medieval Irish spirituality.[9] Pilgrimages associated with Colum Cille,
at places such as Iona in Scotland and Glencolumcille in Donegal, came to be
focussed not on a shrine but on a wider sacred landscape of places associated with
the saint, the pilgrimage taking the form of a *turas*, journeying to, or making a
circuit of related sites.[10] In medieval stories of saints' lives, a common trope was
the saint's visit to Rome, sometimes with the acquisition of relics or papal gifts,
but always with enhanced authority as a result of the pilgrimage. At the same time,
long voyages to the Otherworld were a common narrative thread in the Irish literary tradition. There were similarities between the stories of wandering saints and
the secular voyage tales of medieval Irish literature, such that the two traditions
cannot be totally separated. The liminality associated with pilgrimage was a feature
of these tales also.[11] Among the best known secular stories were the travels to the
Otherworld as narrated in the voyage of Máel Dúin's boat (*Immram Curaig Maíle
Dúin*),[12] a story of conversion, or the voyage of Bran (*Immram Brain*) to the land of
women, an Otherworld journey through which the joys and sorrows of life could
be viewed in another dimension.[13] The story of the voyage of Bran was a product

6 Louis Gougaud, *Les chrétientés celtiques* (Paris, 1911), pp 166–74, cited in Sumption, *Pilgrimage*,
pp 198–9. 7 Louis Gougaud, *Gaelic pioneers of Christianity* (London, 1933), p. 32, note 2; Aidan
Breen, 'Fintan (d. 878)' in *DIB*. 8 Hughes, 'The changing theory and practice of Irish pilgrimage',
143–51; Harbison, *Pilgrimage in Ireland*, pp 33–6. 9 Jan Erik Rekdal, 'The Irish ideal of pilgrimage
as reflected in the tradition of Colum Cille (Columba)' in Ailbhe Ó Corráin (ed.), *Proceedings of the
third symposium of Societas Celtologica Nordica held in Oslo, 1–2 November 1991* (Uppsala, 1994), pp
67–83; Maher, '*Peregrinatio pro Christo*', 11–12. 10 Yeoman, *Pilgrimage in medieval Scotland*, p. 77.
11 Katya Ritari, *Pilgrimage to Heaven: eschatology and monastic spirituality in early medieval Ireland*
(Turnhout, 2016), pp 145–8. 12 H.P.A. Oskamp (ed. & trans.), *The voyage of Máel Dúin: a study
in early Irish voyage literature* (Groningen, 1970). 13 J.M. Wooding (ed.), *The Otherworld voyage in
early Irish literature* (Dublin, 2000); John & Caitlín Matthews, *The encyclopaedia of Celtic myth and
legend* (London, 2002), pp 113–50; Séamus Mac Mathúna, *Immram Brain: Bran's journey to the land of
the women* (Tubingen, 1985). Both of these tales were included in *Leabhar na hUidhre*, an Irish manuscript compiled before 1108 (RIA, MS 23 E 25).

of medieval Christian providential understanding of life and history as 'a meaning-less flow of contingencies, in which significance was attached to particulars only through reference to universal truths'.[14]

The allegory of the *Navigatio Brendani*, telling a story of the journey of St Brendan in search of an island of the Promised Land of the saints, shared aspects of the same Christian and literary tradition. Its theme was a spiritual one.[15] As Thomas O'Loughlin has explained, the intended audience was the monks in a monastery, and the story involved a circular journey, repeated each year for seven years, where 'the only destination actually mentioned is reached when those in the boat have learned to celebrate the perfect Liturgy of the Hours'.[16] There was no actual voyage, transatlantic or otherwise. The story was an allegory. Nonetheless, it has often been supposed that the detail of the sea journey in the voyage of St Brendan, in a small hide-covered boat, reflected the seagoing conditions of his age. It has even given rise to modern imitators on that basis.[17] However, in a recent discussion of the hagiographical literature, Jonathan Wooding suggests that the concept of the fragile boat was a metaphor used to emphasize the intensity of the penitential aspect of the journey undertaken by the saint. He argues that descriptions of boats found in devotional texts such as saints' Lives should be interpreted allegorically rather than being taken literally as evidence of the kind of boats used in real voyages.[18]

IRISH PILGRIMS TO JERUSALEM

The Irish idea of *peregrinatio* in the early church was an informal one. However, what evolved from this, in line with trends elsewhere in Europe, was a more struc-tured form of pilgrimage focussing on a number of particularly appealing sites. The exhortation by Christ to 'Take up your cross and follow me' (Matthew 10:8) was an invitation to live by Christian moral values, but could be interpreted by some as a literal invitation to follow in the physical footsteps of Christ in the Holy Land. Other biblical episodes involving temporary exile – the flight into Egypt or Jesus spending forty days in the desert – prompted comparisons between long

14 Mac Mathúna, *Immram Brain*, p. 240. 15 J.M. Wooding, 'Monastic voyaging and the *Navigatio*' in J.M. Wooding (ed.), *The Otherworld voyage in early Irish literature* (Dublin, 2000), pp 226–45; Harbison, *Pilgrimage in Ireland*, pp 37–43; Clara Strijbosch, *The seafaring saint: sources and analogues of the twelfth-century voyage of Saint Brendan* (Dublin, 2000). 16 Thomas O'Loughlin, *Journeys on the edges: the Celtic tradition* (London, 2000), pp 85, 91–7. 17 Tim Severin, *The Brendan voyage: across the Atlantic in a leather boat* (Dublin, 1978; reprint 2005). For a critique of Severin's dubi-ous interpretation of the medieval evidence, see J.J. O'Meara, 'In the wake of the saint: the Brendan voyage, an epic crossing of the Atlantic by leather boat' in Wooding (ed.), *The Otherworld voyage*, pp 109–12. 18 J.M. Wooding, 'St Brendan's boat: dead hides and the living sea in Columban and related hagiography' in J. Carey, M. Herbert & P. Ó Riain (eds), *Studies in Irish hagiography: saints and scholars* (Dublin, 2001), pp 77–92. For the more mundane journey of St Columbanus via Nantes, see Charles Doherty, 'Exchange and trade in early medieval Ireland', *JRSAI*, 110 (1980), 67–89, at 77.

pilgrimages and the life of Christ.[19] Unsurprisingly, given the challenging nature of the journey, evidence of medieval Irish participation in the pilgrimage to Jerusalem is relatively sparse. The story of St Mac Nise of Connor is a rare account of an Irish saint travelling to Jerusalem, Rome being the more common destination for Irish saints in medieval hagiography. The Latin Life of Mac Nise is preserved in the form of a liturgical office in the fourteenth-century *Codex Salmanticenis* (which probably had an Ulster origin), though the saint himself was depicted as a fifth-century contemporary of St Patrick.[20] We are told that Mac Nise visited the Holy Land and that while there he acquired relics of the stone of the Holy Sepulchre, the hair of the Virgin Mary, the bones of St Thomas the Apostle, vestments of the Apostles and a chalice from the altar at Jerusalem. Unfortunately for the church at Connor, the saint left these relics in Rome on his return journey.[21] This narrative of St Mac Nise indicates that its author and intended audience were familiar with the idea of the Holy Land as a suitable destination for devout Christians and as the authentic place in which to source Christian relics of special significance.

The medieval Irish annals contain some incidental references to prominent people from Ireland having undertaken pilgrimages to the Holy Land. The annals of Inisfallen record that Ua Cinn Fhaelad, king of the Déisí, went to Jerusalem in 1080.[22] Neither the details of his pilgrimage nor the nature of his entourage are recorded. One result of the expansion of crusading and pilgrimage activity was the greater availability of relics, such as fragments of the True Cross, after the siege and capture of Jerusalem by the Crusaders in 1099. Among the manifestations of that devotion in Ireland were the creation of reliquaries for fragments of the True Cross, such as the Cross of Cong, possibly commissioned at Tuam, Co. Galway, between 1123 and 1134. The Cistercian-founded Holy Cross abbey in Co. Tipperary (*c*.1180) developed into a major pilgrimage destination, focussed on its relic of the True Cross. Holy Cross abbey continued to attract pilgrims for centuries, ensuring that it was sufficiently wealthy to fund its rebuilding in the fifteenth century.[23]

The idea of a physical journey to walk in the footsteps of Christ in the Holy Land had undoubted appeal, and found expression in medieval Irish bardic poetry. Whether by choice or circumstance, Muireadhach Albanach Ó Dálaigh became a well-travelled pilgrim poet in the thirteenth century. He was living at Lissadell in Sligo in 1213, but he had to flee to Scotland for his own safety, having killed

19 Horton & Marie-Hélène Davies, *Holydays and holidays: the medieval pilgrimage to Compostela* (Lewisburg, 1982), pp 22–3. 20 Ó Riain, *Dictionary of Irish saints*, p. 419. 21 W.W. Heist (ed.), *Vitae sanctorum Hiberniae ex codice olim Salmanticensi nunc Bruxellensi* (Brussels, 1965), p. 405 (§5–6). 22 *A.Inisfallen*, p. 235. 23 Flanagan, *The transformation of the Irish church*, p. 224; Griffin Murray, *The Cross of Cong: a masterpiece of medieval Irish art* (Sallins, 2014); Bernadette Cunningham & Raymond Gillespie, 'Holy Cross abbey and the Counter-Reformation in Tipperary', *Tipperary Historical Journal*, [IV] (1991), 171–80; Aubrey Gwynn & R.N. Hadcock, *Medieval religious houses: Ireland* (Dublin, 1970), pp 134–5; for the relic collection at Christ Church cathedral, Dublin, see above p. 24.

a steward of Domhnall Ó Domhnaill.[24] From Scotland, it appears he visited the Continent and possibly the Holy Land. In a poem beginning *Déana mo theagasg, a Thrionóid* ('Do thou teach me, O Trinity') he portrayed pilgrimage as a form of repentance and a possible means to salvation:

> May I, sinful man, practise penance and austerity and pilgrimage, let me pour tears from my eyes seeking to possess my Creator thereby.

> *Go ndearnar aithrighe is fheadhbhdhacht*
> *Is oilithre gidh olc mé;*
> *Go léigear sileadh dom shúilibh*
> *ag sireadh ar nDúilimh dhé.*[25]

The poem indicated that he would leave his normal life and go away on pilgrimage to a warm and sunny place, but he understood that the experience would be transient in comparison to the ultimate goal of salvation:

> I will abandon the world and flee to the Creator, Maker of the sun; short-lived the pleasures of that land; I prefer my own true home [Heaven].

> *Tréigfead uile fhir an [domhain]*
> *Ar an Dúileamh ro dhealbh gréin;*
> *Ro-ghearr leam toradh an tíre*
> *Fear ar ndomhan fire féin.*[26]

The same poet composed another poem while on a journey 'far off across the wave-bordered Mediterranean sea' (*tar muir Torr(i)an tonnbruachaig*). When he wrote this poem beginning with the line *Fada in chabair a Cruacain* ('Help from Cruachain is far off'), the poet was near Monte Gargano on the east coast of Italy, probably early in the year 1224. He described himself as 'a palmer good at praising' (*Falmaire maith re moladh*), an indication that the journey was a pilgrimage.[27] Palms were a reminder of the triumphal entry of Jesus to Jerusalem as recounted in the Gospels, and the emblem was familiar to medieval pilgrims from the elaborate ritual of the blessing of the palms performed on the Sunday before Easter.[28] Pilgrims to Jerusalem brought home palms, or metal badges depicting palms, as

24 Lambert McKenna (ed. & trans.), *Aithdioghluim dána* (2 vols, London, 1935–40), i, p. xxxii. 25 McKenna (ed.), *Aithdioghluim dána*, poem 70, stanza 31. 26 Ibid., stanza 28. 27 Gerard Murphy, 'Two Irish poems written from the Mediterranean in the thirteenth century', *Éigse*, 7:2 (1953), 74–9, stanzas 1 & 18. The only known manuscript copy of this poem is in fragmentary form in British Library Add. MS 19,995, fol. 8, a fifteenth-century compilation preserved on scraps of vellum. 28 J. Wickham Legg (ed.), *The Sarum missal, edited from three early manuscripts* (Oxford, 1916), pp 92–8.

evidence of their pilgrimage. The poet expressed his longing to smell the air of Ireland, or to reach Scotland, which was then his home. The journey had been an extended one and not without tragedy. Four men had set out on the long voyage from the coast of Scotland, but the two younger ones had died on the way. The poem referred to a young Ó Conchobair who had died. This may well have been Aodh Ó Conchobair who, according to the annalists, died 'coming from Jerusalem and the River Jordan' in 1224.[29]

Muireadhach Albanach Ó Dálaigh's later poem, *Tomhais cia mise a Mhurchaidh* ('Guess who I am, O Murchadh'), reveals that the poet reached Ireland safely following his pilgrimage. This was a conventional praise poem, addressed to a descendant of Brian Bóramha, with incidental references to overseas adventures. The poet explained that he had come 'from over the bright-surfaced Mediterranean' (*Tar Muir dtaobhsholas dToirrian*), and that he was both 'a palmer and a poet' (*falmaire agus fear dána*). In the final stanza he indicated that he would return to Scotland but would visit Ireland again. Unfortunately this kind of praise poem was never intended as a travelogue and was not the place for him to offer a detailed account of his pilgrim travels.[30]

Another poem preserved in the same medieval manuscript is attributed to Giolla Brighde Albanach. It might have been composed on the outward leg of the voyage experienced by Muireadhach Albanach Ó Dálaigh, or on a similar voyage during the thirteenth century. The poem, *A ghilli gabhus an stiuir* ('Lad who takest the helm'), is set in the autumn, in bad weather in the eastern Mediterranean near Greece.[31] The journey is taking a long time and the seafarers have called at many havens. The poet is traumatized by the journey and unhappy with the helmsman (stanzas 1–2). He and his travelling companions have endured this seemingly unending voyage all autumn – not just for a few nights – and the poet has had enough of sailing (stanzas 8–10). He describes how their ship faced unfavourable easterly winds from the direction of Acre in Palestine. He does not know where they may land. He invokes St Brigid and also prays to Mary: 'my ship sails crosswise and obliquely ... may your intercession avail to set us straight' (*Fiar is tarrsna théid ma long ... do ghuidhe re dirgad dunn*) (stanza 6).

Yet another Irish poem, which may date from the thirteenth century, describes a long pilgrimage by sea:

We have come across three seas to the wave-furrowed Mediterranean Sea, having been put out from Ireland's shore ...

Tángamar tar thrí maraigh
Go Muir dToirrian dtonnchladhaigh
ó chuan Éireann ar n-athchur ...[32]

---

29 Murphy, 'Two Irish poems', stanzas 2; 9–11; *AFM*, iii, p. 215, *A.Conn*, p.7, *A.LCé*, 1224. 30 Bergin, *Irish bardic poetry*, poem 24, stanzas 5 & 7. 31 Murphy, 'Two Irish poems written from the Mediterranean'. 32 Poem edited from RIA, MS 23 D 14, pp 140–1 in Brian Ó Cuív, 'A pilgrim poem', *Éigse*, 13:2 (1970), 105–9, stanza 5.

The poet is not named, but the poem, *Do chros féin duit, a Dhúilimh* ('Thy own cross I offer to thee, O Creator'), survives in a seventeenth-century manuscript from Laois. Carrying a cross from his home, the poet has been away for two years, without meeting anyone from Ireland (stanza 2). In addition to the cross, he has other pilgrim possessions, including a *sclaimhín*, a pilgrim cloak. The use of this term in an Irish poem of the early thirteenth century suggests familiarity with the phenomenon of Continental pilgrimage, and the usual accoutrements that were the international pilgrim's recognized attire. That the poem was still being copied in the seventeenth century may indicate ongoing interest in the theme of overseas pilgrimage.

The Book of Uí Mhaine, a collection of literary and historical texts assembled in the late fourteenth century, preserves a poem on the infancy of Christ by a poet who asserted he was in the Holy Land at the time of writing. In the poem beginning with the line *Sa ráith-se rugadh Muire* ('In this dwelling Mary was born'), the poet offers no description of the pilgrimage journey, but asserts that he is present in the home place of the Virgin Mary.[33]

I give thanks to great Mary for the flagstone which was under the Virgin; the slope on which she trod is now touched by this wretched body.

Ad-lochar do Mhuire mhóir
An leac do bhí fán bhanóigh,
An stuagh-sa do bhí fá a bonn
An chlí thrugh-sa gá tadhall.[34]

Elsewhere, he observes 'On this bare flagstone beside us Christ was made flesh' (*Ar an leic luim-se láimh rinn / táinig Críost ina cholainn*) (stanza 5). When Brian Ó Cuív edited and translated this poem, he doubted that the poet had actually travelled to the site of Mary's home in Nazareth, Elizabeth's house in Judaea or any of the other holy places mentioned, and wondered whether the poet might have based his work on Gospel stories he had heard, pictures he had seen, or older poems in the Irish tradition.[35] Similar works consisting of meditations on the sacred sites of the Holy Land, as a form of spiritual pilgrimage, are found in other medieval literary traditions also.[36]

Goffraidh Ó Cléirigh, writing prior to the end of the fourteenth century, contemplated walking on the sacred soil of the Holy Land and deemed it a fitting place to die. His poem, *Dlighid iasacht a iodlacudh re athtarbha* ('To restore with interest the loan'), is also preserved in the Book of Uí Mhaine:

33 Brian Ó Cuív, 'A poem on the infancy of Christ', *Éigse*, 15:2 (1973), 93–102. The poem can be found at fol. 58 of the Book of Uí Mhaine (RIA, MS D ii 1).   34 Ó Cuív, 'A poem on the infancy of Christ', p. 101, stanza 31.   35 Ibid., pp 93–4.   36 Colin Morris, 'Pilgrimage to Jerusalem in the Middle Ages' in Morris & Roberts (eds), *Pilgrimage: the English experience from Becket to Bunyan*, pp 141–63, at pp 159–60.

May I in all observance prostrate myself in Solomon's Temple; may I be known as a pilgrim to that smooth-polished castle.

In reward for a journey to the Holy Land I should gladly receive Heaven from Him; woe to him who should wear a shoe there, for God is present on every sod I should tread on.

Teampall Solmha
go sléachtar ann go hoirichleach
cloch gan ghné ngairbh
go rob hé m'ainm a hoilithreach.
Tocht sa tír naoimh
Neamh uadha is air [do bhinnghéabhainn]
Mairg fa mbia bróg
Is Dia ar gach fhód dá [n-imdhéaghainn].

...

The stream (Jordan) of Jesus and John – may its waters wash me; may my soul be cleansed by that rapid winding stream.

May the road-hostelry of life beyond the grave await me in the fair City; may I, never returning home, have a tomb raised over me in the East.

May God who stands upon the sea, the shoal and the frozen water, cause no sad delay to the man who rides over the waves.

Sreabh Íosa is Eoin
A huisce go dtí tharumsa
Sruth cithmhear cas
Go nighthear as an t–anamsa.
Go dtí i bport fhionn
Na héigbheathadh riom ródbhruighean;
Gan teacht dom thoigh
Mo leacht gurab thoir tógbhuighear.
Marcach na dtonn
Ná tabhradh duine ar déarchairde
Dia ar muin mhara
Idir mhuir thana agus théachtfhairrge.[37]

Whether or not these poets ever ventured on the long journey east, it is evident that information about the special places of the Holy Land was available to them and to their audiences in medieval Ireland. The possibility of pilgrimage to such

---

37 McKenna (ed.), *Aithdioghluim dána*, poem 61, stanzas 13–14; 16–18.

places was real if remote, and people could have a sense of the spiritual value of the journey to such a holy place.

Aside from poets who might have contemplated or completed personal pilgrimages, some of the Gaelic political elite also embarked on journeys to the Holy Land. In the early thirteenth century, the Annals of Connacht record the death in 1231 of Ualgarc Ó Ruairc, king of Breifne, while on pilgrimage to the River Jordan. It seems he may have died on the outward journey.[38] Aodh Ó Conchobair, son of a former king of Connacht, died on his way home from Jerusalem and the River Jordan. His death was noted by chroniclers in 1224 because it was a significant event in the history of the province. Had he lived, he would have been among the contenders for the kingship of Connacht following the death of his grand-uncle, Cathal Crobderg Ó Conchobair, in the same year.[39] The reasons for Aodh Ó Conchobair's pilgrimage are not recorded – personal motivations were rarely mentioned in the annals. However, in theological terms, by the thirteenth century the concept of pilgrimage had become 'an extension of the sacrament of Penance',[40] and Aodh Ó Conchobair as a prominent member of the Gaelic elite could evidently afford the most public and elaborate form of repentance that money could buy. Thus, the explicit reference to the River Jordan is noteworthy. Bathing in the waters of the Jordan was the traditional concluding element of the pilgrimage rituals in the Holy Land. It symbolized purification from sin and rebirth in Christian life.[41] In the New Testament, it was recorded that John the Baptist preached on the banks of the Jordan, and that Jesus was baptized there (Matthew 3:13). In this way the place became associated with the attainment of purity and freedom from sin.[42] The specific reference to the river in these accounts of Irish pilgrims in the Holy Land suggests a spiritual motivation to do with repentance.

For those seeking redemption, the Holy Land was a particularly attractive, if difficult to reach, pilgrimage destination. Two Franciscan pilgrims from Ireland, Simon Semeonis (from Clonmel) and Hugo the Illuminator, undertook the journey in 1323, and one of them wrote an account of their Jerusalem pilgrimage. Being members of a religious order eased their journey; they could rely on a network of friaries to offer them shelter and sustenance. They first crossed the Irish Sea from Dublin, and subsequently the English Channel, before continuing overland as far as Venice, visiting shrines at Amiens, Paris, Padua and elsewhere on the way. From Venice they began a voyage that eventually took them to the major port of Alexandria in Egypt. From there they crossed the Sinai desert towards their destination.[43] It is not possible to know how many others from Ireland emulated their journey in the fourteenth century, but Simon's story is probably typical.

38 *A.Conn*, p. 43. **39** *AFM*, iii, p. 215, *A.Conn*, p. 7, *A.LCé*, i, pp 268–71. **40** Turner & Turner, *Image and pilgrimage in Christian culture*, p. 232. **41** A.H. Bredero, *Christendom and Christianity in the Middle Ages* (Grand Rapids, 1994), p. 99. **42** Cross & Livingstone (eds), *Oxford dictionary of the Christian church*, p. 900. **43** Malgorzata Krasnodebska-D'Aughton, 'Relics and riches: familiarizing the unknown in a fourteenth-century pilgrimage account from Ireland' in M. Boulton & J.

IRISH PILGRIMS TO ROME

While the Holy Land remained the pinnacle of Christian pilgrimage, at least at an aspirational level, difficulties of access, particularly during the Crusades, meant that places like Rome and Santiago prospered as alternatives. A predominantly overland route from Ireland to Rome was well established by the twelfth century. Early pilgrims from Ireland, travelling via southern England before crossing the English Channel, often disembarked on continental Europe at or near Wissant, a fishing village 20 km south-west of Calais, on the north coast of France. Such was the volume of traffic that a cemetery specifically for 'Scots, Irish and other pilgrims' was established at Wissant about 1177.[44] From there, pilgrims destined for Rome might have headed first for Paris and then southwards towards Lyon. Later in their journey, having reached the Italian peninsula, Irish pilgrims could have availed of hostels founded for them at Vercelli and Piacenza on the Via Francigena, while the monastery of Sancta Trinitas Scottorum in Rome was home to Irish monks who supported pilgrims arriving from Ireland in the twelfth century.[45] The monastic infrastructure was much altered in later centuries, but the Via Francigena remained a major routeway.

Deaths of Irish pilgrims in Rome are recorded with surprising frequency in the medieval Irish annals, particularly in the eleventh and twelfth centuries, and it seems that in many instances pilgrims set off when they were relatively old.[46] Céile, the abbot of Bangor (Bannagher), whose pilgrimage and death was recorded twice in the Annals of Ulster, for the years 928 and 929, died in Rome.

> Céile, comarb of Comgall, and Apostolic doctor of all Ireland, went into
>   pilgrimage.
> Thrice nine, nine hundred years, are reckoned by plain rules,
> Since the birth of Christ, a deed of fame, To the death of chaste
>   Céile-clerigh.

> *Ceile comarba Comgaill, et apostolicus doctor totius Hibernie do dul i*
>   *n-ailithri.*
> *Tri noi, noi ced do bliadnaib,*
> *Rimthir fo rialghlaibh reilibh,*
> *O gein Crist gnim cen den,*
> *Co bas caidh Ceili clerig.*[47]

Hawkes, with M. Herman (eds), *The art, literature and material culture of the medieval world* (Dublin, 2015), pp 111–24. For an edition of the narrative by Simon Semeonis, see Mario Esposito (ed. & trans.), *Itinerarium Symonis Semeonis ab Hibernia ad Terram Sanctam* (Dublin, 1960). **44** Flanagan, *Transformation of the Irish church*, p. 152. **45** Ibid., pp 230–1. **46** Harbison, *Pilgrimage in Ireland*, pp 29–31. **47** *AU*, i, pp 450–1.

Céile, comarb of Comgall, a scribe and anchorite, and Apostolic doctor of all Ireland, rested happily at Rome, on his pilgrimage, on the 18th of the Kalends of October, the 59th year of his age.

Céile comarba Comgaill, scriba et anchorita et apostolicus doctor totius Hibernie, lix° anno etatis sue, xviii°, die Kl Octimbris, in perigrinatione feliciter Romae quieuit.[48]

In the early seventeenth century, the Four Masters recorded the text of a poem composed by this tenth-century pilgrim abbot, as he set out on his journey to Rome. The poem equates the pilgrimage with entering a monastery so as to end one's days in a state of holiness: 'to remain under holy rule in one place'.

Time for me to prepare to pass from the shelter of a habitation,
To journey as a pilgrim over the surface of the noble, lively sea.
Time to depart from the snares of the flesh, with all its guilt,
Time now to ruminate how I may find the great son of Mary.
Time to seek virtue, to trample upon the will with sorrow,
Time to reject vices, and to renounce the Demon.
Time to reproach the body, for of its crime it is putrid,
Time to rest after we have reached the place wherein we may shed our
    tears.
Time to talk of the last day, to separate from familiar faces,
Time to dread the terrors of the tumults against the day of judgment.
Time to defy the clayey body, to reduce it to religious rule,
Time to barter the transitory things for the country of the King of
    Heaven.
Time to defy the ease of the little earthly world of a hundred pleasures,
Time to work at prayer, in adoration of the high King of angels.
But only a part of one year is wanting of my three score,
To remain under holy rule in one place it is time.

Mithigh damh-sa tairir do thriall o thoraibh teghlaigh,
do asccnamh imm ailither, tar tuinn mara muaidh menmnaigh.
Mithigh anadh d'inntladhadh collna co líon a caire,
    mithigh iaramh imradhadh co ro fríth Mac mór Maire.
Mithigh asccnamh sualach, saltradh for toil co treamhon,
    mithigh freiteach n-dualcha, agus derna fri deamhon.
Mithigh corp do chairiucchadh, daigh isa cion ron-brena,
    mithigh foss iar t-taiririudh airm i t-telccmís ar n-déra.

---

48 Ibid. His pilgrimage to Rome is also recorded in AFM, with the correct date of death, AD 927, as in the verse cited by the Ulster annalist.

Mithigh focuil tigh-láithi, terbhadh frí gnúisi gnátha,
  mithigh omhan indnaidhe treasa luain láithe brátha.
Mithigh lámh corp crédbhaidhe, costadh im chrábhaidh n-glinne,
  mithigh reic na n-earchraidhe ar thír na flatha finne.
Mithigh lámh fri turbhaidhe domhnain cé cétaibh caingen,
  mithigh grés fri h-irnaighe, icc adradh airdrigh aingeal.
Acht inge di aen-bliadhain, ní thesta dom trí fichtibh.
  Airisemh fo naomh-riaghail in nách maighin ba mithigh.[49]

In contemplating an extended pilgrimage, as his life drew to a close, Céile focussed on the idea of embarking on a spiritual journey and abandoning 'the little earthly world of a hundred pleasures'.

The phenomenon of pilgrimage to Rome features more frequently in Irish annals in the eleventh century. In 1026 Mael Ruanaid Ua Maíl Doraid, king of the North, went first to Clonfert and proceeded from there to Iona. He later went to Rome.[50] In the surviving account of this pilgrimage contained in the Annals of Inisfallen, Clonfert was explicitly associated with St Brendan, and Iona with St Colum Cille. Rome required no explanation or specific saintly association. Its status was understood, as was the fundamental idea of prolonged pilgrimage to places of special sanctity. When Cellach Ua Selbaig, coarb of Barre, who had also made a pilgrimage to Rome, died in 1036, he was described as the 'chief anchorite of Ireland', someone who separated themselves from society for reasons of spiritual devotion. Such a lifestyle, set apart from the Christian community but still within it, was seen as an extended form of spiritual pilgrimage.[51]

A different approach to pilgrimage was taken a few years later by Laidhcenn, son of Maelan Ua Leocain, lord of Gaileanga (in Meath), and his wife, the daughter of Gott Ó Maeleachlainn who travelled together on their pilgrimage to Rome in the mid-eleventh century. As elite members of society they had probably gone with an entourage of servants and protectors but, while they reached Irish shores on the return journey, they did not survive an illness they had contracted. The Annals of the Four Masters record that the family died in the east of Ireland on their return from Rome in 1051, but say nothing more of their pilgrimage.[52]

One particularly prominent pilgrim to Rome was Donnchadh Ó Briain, son of Munster king Brian Bóromha, who went on pilgrimage in 1063–4, and died there soon afterwards.[53] This pilgrimage was embarked on after his political career had ended, an example of a pilgrimage being undertaken late in life. The Annals of Clonmacnoise explained that he went to Rome

---

49 *AFM*, ii, pp 618–19. 50 *A.Inisfallen*, p. 193. 51 Ibid., p. 203; Colmán Ó Clabaigh, 'Anchorites in late medieval Ireland' in L. Herbert McAvoy, *Anchoritic traditions of medieval Europe* (Woodbridge, 2010), pp 153–77. 52 *AFM*, ii, p. 861. 53 *A.Inisfallen*, *s.a.* 1064, p. 223. For discussion of the historical context, see Aubrey Gwynn, 'Ireland and the Continent in the eleventh century', *Irish Historical Studies*, 8:31 (1953), 193–216.

to doe pennance because hee had a hand in the killing of his owen eld-
est brother Teige McBryan. Hee brought the Crowen of Ireland with him
thither, which remained with the popes until Pope Adrean gave the same to
King Henry the second that conquered Ireland. Donnough McBrian died
in pilgrimage in the abby of St Stephen the protomartyre.[54]

A Latin inscription in the church of Santo Stefano Rotundo in the south of Rome
records the death of this particularly prominent Irish pilgrim:

> Year of the Lord 1064. Donnchadh Ó Briain, king of Cashel and Thomond,
> son of Brian Bóromha king of all Ireland, is buried in this church.

> *Anno Domini MLXIIII Depositus est in hac ecclesia Donatus O Brienus,
> Casheli Thomondique Rex, Briani Borui Totius Hiberniae Monarchae Filius.*[55]

Perhaps 300 years later, his pilgrimage and death were the subject of a verse eulogy,
Dursan toisg Dhonnchaidh mheic Briain ('Alas the journey of Donnchadh son of
Brian') by a Clare poet, Cam Cluana Ó Duibhgeannáin:

> Alas the journey of Donnchadh son of Brian on his pilgrimage owing to its
> great sadness, it is sad that he did not return home, though it be good for
> his soul.

> *Dursan toisg Dhonnchaidh mheic Briain
> da oilithre da hairdchiaigh,
> ionnsa gan a theacht da thoigh,
> acht ciodh maith é da anmain.*[56]

This stanza indicated familiarity with the idea that a plenary indulgence could
be gained by one who died in Rome on pilgrimage. Such an indulgence was considered priceless for one on the threshold of death; it would free his soul from
Purgatory, allowing him entry into the heavenly kingdom.

> An exact half of Ireland – great the honour – Donnchadh had after Brian, so
> that he agreed to go across the sea for the sake of his pure soul.

> *Ceirtleath Éireann – mór an modh –
> D'éis Briain do bhí ag Donnchadh,*

---

54 *A.Clon*, p. 179. 55 The inscription was recorded in 1986 by Cardinal Tomás Ó Fiaich. See
Tomás Ó Fiaich, *Gaelscrínte san Eoraip* (Baile Átha Cliath, 1986), p. 170. 56 Meidhbhín Ní Urdail,
'A poem on the adventures abroad and death of Donnchadh son of Brian Bóraimhe', *ZCP*, 59 (2012),
169–99, at 180–1. The poet may be the person of that name who was killed in Dublin in 1394 (*AFM*,
iv, p. 733).

> Gur aontaigh sé dul tar muir
> Ar mhaith da anmain iodhain.[57]

His supporters tried to dissuade him from going on the onerous pilgrimage, but Donnchadh insisted, saying

> 'To wander around Peter's burial place, to be in it in its chief resting place: I would not abandon it one by one for the very fierce people of Ireland.'

> 'Dul timcheall reilge Peadair,
> bheith innte 'na hairdleabaidh:
> ni threigfinn í ceann i gceann
> ar shluagh iomthnúthach Éireann'.[58]

The poem combined the story of a pilgrim king with a supernatural interlude telling of his journey to and from the Otherworld, thereby presenting him as a typical hero of an Irish romantic tale. The poem is as much about the kingship of Ireland as it is about pilgrimage, but it illustrates that the spiritual significance of his death in Rome was understood. Donnchadh Ó Briain's death abroad was also alluded to in a poem about a Santiago pilgrim composed in 1428, indicating that the death of this prominent Irish king while on pilgrimage was still remembered in later centuries, and the pilgrimages to Rome and Santiago were linked in the poet's mind.[59]

While the Gaelic lords who went to Rome were probably there primarily as pilgrims, bishops were more regular visitors, often for reasons of ecclesiastical politics or administration. Newly appointed archbishops were expected to travel to receive the *pallium* directly from the pope.[60] Among the prominent ecclesiastics from Ireland who had visited Rome in the twelfth century was Imhar Ua hAedhagáin, who died in Rome in 1134. He built the church of SS Peter and Paul at Armagh,[61] and the church dedication recalled the Roman connection. A few years later his pupil, Malachy, who had been installed as archbishop of Armagh in 1134 but later opted to become bishop of Down, went to Rome in 1139. We know something of the route he took. Malachy travelled through England, where he visited York, before proceeding southwards through France. While there he stayed at Clairvaux and met St Bernard, who would later become his biographer. Malachy's primary business in Rome related to episcopal appointments rather than pilgrimage, but travelling to the shrine of St Peter was an intrinsic element of his journey. His second journey to the Continent, again via England, was in 1148, but he died at Clairvaux before he could reach Rome on that occasion.[62]

57 Ní Urdail, 'A poem on the adventures abroad', 180–1. 58 Ibid. 59 See below, p. 133. 60 A *pallium* was a band of white woollen material with six black crosses and symbolized the archbishop's power in his ecclesiastical province (Cross & Livingstone, *Oxford dictionary of the Christian church*, p. 1211). 61 *AFM*, ii, p. 1047. 62 Flanagan, *Transformation of the Irish church*, pp 121–3; Cross & Livingstone, *Oxford dictionary of the Christian church*, p. 1023.

There are many other recorded instances of bishops from Ireland making the journey to Rome to deal with ecclesiastical matters. Conor Mac Concoille, another Armagh ecclesiastic, died in Rome in 1175, having travelled 'to confer with the successor of St Peter'.[63] In 1247/8 Raighned, a Dominican who was appointed archbishop of Armagh, 'came from Rome, bringing with him a *pallium*, in which he said Mass at Armagh on the festival of SS Peter and Paul'.[64] His first visit to Rome was part of his appointment process, but he made at least two subsequent visits. He went on pilgrimage in 1251,[65] and then, in June 1253, he obtained a licence from the king to travel there again for five months to deal with the affairs of his church. He died in Rome in 1256.[66]

It was possible for many Irish bishops to attend the Fourth Lateran Council held in Rome in 1215.[67] Those who went included Donnchad Ua Lonngargáin, archbishop of Cashel, who died while in Rome, and Conchobar Ua hÉnna, bishop of Killaloe, who died in 1216 following his return.[68] In all of these annalistic records, death in Rome was incidental to the narrative. The presence of an Irish bishop in Rome was not considered unusual and the extent of ecclesiastical travel is certainly under-recorded in the largely secular annals. There are enough references to indicate that such journeys were feasible for anyone with the necessary resources and motivation. It remained, however, a hazardous undertaking. Malaria was among the diseases prevalent in medieval Rome that may have caused the deaths of some Irish visitors there, both clerical and lay. Some devout early medieval pilgrims may have perceived death in Rome or Jerusalem as the ultimate purpose of their journey, believing it brought them physically closer to the gates of paradise, but in the later medieval era those bishops and others who went to Rome on ecclesiastical business or on pilgrimage certainly hoped to return home alive.[69]

In the later Middle Ages, the granting of indulgences to the faithful who had completed specific pilgrimages was a powerful encouragement to undertake the journey. By 1450 the phenomenon of lay Irish pilgrimage to Rome had become particularly noteworthy in jubilee years. Even the first jubilee year of grace announced by Pope Boniface VIII in 1300 did not go unnoticed in Ireland. In an entry for that year the Annals of Connacht recorded that notification from Rome had been widely disseminated, though no Irish pilgrim was mentioned:

> A general proclamation came from Rome throughout Christendom in the time of Pope Boniface VIII. This proclamation comes every hundredth year and that year is called the Year of Grace. And a countless host from all the

63 *AFM*, iii, p. 23. 64 Ibid., p. 331. 65 Ibid., p. 341. 66 Ibid., including O'Donovan's notes. 67 P.J. Dunning, 'Irish representatives and Irish ecclesiastical affairs at the Fourth Lateran Council' in J.A. Watt, J.B. Morrall & F.X. Martin (eds), *Medieval studies presented to Aubrey Gwynn, SJ* (Dublin, 1961), pp 114–32. 68 *AFM*, iii, pp 184–5; for other medieval bishops of Killaloe and their officials in contact with Rome, see Aubrey Gwynn & D.F. Gleeson, *A history of the diocese of Killaloe* (Dublin, 1962), p. 515. 69 Norbert Ohler, *The medieval traveller* (Woodbridge, 2010), p. 184.

lands of Christendom went on pilgrimage to Rome in answer to this sum-
mons and there obtained remission of all their sins through this indulgence.

*Gairm cotchend do techt on Roim ind amsir Bonabatius Papa viii fan Cristaigecht
uli, 7 cecha cetmad bliada[i]n tig an gairm-sin 7 bliadain ratha a hainm-side, 7
sluag diarmide a hule tirib na Cristaidechta do dol fon gairm-sin da n-oilithri co
Roim 7 locad na n-uli peccad d'fagbail doib triasan rath-sin inti.*[70]

The 1300 jubilee does not appear to have been planned far in advance; rather it was
a response to a popular movement, with increased numbers of pilgrims arriving in
Rome from the beginning of the millennial year. That this was so is a reminder that
pilgrimages tend to take on a life of their own, beyond the control of ecclesiastical or
secular authorities. In February 1300 the pope announced a plenary indulgence for
all pilgrims to Rome in that year, offering 'the most full pardon of all their sins'.[71]
This was designed to promote Rome as the new Jerusalem. The popularity of Rome
had increased from the late thirteenth century following the loss of the Crusader
states including Jerusalem in 1244. Such fluctuations in the fortunes of the Roman
pilgrimage continued to be affected by the feasibility of access to Jerusalem.[72]

A jubilee year in Rome would probably happen only once in a medieval adult's
lifetime. In respect of the jubilee in 1450 the Annals of Lecan recorded that 'many
Irish went to Rome, to wit, Maguire King of Fermanagh, and O'Flanagan of
Tuaraha, et alii'.[73] Other annals record that Muircertach Ua Flannagáin, chief of
Tuath Ratha, died at Rome in the course of the 1450 pilgrimage.[74] The head of
the Fermanagh lordship mentioned in connection with that same jubilee year pilgrimage to Rome was Tomas Óg Mág Uidhir (d. 1480), also known for his two
pilgrimages to Santiago.[75] Among those others who went to Rome for that jubilee
year of 1450 was Nioclás Ua Flannagáin, a priest associated with the monastic
house at Devenish, in Fermanagh. He died in Rome.[76] William Mac Fheorais died
in 1451 on his way home from Rome after having been appointed to the arch-
bishopric of Tuam.[77] He had probably combined a jubilee-year pilgrimage with
a journey to receive the *pallium* from the pope. Yet another prominent pilgrim
who failed to return home was Cathal Rua Ó Conchobair, who died 'on the way
of Rome' in 1451.[78] The occasional penitential pilgrimage overseas continued also.
In 1491, we learn from the Annals of the Four Masters that Henry Dillon, son of
Hubert, committed patricide. The annalists recorded that Henry 'killed his own
father, Hubert, by the cast of a knife; in consequence of which he himself went
to Rome.' (*Hanri mac Hoiberd mic Semais Diolmhain do mharbhadh a athar feisin
Hoberd derchor do sgin 7 é fein do dol do chum na Romha as a los.*)[79]

70 *A.Conn*, pp 200–1. 71 D.J. Birch, *Pilgrimage to Rome in the Middle Ages: continuity and change*
(Woodbridge, 1998), pp 197–8. 72 Birch, *Pilgrimage to Rome*, p. 205. 73 *A.Lec*, p. 225. 'Tuaraha'
is Tuath Ratha, a territory in Fermanagh. See 'Index locorum', *AFM*, vii, p. 114. 74 *AFM*,
iv, p. 969. 75 See below, pp 133–42. 76 *AFM*, iv, p. 967. 77 Ibid., p. 971. 78 *A.Lec*, p.
230. 79 *AFM*, iv, pp 1188–9.

CONCLUSION

There is a wealth of early evidence to show that there was a long tradition of overseas pilgrimage from Ireland to Europe and the Near East before and after the shrine of St James in Galicia became widely known in the twelfth century. Jerusalem and Rome continued to be attainable, if challenging, destinations and journeys to Rome became increasingly routine after 1300. Both ecclesiastical and lay pilgrims from Ireland are known to have reached Rome and Jerusalem long before that, but overall numbers making such journeys were probably very low. The next chapter will explore why Santiago de Compostela developed as an alternative to Rome and Jerusalem within the medieval Christian world, and how the Irish came to know about it.

3

The image of Santiago de Compostela

For those who engaged in it, the act of pilgrimage was not a rash act but a supremely rational one. It was based on an understanding of the economy of salvation that was both pragmatic and profound. The idea that a practical initiative involving a journey to a sacred place, however physically challenging, could transform one's life forever in the hereafter was inherently attractive, despite the known dangers of travel to distant places. Many deemed it worth the considerable effort involved. Overseas pilgrimage was the subject of careful planning and preparation. Those wishing to invest time and money in salvation through pilgrimage wanted to choose the best option. This could only be done by assembling as much information as possible not only to plan the logistics of the journey but to weigh up the advantages of different pilgrimage destinations. Information came in many forms: sermons about the saint whose shrine it was, stories from returned pilgrims who had already made the journey, and to a much lesser extent (if at all) from written sources. In a society with minimal literacy, personal reports of travel, and information supplied by merchants who were regular visitors to distant places, were probably far more influential that any written texts.

ST JAMES IN THE BIBLE

Perhaps the most common way of learning about the traditions associated with Santiago de Compostela was through stories about St James the Great. Those stories circulated both in oral and written forms and around them were built other elements of the narrative. It was difficult to avoid St James. As one of Christ's Apostles he featured both in the liturgy and in more informal devotional contexts. Most of what could be reliably found out about the life of the saint was contained in the New Testament.

The Apostle, James the Great, was elder brother of John the Evangelist, reputed author of the Fourth Gospel. They were both sons of Zebedee. According to Mark's Gospel, when Christ chose the twelve Apostles, he named James and his brother John *Boanerges* or 'Sons of Thunder' (Mark 3:17), possibly because of their tempestuousness. Several instances were recorded of the brothers being overzealous. When messengers were making preparations for Jesus on the road to Jerusalem they were not welcomed in a Samaritan village. James and John asked, 'Lord, do you want us to call down fire from Heaven to burn them up?' (Luke

9:53–56), but he rebuked them for this.[1] They continued the journey through a different village. On another occasion, as recorded in Mark's Gospel, James and John requested the special favour of Jesus that they would be on either side of him in Heaven. He replied, 'The cup that I must drink you shall drink, and with the baptism with which I must be baptized you shall be baptized, but as for seats at my right hand or my left, they are not mine to grant; they belong to those to whom they have been allotted' (Mark 10:37–40). Jesus then gathered the Apostles together and explained:

> You know that among the pagans their so-called rulers lord it over them, and their great men make their authority felt. This is not to happen among you. No; anyone who wants to become great among you must be your servant, and anyone who wants to be first among you must be slave to all. (Mark 10:42–43)

The Gospel of St Mark recorded that James and his brother John, along with Peter, were the only people permitted to be present at the miracle of the raising of the daughter of Jairus (Mark 5:35–43). The same three Apostles witnessed the Transfiguration (Mark 9:2–13) and they also accompanied Jesus in the garden of Gethsemane (Matthew 26:37), shortly before his betrayal and crucifixion. The thirteenth-century poet, Muireadhach Albanach Ó Dálaigh, in a devotional poem addressed to the Virgin Mary, while contemplating the three Marys, made the connection between the mother of Jesus and the mother of the Apostles James and John.

> The mother of James was one of these women, she got a protection from every trial; One of them was Mary the mother of John, tidings which nobody has made known in poetry.

> *Máthair Iacóibh inghean díbh,*
> *Sgiathdóigh ar gach n-imneadh fhuair,*
> *Bean díobh Muire máthair Eóin,*
> *Sgeóil nár ghnáthaigh duine i nduain.*[2]

For an Irish audience the idea expressed in the poem would have enhanced the status of James, making him a cousin of Christ and therefore a uniquely powerful intercessor.

James was martyred in AD 44, the first Apostle to die for their Christian faith (Acts 12:1–2). However, there is no intimation in the Bible that James the Great preached in Spain before his martyrdom. On the contrary, Romans 15 expressly

---

1 Biblical quotations are from *The Jerusalem Bible: popular edition* (London, 1974). 2 Osborn Bergin, *Irish bardic poetry* (Dublin, 1970), poem 21, stanza 8.

mentioned Paul's intention of going to preach in Spain, explaining that no one had yet done so (Romans 15:20–21; 28). This is reinforced by an early Christian tradition that the Apostles did not leave Jerusalem until after the death of James the Great.[3] Despite this, by the seventh century people in northern Spain began to tell stories of St James having preached in Spain. The narrative was elaborated and embellished in later centuries. By the tenth century, a Spanish tradition claimed that not only had James preached in Spain but that after his martyrdom in AD 44, the body of St James had been miraculously translated to Spain. This tradition eventually came to form the core of the story of the shrine of Santiago de Compostela.

Some, such as a well-travelled German pilgrim Arnold von Harff in the 1490s, doubted whether the body of St James was in Santiago, and he was equally sceptical of some claims made about relics at other shrines.[4] There was certainly scope for confusion about St James since the abbey of St Denis in Paris had the arm of St James mounted in a crystal-and-gold reliquary in 1122, his hand was reputed to be in Reading Abbey in England from the 1130s, and in the 1320s a Franciscan pilgrim from Ireland who visited Jerusalem was told that the head of St James, son of Zebedee, was in the Armenian church on Mount Sion.[5] The Armenian custodians still retain that relic for veneration, alongside relics of St James the Less.[6]

Although the New Testament was not available in print in the Irish vernacular before the seventeenth century, James's status ensured that he featured in liturgical and devotional works. The ninth-century Irish martyrology known as the *Félire Oengusso* included the Passion of James, brother of John, at 25 July, and made reference to the translation of the body of St James to Spain.[7] More routinely, sermons on aspects of the life of Jesus, in which the Apostles figured, were probably commonplace. The leading Apostles, Peter, James and John, could have featured prominently in such sermons. Thus, the account of the Transfiguration and the story of Jesus and his sleeping companions in the Garden of Gethsemane were probably reasonably well known in medieval Ireland, and James had been an eye-witness at each of those events.

Connections between St James and Ireland were probably being made as early as the twelfth century as the Irish church appropriated the Apostle for its canon of saints. A text on the Irish saints preserved in the Book of Leinster, compiled in Co.

---

3 Cross & Livingstone (eds), *Oxford dictionary of the Christian church*, p. 857. 4 Sumption, *Pilgrimage*, pp 195–6, 216, 291. 5 Esposito (ed.), *Itinerarium Symonis Semeonis ab Hybernia*, pp 109–11. 6 Tom Bissell, *Apostle: travels among the tombs of the twelve* (London, 2016), pp 100–1. 7 William Stokes (ed.), *Félire Óengusso Céli Dé: the martyrology of Oengus the Culdee*, Henry Bradshaw Society, 29 (London, 1905), pp 171–2; John Hennig, 'Studies in the Latin texts of the Martyrology of Tallaght, of *Félire Oengusso* and of *Félire hUi Gormain*', *Proc. RIA*, 69C4 (1970), 45–112, at 67; the same feast would also have been included in the Martyrology of Tallaght, even though it is now missing from the surviving manuscripts (ibid., 82). For the surviving manuscripts, see Donnchadh Ó Corráin (ed.), *Clavis Litterarum Hibernensium: medieval Irish books and texts (c.400–c.1600)* (3 vols, Turnhout, 2017), i, pp 353–5.

Laois in the mid-twelfth century, linked various Irish saints with specific Apostles and fathers of the church. Two prominent Irish saints, Comgall of Bangor and Finnian of Movilla (both associated with east Ulster), were linked with the Apostle James.[8] James was named in the context of all the other Apostles, and it seems that Finnian was being linked with James the Great, with Comgall being associated with James the Less. There is no implied connection to the shrine at Santiago de Compostela in this source.

SERMONS ON THE FEAST OF ST JAMES

One route towards understanding what Christian communities in Ireland may have known about St James is through the sermons they would have heard preached on his feast day, 25 July. In the liturgical calendar, 25 July was a holy day on which a fast was to be observed on the eve of the feast, and attendance at a church liturgy was expected on the feast day itself. A compilation of sermons known as the *Festial* of John Mirk, an English Augustinian canon, was in use among the Anglo-Irish clerical community in late medieval Ireland. The work was composed *c*.1382–90, and a mid fifteenth-century copy from Ireland survives in Trinity College, Dublin, MS 201.[9] Mirk's *Festial* owed its popularity to the range of vivid and sometimes sensational moral tales (*exempla*) it contained. These stories were designed to enliven sermons and make the preacher's words more memorable. John Mirk's compilation included a sermon for the feast of St James the Apostle.

The account of the life of St James in Mirk's *Festial* began with some genealogical information, noting that James was son of Mary's sister, and was a brother of John the Evangelist. He was sent into Spain 'by ordnance of all the Apostles' to preach God's word. However, he only managed to convert nine people, seven of whom he brought back to the Holy Land, leaving just two to preach in Spain. Next came a tale of a contest between good and evil back in Judaea with James pitted against Hermogenes and Philetus. Eventually James converted his opponents to Christianity before he was put to death by King Herod. After James's death, the ship containing his body was guided to Spain. The sermon then told of strange encounters with a wicked king and Queen Lupa, a she-wolf, and gave a lively if far-fetched account of James in Spain and of the miracles worked there. The miracle stories included the protection of individuals recognizable as pilgrims from their scrip and their staff.[10]

---

8 Pádraig Ó Riain (ed.), *Corpus genealogiarum sanctorum Hiberniae* (Dublin, 1985), pp 160–1.   9 This manuscript, in English, appears to have been owned by Thomas Norreys, a chaplain or warden of the Guild of St Anne in Dublin. Like John Mirk, Norreys may have been an Augustinian canon. See Alan J. Fletcher, 'Preaching in late-medieval Ireland: the English and the Latin tradition' in A.J. Fletcher & R. Gillespie (eds), *Irish preaching, 700–1700* (Dublin, 2001), pp 56–80, at pp 73–4.   10 Susan Powell (ed.), *John Mirk's Festial: edited from British Library MS Cotton Claudius A.II.*, EETS original ser., 335 (2 vols, Oxford, 2011), ii, pp 189–93.

There is a strong similarity between the stories of St James told in Mirk's *Festial* and those found in James of Voragine's Golden Legend (*Legenda aurea*). Indeed, John Mirk's work could be described as an abridged version of the *Legenda aurea*, omitting most of the later Spanish elements of the narrative of St James that might have seemed too unfamiliar for an Irish or English audience. The late thirteenth-century compilation of saints' Lives that became known as the *Legenda aurea* was the work of James of Voragine (*c*.1229–98), a Dominican archbishop of Genoa on the Mediterranean coast. It was intended as an orthodox work, containing stories of the saints venerated in the church in the course of the liturgical year. The *Legenda aurea* was translated into almost every Western European language and it is said that it was more widely read than the Bible in the Middle Ages.[11] While no full Irish-language translation is known to survive, the small fragment of the Irish Life of Pilate in Oxford, Bodleian Library, MS Rawlinson B 513, fol. 13b, an Offaly manuscript dated to the last quarter of the fifteenth century, may be a remnant of a full Irish translation of that work.[12] A Latin version of the story of Pilate was contained in chapter 53 of the *Legenda aurea* on the Lord's Passion. Another version of the same story occurs in the compilation of hagiographical and devotional tracts in the early sixteenth-century manuscript known as *Leabhar Chlainne Suibhne* (Book of the MacSweeneys).[13] This Irish translation was probably based on an English rather than a Latin version.[14]

The *Legenda aurea* narrative of the life of St James the Great had a particular focus on the Spanish dimension. Having recounted aspects of the life of St James that were partly biblical, it then proceeded to tell stories of various pilgrims who had encountered St James in different guises. James of Voragine drew these stories from a range of written sources, not least the *Codex Calixtinus*, the pre-eminent collection of medieval propaganda about the shrine of St James in Galicia. The stories usually contained an element of miraculous assistance provided to individual pilgrims by St James in the form of provision of food or even a donkey for transport as they made their way to Compostela.[15]

The kind of moral tale recounted in the *Legenda aurea* included this one of St James lending a donkey to a struggling pilgrim:

Pope Calixtus tells us that about the year 1000, a certain Frenchman set out with his wife and children to go to the tomb of Saint James, partly to escape

11 Jacobus de Voragine, *The Golden Legend: readings on the saints*, trans. W.G. Ryan (2 vols, Princeton, NJ, 1993), i, pp xiii–xiv.   12 Gearóid Mac Niocaill, 'Dhá leagan de scéal Phíoláit', *Celtica*, 7 (1966), 207–13. The suggestion that the Rawlinson fragment might be a portion of a complete translation is found in *Cat. Ire. MSS in BL*, ii, p. 553; for the date of the manuscript, see Brian Ó Cuív, *Catalogue of Irish manuscripts in the Bodleian Library at Oxford* (2 vols, Dublin, 2001), i, pp 255–60.   13 *Leabhar Chlainne Suibhne* (RIA, MS 24 P 25), fol. 64v contains a story of how Veronica procured the death of Pontius Pilate.   14 Mac Niocall, 'Dhá leagan de scéal Phíoláit', 205.   15 Jacobus de Voragine, *Golden Legend*, trans. Ryan, ii, pp 3–10.

the plague that was raging in France, but also out of a pious wish to visit the saint. When they reached the city of Pamplona, his wife died, and the inn-keeper stole all his money and even the ass his children rode on. Grieving for his lost wife he continued his journey, carrying some of his children on his shoulders and leading the others by the hand. A man came along leading an ass, was moved to compassion by the pilgrim's plight, and lent him the beast to carry the children. When he came to the shrine of Saint James and was watching and praying beside the Apostle's tomb, the saint appeared to him and asked whether he recognised him. The man said no, and the saint said: 'I am the Apostle James, who lent you my beast on your way here, and now I lend it to you for the return journey; but you should know in advance that the innkeeper will fall off the roof and die, and all he stole from you will be returned to you!' Everything happened as the saint had foretold. The man got home safe and happy, and when he lifted his children from the ass's back, the animal vanished.[16]

The idea being conveyed through such stories was that those who showed devotion to St James would be protected and rewarded by him, while those who behaved unfairly towards pilgrims would be punished. Pilgrims to the shrine would have heard stories such as these. When embarking on their journey they are likely to have cultivated their devotion to St James, as guide and protector of pilgrims.

One other source of Irish material on St James that some preachers in medieval Ireland had available is the *Liber exemplorum* now in Durham University Library.[17] This book of moral tales – intended as a handbook for preachers – was the work of an English Franciscan friar working in Ireland in the thirteenth century. St James featured in a story about the miraculous protection the saint would offer virtuous pilgrims, a story the narrator explained had been obtained from eyewitnesses.

A pilgrim going to pray at the shrine of St James had stopped in the same place. As is the custom of travellers, he got up in the night, before dawn, and went from the village into the wood nearby. There, as sometimes hap-pens, he by mischance lost his companions and began to stray from the path. And when he had gone some way, he met a man of august bearing and countenance; when asked who he was and where he came from, he told him his name, the place that he came from and the reason for his journey. The stranger claimed that he was St James, to whom the man was going, and that he already knew all about him. Then he praised the man's devo-tion as if truly pleased that they met, commended his pious intentions and said that a great prize had been prepared from him and that his reward was not far away. Then, with words which assailed the man from all sides, he

16 Jacobus de Voragine, *Golden Legend*, trans. Ryan, ii, pp 8–9.   17 Durham University Library, MS Cosin B.IV.19, dates from the mid-fourteenth century, and is based on a source dated *c*.1275.

eventually described the miseries and sorrows of this life, how everything we love in this life is short-lived and in like fashion how all things which we fear or cause us pain pass without delay. Meanwhile, with what seemed like reasonable arguments of this sort, he gradually began to plant a contempt for life in the mind of the man, who suspected nothing untoward, and to remove his fear of death. In the end, he said that no virtue would help the man, that instead he should hasten from this life and, if he could find no other route, that he should take his own life, for he should not allow himself to be long detained among these sorrows but that he should hasten to the joy prepared for him. What more? Tricked, he gives his assent to the deceiver's arguments, seizes his sword and cuts his own throat. His companions, who had looked everywhere for him, eventually find his dead body. The corpse is carried to the village that they had left. And, because the man with whom they had stayed that night seemed to know something about this kind of crime, they falsely accuse him and demand that he pays the penalty. The man saw that his innocence was impugned without cause and begged with all his heart for divine aid, when behold the man who had been dead suddenly arose and, to the amazement of everyone present, showed that the man was innocent. He told them how he had been led down to Hell by the same evil angel who had persuaded him to take his life; but on the way they met a man of radiant countenance and he said that he was St James. The saint snatched him away up to Heaven and led him to the throne of the Supreme Judge and there, pouring out prayers on his behalf, secured his restoration to life.[18]

The same collection of moral tales included one set in Ireland, composed to illustrate the efficacy of relics when used by virtuous people.[19] Given the use of an Irish setting in part of this handbook it seems likely that the story of St James as protector and encourager of pilgrims was also used by preachers active in Ireland.

PASSION OF ST JAMES

The evidence of these sermons and *exempla* demonstrates that the residents of Anglo-Norman Ireland would have heard of St James, whereas the evidence from Gaelic regions is less clear. As an Apostle, James certainly attracted some attention from the learned orders of Gaelic Ireland, but without any indication of a link with the shrine at Santiago de Compostela. For example, a late medieval Irish-language version of the story of the sufferings of St James is preserved in the *Leabhar Breac*,[20] an early fifteenth-century Irish manuscript miscellany. The

18 Translated from the *Liber Exemplorum* in Jones (ed.), *Friars' tales*, pp 62–3. 19 Jones (ed.), *Friars' tales*, pp 126–7. 20 *Leabhar Breac* (Speckled Book) is now RIA, MS 23 P 16.

Leabhar Breac is a compilation of predominantly religious material, penned by Murchadh Riabach Ó Cuindlis in north Tipperary. It includes biblical and other devotional texts translated from Latin. There are stories of the lives of prominent saints, as well as litanies and martyrologies. Also included in the manuscript are Irish-language versions of some secular tales of Continental origin.[21] The *Leabhar Breac* preserves one of the rare examples of the Passion of St James in the Irish manuscript tradition, but it is not evidence of a particular Irish cult of St James associated with the pilgrimage to his shrine in Galicia. It merely indicates a general awareness of the story of the Apostle, James the Great. Among the other non-Irish saints who feature in the same section of the *Leabhar Breac* are Apostles Peter and Paul, Andrew and Philip. The passions of Stephen, Marcellinus and Longinus are also included.[22] The passions of the Apostles are preceded by an account of the Passion of Christ and homilies on Good Friday and on the Resurrection.[23] The apostolic narratives are followed by a short tract on the pedigrees and manners of death of the Apostles.[24] Thus, the selection and arrangement of texts in the *Leabhar Breac* is such that James is presented simply as a prominent Apostle, and the idea of a particular cult associated with St James in Spain does not feature.

Another version of this text is found in a collection of devotional prose texts assembled by scribe Tadg Ua Rigbardáin in 1473, and may have been owned by the Mac Aodhagáin family of Redwood Castle, Co. Tipperary.[25] The same scribe was also responsible for two other devotional compilations, comprising homilies, monastic rules and the Irish version of the *Meditationes Vitae Christi*.[26] In Ua Rigbardáin's copy of the Passion of James son of Zebedee, the text is preceded by a similar narrative of the persecution of Peter and Paul, and is followed by the Passion of St Andrew.[27] It would seem from the way St James features in Irish collections of devotional texts in the fifteenth century that the Apostle awakened little special interest. His feast was dutifully recorded in the Irish martyrologies, together with those of other major Christian saints. He was sometimes described as 'brother of John' to distinguish him from the other Apostle, James the Less, without further elaboration.[28] Where the Passion of St James is recorded in Irish sources it is in the context of the passions of other Apostles. No prose Life of St

---

21 For a detailed listing of the contents see *Cat. Ire. MSS in RIA*, pp 3379–404. 22 *Cat. Ire. MSS in RIA*, pp 3395–400; RIA, MS 23 P 16, fols 172v–179v. 23 RIA, MS 23 P 16, fols 160v–172. 24 Ibid., fol. 180v. 25 RIA, MS 24 P 1; Westley Follett, 'Religious texts in the Mac Aodhagáin library in Lower Ormond', *Peritia* 25 (2014), 213–29. 26 RIA, MSS 3 B 22, 3 B 23. 27 Robert Atkinson, *The passions and the homilies from Leabhar Breac*, Todd Lecture Series, 2 (Dublin, 1887), pp 106–10; the text is found in *Leabhar Breac*, pp 177–8 and RIA, MS 24 P 1, pp 66–70. For other copies, see Charles Plummer (ed.), *Miscellanea hagiographica Hibernica* (Brussels, 1925), p. 256; *Cat. Ire. MSS in RIA*, pp 1264, 3367 & 3399; for the scholarly context in which many of these manuscripts circulated, see Follett, 'Religious texts in the Mac Aodhagáin library', 213–29. 28 Pádraig Ó Riain (ed.), *Four Irish martyrologies: Drummond, Turin, Cashel, York* (London, 2002), p. 81, 152, 193. (His feast is not included in the Martyrology of Cashel.)

James survives in Irish in the medieval manuscript tradition, whether translated from another source or as an original composition.[29]

ST JAMES IN BARDIC POETRY

Just as St James has left a very weak footprint in Irish hagiographical literature, the saint and his Galician shrine was scarcely noticed by the bardic poets.[30] One of the few references to north-west Spain comes in the work of a fifteenth-century poet who had almost certainly been to Santiago, Domhnall Ó hUiginn, son of Brian, who was a member of a Connacht poetic family and was described as head of an Irish school of poetry at the time of his death in 1501/2. Ó hUiginn spent time in Scotland and his sole surviving poem was in praise of Eoin Mac Domhnaill, Lord of the Isles. In the poem, *Meisde nach éadmhar Éire* ('Alas that Ireland is not envious'), the poet sought to entice the Lord of the Isles to extend his interest to Ireland. He claimed that Scotland owed its origins to the Gaeil, and he dismissed the geographical distance separating them, claiming there was not a day's journey by sea between them (stanza 13). The poet drew an analogy between the Gaeil discovering Scotland – having seen it from a high vantage point in their own land – and the earlier discovery of Ireland from Spain. Here, Ó hUiginn was recalling the origin myth linking Ireland with Spain that would have been well known to him from *Leabhar Gabhála Éireann* (Book of Invasions of Ireland). It recounted that the sons of Míl, from whom the Gaeil were descended, had seen Ireland from Breóghan's Tower, a Roman lighthouse on a prominent headland at A Coruña on the north coast of Galicia, a theme taken up in other historical contexts.[31]

> From the top of Breóghan's Tower (famous is its omen) a man sees an island like a ship from beyond the clouds.

> *Do Thur Bhreógain (bladh dá shéan)*
> *samhail éanluinge d'oiléan,*
> *an fear do bhí i mbarr an tuir*
> *do-chí a-nall idir néallaibh.*
> ...

> Just as Ireland's location was originally discovered from Breóghan's Tower in the eastern land, we in turn, spotted Scotland from Ireland's heights.

> *Mar fríoth a hiúl san tír thoir,*
> *Éire ar tús do Thur Bhreóghain;*

---

29 For a list of the surviving Irish Lives and Passions of non-Irish saints, see Plummer (ed.), *Miscellanea hagiographica Hibernica*, pp 254–71. **30** Bardic poetry database: www.bardic.celt.dias.ie, accessed 17 May 2017. **31** See below, pp 78–82. This Roman lighthouse is known locally as Torre de Hercules.

iúl ar Albain do-uair sionn
ar n-uair a hardaibh Éireann.[32]

The link with Spain was more than just a legend for Domhnall Ó hUiginn. His poem has many echoes of his experience of sea travel, of venturing to new lands and seeing distant places. The renowned Roman tower at A Coruña seems to have left a lasting impression, but curiously Ó hUiginn failed to mention the shrine at Santiago.[33]

In contrast, there is more direct evidence of the Santiago pilgrimage in Welsh poetry of the same period. In the fourteenth century, Gruffudd Gryg composed a poem to the moon, inspired by his voyage to Santiago,[34] while Robin Ddu of Anglesey addressed a poem to the ship in which he would go on pilgrimage in a jubilee year.[35] The fifteenth-century poet Ieuan ap Rhydderch, when describing the enthusiastic use of incense at the cathedral of St Davids in south-west Wales, compared it to the cathedral at Santiago de Compostela, a comment most likely made by one who had been to Santiago. The same poet also sought to rank St Davids in comparison to Jerusalem and Rome, saying that three pilgrimages to St Davids was equivalent to one to Jerusalem, while two pilgrimages to St Davids was as good as one to Rome.[36] A fifteenth-century Welsh poet, Lewis Glyn Cothi (*c.*1420–89), described the ship that brought a Welsh pilgrim, Elliw of Glyn Aeron, from Santiago to Pembroke, from where she would board another ship to take her home to Cardiganshire.[37] This is one of several poems that reflect on the jour-ney rather than the spiritual purpose of pilgrimage. The same poet recorded the journey of Dafydd ap John of Gower who had gone to Rome to obtain parchment indulgences for others. The poet wished for Dafydd's safe return as he crossed

---

32 M.B. Ó Mainnín, 'Dán molta ar Éoin Mac Domhnaill, "tiarna na nOilean" (+1503)' in M. Mac Craith & P. Ó Héalaí (eds), *Diasa díograise: aistí i gcuimhne ar Mháirtín Ó Briain* (Indreabhán, 2009), pp 413–35. 33 Bernadette Cunningham, 'The view from Breóghan's Tower' in S. Ryan (ed.), *Treasures of Irish Christianity, III: to the ends of the earth* (Dublin, 2015), pp 46–9. For Scottish pilgrims to Santiago, see Phinella Henderson, *Pre-Reformation pilgrims from Scotland to Santiago de Compostela*, CSJ Occasional Paper 4 (London, 1997). 34 Eurys Rowlands, 'The continuing tradition' in A.O.H. Jarman & G. Rees Hughes (eds), *A guide to Welsh literature, 1282–c.1550* (Cardiff, 1997), pp 275–97, at pp 283–4. 35 Rowlands, 'The continuing tradition', p. 284. 36 Glanmor Williams, 'Poets and pilgrims in fifteenth- and sixteenth-century Wales', *Transactions of the Honourable Society of Cymmrodorion* (1991), 69–98, at 70; J. Wyn Evans, 'St David and St Davids: some observations on the cult, site and buildings' in J. Cartwright (ed.), *Celtic hagiography and saints' cults* (Cardiff, 2003), pp 10–25, at pp 10–11. For medieval Welsh pilgrims to Rome, see K.K. Olson, '"Ar ffordd Pedr a Phawl": Welsh pilgrimage and travel to Rome, *c.*1200–*c.*1530', *Welsh History Review*, 24:2 (2008), 1–40. 37 E.D. Jones, 'Lewis Glyn Cothi' in Jarman & Rees Hughes (eds), *A guide to Welsh literature, 1282–c.1550*, pp 222–39, at p. 232. See also Jane Cartwright, 'The harlot and the hostess: a prelimi-nary study of the Middle Welsh Lives of Mary Magdalene and her sister Martha' in Cartwright (ed.), *Celtic hagiography and saints' cults*, pp 77–101, at p. 96, citing D.R. Johnston (ed.), *Gwaith Lewys Glyn Cothi* (Cardiff, 1995), p. 189, ll 53–6.

the Alps and journeyed along the banks of the Rhine.[38] The scarcity of equivalent poems in relation to the Santiago pilgrimage from late medieval Ireland might be interpreted as indicating that Irish pilgrims were outnumbered by those from Wales.

One of the explanations for the absence of St James from the Irish bardic corpus lies in the political character of the poetic source rather than a lack of interest in the saint. The Mág Uidhir territory in Fermanagh was among the Gaelic regions in which a cult of St James had developed in the fifteenth century, and from where known pilgrims went to Santiago. Just one surviving poem, in a sixteenth-century Mág Uidhir poem-book, invokes St James the Great. The poem beginning with the line *Gabh m'eagnach a Chú Chonnacht* ('Receive my complaint, Cú Chonnacht') was addressed by Conchobhar Crón Ó Dálaigh to Cú Chonnacht Mág Uidhir, who died in 1589.[39] The poem originally ended with this stanza:

> May Saint James and the angelic Virgin obtain from the Prince of Heaven that I should not be sued for the guilt of the spear-wound which saved the world from its plight.

> *Faghthar leo ó Fhlaith nimhe*
> *San Sém 's an Ógh ainglidhe,*
> *Gan m'agra a ccóir guine an gha,*
> *Do fhóir an chruinne a cumhga.*

That there are so few traces in the bardic poetry emanating from that region suggests that the pilgrimage had little bearing on the political functions served by the work of the poets.[40]

WARS OF CHARLEMAGNE, AND OTHER CONTINENTAL TALES

The ecclesiastical cult of St James concentrated on the biblical stories of the Apostle, but there was another route through which stories of St James could enter the Irish tradition. Retellings of the military exploits of Charlemagne in Spain, containing material on St James, could certainly have helped increase awareness of Santiago de Compostela. Stories of the conquests of Charlemagne, emperor of the West (742–814), derived from Continental sources, were in circulation in fifteenth-century Ireland as elsewhere in Europe. Indeed, the death of

---

38 Jones, 'Lewis Glyn Cothi', p. 232. 39 David Greene (ed. & trans.), *Duanaire Mheig Uidhir* (Dublin, 1972), poem 19. 40 On the role of professional poets in Gaelic society see P.A. Breatnach, 'The chief's poet', *Proc. RIA*, 83C (1983), 37–79; for the Fermanagh context, see Katharine Simms, 'Medieval Fermanagh' in E.M. Murphy & W.J. Roulston (eds), *Fermanagh history and society* (Dublin, 2004), pp 77–103.

Charlemagne was among the few overseas events recorded for the ninth century in the Annals of Ulster.[41] A Latin version of Charlemagne's adventures found in an Irish context is preserved in TCD, MS 667, a Co. Clare manuscript with Franciscan associations that dates from 1445 and may have been used as a source for sermons.[42] Variant versions of the story of his exploits can be found in a number of medieval Irish-language manuscripts, the best known of them being the late fifteenth-century Book of Mac Carthaigh Riabhach, a Munster manuscript now better known as the Book of Lismore.[43] An Irish version is also found in BL, MS Egerton 1781, a manuscript associated with Cavan and Leitrim, dating from *c*.1484–7. Yet another Irish vellum manuscript containing the text is UCD-OFM, MS A 9, which again dates from the late fifteenth century and was in the Irish Franciscan college of St Anthony at Louvain in the mid-seventeenth century. Other later fragments survive in King's Inns, Dublin, MS 10; TCD, MS 1304; and BL, MS Egerton 92.

The fifteenth-century Irish version of the story of the wars of Charlemagne against the Moors of Spain, *Gabhaltais Shearlais Mhóir,* is an abridged version, possibly translated from a Middle English version rather than the Latin original.[44] Many of the local names of Spanish places were omitted in the Irish version, the story being customized to suit the interests of local audiences who might not have appreciated too much unfamiliar topographical detail. In the Irish narrative of the wars of Charlemagne the story opens with St James in Galicia, preaching there in his lifetime. The story relates that after he was killed by Herod his body was put in a ship and guided by an angel back to Galicia. The people of Galicia later drove out those who espoused Christianity, until Charlemagne came along many centuries later guided by a star to the place where St James was buried.[45] According to this story, James appeared three times to Charlemagne and inspired him to resist the Moors in Galicia. In the vision, James explained that he was an Apostle of Christ,

> whom my Lord sent to preach with great grace to the various peoples; and it is I whom Herod killed with a sword, and it is my body that is resting in Galicia in bondage at the hands of the Saracens.

41 *AU*, s.a. 813.   42 TCD, MS 667, pp 107–30; Colmán Ó Clabaigh, *The Franciscans in Ireland, 1400–1534* (Dublin, 2002), pp 138–40.   43 The Book of Lismore is in private hands. A digitized version is available at www.isos.dias.ie (accessed 29 Nov. 2017). There is also a printed facsimile edition by R.A.S. Macalister (ed.), *The Book of Mac Carthaigh Riabhach otherwise the Book of Lismore* (Dublin, 1950), and an edition and translation of the text from Douglas Hyde (ed.), *Gabhaltais Shearluis Mhóir: the conquests of Charlemagne: edited from the Book of Lismore and three other vellum MSS,* Irish Texts Society, XIX (London, 1917).   44 For the significant similarities between the Irish and the Middle English versions, see S.H.A. Shepherd (ed.), *Turpines story: a Middle English translation of the Pseudo-Turpin Chronicle,* EETS original ser., 322 (Oxford, 2004), pp xxxviii–xl; S.H.A. Shepherd, 'The Middle English Pseudo-Turpin Chronicle', *Medium Aevum,* 65:1 (1996), 19–34, at 23–5.   45 Hyde (ed.), *Conquests of Charlemagne,* pp 2–5.

do chuir mu thighearna do shenmoir maille na grásaibh mora dona popluib ocus is me do mharbh Iruath do chlaidiumh ocus asé mu corp ata a cumsanad isin Ghailinnsi fo dhaeirsi ag na Seirisdinibh.[46]

James explained to Charlemagne:

And the path which you saw in the air, that is a sign that you shall go with great hosts to fight with the Pagan peoples and to save my country and my land, and to visit the place where my body was buried, from the border of this country to Galicia; and let every people come after you on pilgrimage from sea to sea, to that place, to get remission of their sin from God, and to tell the praises of the Lord and the virtues and miracles which He performed from the period of your own life to the end of the world.

Ocus in tslighi ad chonncais isin aier as comurtha sin co ragha-sa maille re slua-ghaib móra do chathughadh ris na cineadhuibh padhanda ocus do shaeradh mu thíre ocus mo thalman ocus d'fisrughadh an inaidh ar cuireadh mu chorp ó imeal na crichi so gusin nGailinnsi, ocus ticedh ad diaig an uili phobal chum oilitri o muir cu muir, isin inad sin d'fhaghail logaid an a phecadh i Dhia ocus ag innisin admolta in tighearna ocus na subalche ocus na mirbuiledh do rinne se o aimser do betha-sa cu deredh in domain.[47]

This opening section of the Irish narrative concluded in the form of a sermon, extolling the virtues of love, charity, humility, chastity, prayer and silence (as against anger).[48]

The oldest part of the Latin narrative, from which the Irish version ultimately derives, is the first five chapters and these were written by a cleric of Compostela *c.*1020, probably to encourage pilgrims to visit the burial place of St James.[49] Later sections were added down to AD 1150 and included an adaptation of the story of the death of Roland, derived from the French *Chanson de Roland*. In the Middle Ages, however, this textual history was not widely known and the entire story was usually taken at face value. The poem portrayed Charlemagne in a favourable light, a restrained leader as compared with the impetuous Roland. Juxtaposing triumph and loss, it told a tragic story of war and human suffering, in which Roland and others were destined to die, while Charlemagne, the real hero of the poem, survived.[50] This addition to the story of Charlemagne in the Iberian peninsula told of the death of Roland, commander of the rearguard of Charlemagne's army, which was attacked at the Ibañeta pass in the Pyrenees in 778. The attack had been carried out by a Basque army, but the twelfth-century story blamed the Moors for the death of Roland and other knights, and portrayed Charlemagne as the leader

46 Ibid., pp 4–5. 47 Ibid., pp 4–5. 48 Ibid., pp 20–1. 49 Ibid., p. vi. 50 J.D. Niles, 'The ideal depiction of Charlemagne in "Le Chanson de Roland"', *Viator*, 7 (1976), 123–39.

of Christendom against the Moors.[51] The later parts of the story were originally ascribed to Turpin, archbishop of Rheims, who lived in the late eighth century, but that anachronistic attribution has long been discredited. The prose text is now generally referred to as the Pseudo-Turpin Chronicle.[52]

In terms of the hierarchy of pilgrimages in the known world, the Pseudo-Turpin Chronicle, as transmitted to Irish audiences, ranked Santiago de Compostela second after Rome among the great centres of Christianity, with Ephesus in third place. This view of the geography of medieval Christianity placed the shrines of Peter and Paul at Rome at the centre; Santiago in the west, associated with St James, was supposedly established by Turpin as the premier ecclesiastical establishment in the Western world; and Ephesus, traditionally believed to be where John the Evangelist lived in old age, was accorded a similar place in the Eastern known world. In this way, the shrines of the three Apostles that were portrayed in the Gospels as being closest to Jesus were each used as focal points for major Christian pilgrimages.[53] The Irish-language version of the story of Charlemagne presented an ideological reading – part history, part entertainment, part moral tale – about the power of St James. The final section of the Irish text retold the later history of Spain after the death of Charlemagne and the eventual triumph of Christianity through the power of God and the intercession of St James: 'And the miracles of God and St James were told, and they were worshipped' (*Ocus do innisedh mirbhuili Dé ocus San Sem ocus do adhrad doibh*).[54]

The same story is known from other vernaculars much earlier. A Welsh version of the Pseudo-Turpin Chronicle was commissioned by Gruffydd ap Maredudd in 1265–83, while a Welsh version of the Song of Roland was prepared by *c.*1220, possibly popularized in the context of the Crusades, and reused later in the context of wars between Christians. Its militaristic overtones would have appealed to the nobility in Wales, who were involved in the Crusading movement, but no evidence survives of an equivalent appetite in thirteenth-century Ireland for literature associated with the Crusades.[55] The Irish interest in the text in the fifteenth century may be associated with the upsurge in the Gaelic Irish interest in pilgrimage to Santiago at this time.

Other romantic tales originating outside Ireland and involving adventurous journeys were also translated into Irish in the fifteenth century and may have

51 Cordula Rabe, *Camino de Santiago: Way of St James from the Pyrenees to Santiago* (Munich, 2007), p. 53; for the religious rather than political nature of Muslim opposition to Christians in medieval Iberia, see Ana Maria Carballeira Debasa, 'The pilgrims' Way of St James and Islam: pilgrimage, politics and militias' in A. Pazos (ed.), *Pilgrims and politics: rediscovering the power of the pilgrimage* (Farnham, 2012), pp 9–27. 52 See Shepherd, 'The Middle English Pseudo-Turpin Chronicle', 19–34. 53 Hyde (ed.), *Conquests of Charlemagne*, pp 69–73. 54 Ibid., pp 114–15. 55 Daniel Huws, *Medieval Welsh manuscripts* (Aberystwyth, 2000), pp 216–17; Kathryn Hurlock, *Wales and the Crusades, c.1095–1291* (Cardiff, 2011), pp 44–57; Kathryn Hurlock, *Britain, Ireland and the Crusades, c.1000–1300* (London, 2013), pp 133–5; James Carney, 'Literature in Irish, 1169–1534' in *NHI*, ii, pp 688–707, at p. 702. Irish evidence is incomplete as no manuscript written in Irish in the thirteenth-century is known to survive.

fed into the interest in overseas travel. Marco Polo's adventures in the 'Orient' could be read in Irish by the late fifteenth century, having been translated by or for Finghín Ó Mathghamhna (d. 1496), a Gaelic chieftain living near Schull in west Cork.[56] Another tale of foreign travel, the fabricated story of Sir John Mandeville's travels to Jerusalem and beyond, was translated into Irish by or for the same Finghín Ó Mathghamhna in 1475.[57] Of the surviving copies, the oldest was written at the Franciscan friary at Kilcrea, Co. Cork, while another variant version was copied in Breifne no later than 1484. The Irish version was translated from English and was considerably abridged, omitting much of the detail of travel in Asia while adding detail about local Irish chiefs.[58] Those in the translator's immediate cultural circle were well aware of the cult of St James since a scribe, Cairbre Ó Cendamháin, who was working on a medical manuscript in the house of Finghín Ó Mathghamhna in August 1478, made reference to 'the year of St James' (*bliaduin San Sem*) in a note about the place and date of writing.[59] The concept of a jubilee year of St James appears to have become a thoroughly familiar one in fifteenth-century Ireland. These texts prompted curiosity about exotic lands and might have encouraged those who could afford it to see more of the world for themselves.[60]

Thus, Irish enthusiasm for the pilgrimage to Santiago was not shaped exclusively by the desire for indulgences; a wider range of cultural influences can be detected that could have broadened people's horizons. The literary pattern alluded to by James Carney, of 'a consistent picture of increasing external influence on Irish from at least the beginning of the fifteenth century onwards',[61] was mirrored by an increased involvement in overseas travel by the Irish consumers of that international literature. Instances of devotion to St James can be detected, but the cult cannot be held to have been a prominent feature of the Irish tradition. It may well be that 'tourism, lightly disguised as pilgrimage', was a factor in many an overseas 'pilgrimage' from Ireland in the Middle Ages.[62]

IRELAND AND IBERIA

While those planning to visit Santiago on pilgrimage were concerned with what St James might achieve for them as patron, they were also interested in the secular world of north-west Spain through which they would travel to reach the saint's

---

56 Carney, 'Literature in Irish, 1169–1534', p. 706, citing Whitley Stokes, 'The Gaelic abridgement of the Book of Ser Marco Polo', *ZCP*, 1 (1896–7), 245–73, 362–408, 603; 2 (1898), 222–3. The Irish text survives only in the Book of Lismore.   57 Whitley Stokes, 'The Gaelic Maundeville', *ZCP*, 2 (1898), 1–63, 226–312, 603–4. For an English version of the same tale, see *The travels of Sir John Mandeville*, trans. C.W.R.D. Moseley (London, 2005).   58 *Cat. Ire. MSS in BL*, ii, pp 540–1.   59 RIA, MS 24 P 15, p. 126. See *Cat. Ire. MSS in RIA*, pp 1181–2. The feast of St James (25 July) fell on a Saturday in 1478, but plans were being made for a pilgrimage from Co. Cork to arrive in Santiago in the jubilee year of 1479. See above, p. 25.   60 Sumption, *Pilgrimage*, p. 258.   61 Carney, 'Literature in Irish, 1169–1534', p. 707.   62 Sumption, *Pilgrimage*, p. 257.

shrine. As already mentioned, familiarity with possible Irish links with Iberia was nurtured by a long-established literary tradition, that of the *Leabhar Gabhála* (Book of Invasions),[63] an origin legend for the peoples of Ireland already popular in the eleventh century and preserved in a variety of medieval Irish manuscripts.[64] The *Leabhar Gabhála* comprised a series of stories in prose and verse on the waves of settlers who came to the island of Ireland, culminating in the arrival of the Clann Mhíleadh (sons of Míl) ancestors of the Gaeil. It was an elaborate account of Ireland's place in the world from earliest times down to the eleventh century, incorporating genealogical material drawn from the Bible and other sources. This origin legend continued to be updated by later historians and it provided the essential chronological structure of early Irish history for many generations.[65] Links between Ireland and Galicia featured prominently. The literary tradition of the Book of Invasions included the story of the adventures of the Clann Mhíleadh, who reputedly came to Ireland from Egypt via Spain, an adaption of the Old Testament story of the wandering of the children of Israel.[66] There are variant versions of the narrative, in both prose and verse, telling the story of Íth, son of Breóghan, who saw the promised land of Ireland from A Coruña on the north coast of Galicia. In one prose version, it was

> Íth son of Breogan who saw Ireland at the first, on a winter's evening, from the top of Breogan's Tower; for thus is a man's vision best, on a clear winter's evening. Íth, with thrice thirty warriors, came to Ireland, and they landed on the 'fetid shore' of the headland of Corcu Duibne, what time they arrived.

> *Íth mac Bregoin atchonnairc hÉrinn ar tús, fescor gaimrid, a mulluch Túir Bregoin; dáig is amlaid is ferr radharc duine, glan-fhescor gaimrith. Tánic Íth, trí trichait láech, dochum hÉrenn, 7 gabsat Bréntrácht Irruis Chorco Duibne, in tan sain táncatar.*[67]

Other versions mention different landing places in Ireland, but the link with Breóghan's Tower is consistent.

A variant account of the early links between Ireland and Spain was included by Raphael Holinshed in the first book of his *Historie of Ireland*, published in 1577. In his story, Gathelus, descendant of a Greek lord and ancestor of the Gaeil, settled

63 R.A.S. Macalister (ed.), *Lebor Gabála Érenn: the book of the taking of Ireland* (5 vols, Dublin, 1938–56). 64 John Carey, 'Lebor Gabála and the legendary history of Ireland' in H. Fulton (ed.), *Medieval Celtic literature and society* (Dublin, 2005), pp 32–48. 65 Bernadette Cunningham, *The Annals of the Four Masters: Irish history, kingship and society in the early seventeenth century* (Dublin, 2010), pp 63–4. 66 Macalister (ed.), *Lebor Gabála Érenn*, i, pp xxvii–xxviii. 67 Macalister (ed.), *Lebor Gabála Érenn*, v, pp 10–13.

3.1 Breóghan's Tower/Torre de Hercules, a former Roman lighthouse on the coast at A Coruña.

in Galicia with his followers, founding the city of Brigantium, now A Coruña, and later when that place had grown too populous, some of them migrated to Ireland.[68] Holinshed made no mention of Breóghan.

The stories of Irish links with Galicia long predate the oldest manuscript versions of the *Leabhar Gabhála* in existence. The idea of the Irish being descended from Breóghan found literary expression in Irish poetry by the ninth century in a poem beginning *Can a mbunadas na nGoídel* ('Whence is the origin of the Gaels') by Máel Muru Othna (d. 887), a work that probably predates the *Leabhar Gabhála* as currently organized by more than a century. Máel Muru's poem traced the ancestors of the Irish as they moved from Egypt through Scythia before reaching the Iberian peninsula, where they founded the city of Brigantium and Breóghan's Tower was built. The poem told of Íth son of Breóghan setting out for the land they saw from the tower, his death, and the later arrival of other descendants of Breóghan, who divided Ireland among them. In affirming the truth of his history,

---

68 *Holinshed's Irish chronicle*, ed. L. Miller & E. Power (reprint, Dublin, 1979), pp 123–4.

the poet concluded by describing the Gaeil as 'the people of Breóghan' (*muintir Bregoin*).[69]

Stories adapted from the *Leabhar Gabhála* origin legend were commonplace in early seventeenth-century historical writing about Ireland, and in a Renaissance-style biography of Aodh Ruadh Ó Domhnaill, written some years after his death in 1602, the narrator took a special interest in the visit the Irish earl made to Breóghan's Tower in A Coruña on his arrival in Spain. He recalled in some detail the legend of the peopling of Ireland from Spain, and observed how fitting it was that a leader of the Irish people had now returned to the very same place.[70] The author, Lughaidh Ó Cléirigh, made no mention of Ó Domhnaill's visit to Santiago in the same month; the story that resonated with the professional Irish historian was the Irish origin legend, rather than the cult of St James, perhaps because the political image of the Irish earl was the focus of the biography.

The Breóghan's Tower story persisted through the early seventeenth century. Florence Mac Carthy, who recounted the ancient history of Ireland for the earl of Thomond before 1624, recorded a version of it. In his discussion of Brigantium, founded by Breóghan, Mac Carthy took care to point out that the place being referred to was not Santiago de Compostela but the northern Galician port of A Coruña.[71] Mac Carthy wrote with the authority of one who had been to A Coruña, or at least knew something of its geography:

> Breogan or Breghan founded Brigancia which (as divers holde & write) is not St James called Compostella but Corunna, as some of the ancientest of Spanish writers holde, and ours also who write Brigancia to be upon the sea, as St James's is not, nor nere it, and make mention of a tower which he built near the city upon the sea, the ruins of which tower that stands within half a mile of Corunna down towards the sea on the west side of the haven or bay is called still Tower of Brighan.[72]

The story was also included in Conall Mageoghegan's English translation of the Annals of Clonmacnoise in 1627, and he sought to date the events described in the traditional sources, drawing on both manuscripts and printed books to which he had access.[73] More influential than Conall Mageoghegan or Florence MacCarthy was Geoffrey Keating, whose *Foras feasa ar Éirinn* (completed *c*.1634) circulated

---

69 For discussion of this and related poems, see Katja Ritari, '"Whence is the origin of the Gaels?" Remembering the past in Irish pseudohistorical poems', *Peritia*, 28 (2017), 155–76, at 160–5. 70 Paul Walsh (ed.), *Beatha Aodha Ruaidh Uí Dhomhnaill: the life of Aodh Ruadh Ó Domhnaill transcribed from the book of Lughaidh Ó Cléirigh* (2 vols, London, 1948–57), i, pp 340–3. 71 Raphael Holinshed, whose Irish chronicle was published in English in 1577, had already correctly situated this section of the Irish origin legend in A Coruña. See *Holinshed's Irish chronicle*, p. 123. 72 John O'Donovan (ed.), 'Letter of Florence MacCarthy to the earl of Thomond on the ancient history of Ireland', *Journal of the Kilkenny and South-East of Ireland Archaeological Society*, 2nd ser., 1:1 (1856), 203–29, at 214. 73 *A.Clon*, pp 23–5.

widely in manuscript in the seventeenth century. Keating also showed an interest in the traditional story of Breóghan as part of the origin legend of the Gaeil. He recorded that

> It was this Breoghan, too, who defeated Spain in many battles; and it was he who finished or built Brigansia near Coruna, and the tower of Breoghan in Corunna itself.

> *Is é fós an Breoghan soin do bhris iomad cath ar an Easpáinn, agus is é do chumhduigh nó do thógaibh Brigansia láimh ris an gCruinne, agus tor Breoghain san gCruinne féin.*[74]

Keating was not writing from personal knowledge of the place, however. His sources ranged from an eleventh-century Irish poem by Gilla Cóemáin to a modern printed history of Spain in English, the work of translator Edward Grimston, published in 1612. Keating's interest was in the origin legend of the Gaeil, which linked back to Gallamh, known as Míl of Spain, grandson of Breóghan. Indeed Grimston, too, mentioned the famous lighthouse in A Coruña and explained its Roman origins, attributing it to Octavius Caesar.[75] It was a well-known story but there was no mention of St James the Great in either the poem of Gilla Cóemáin or in Geoffrey Keating's prose narrative.[76] Nor was Keating prepared to accept the myth that the link between Galicia and Ireland owed its origin to the island having been seen from the top of Breóghan's Tower, as the *Leabhar Gabhála* recorded. Rather, he asserted that the Irish links with the Iberian peninsula were based on trade, an entirely plausible and realistic claim.

> They thus had been in the habit of trading with one another, and of exchanging their wares and valuables, so that the Spaniards were familiar with Ireland, and the Irish had a knowledge of Spain before Ioth son of Breoghan was born. Hence it was not from a view obtained in a single night from the summit of the tower of Breoghan that Ioth, or the children of Breoghan, acquired a knowledge of Ireland, but from there having been intercourse for a long time previously between Spain and Ireland.

> *Do chleachtdaois trá leath ar leath bheith ag ceannaidheacht is ag malairt a n-earradh is a seod ar gach taoibh ré chéile, ionnus go raibhe aithidhe na hÉireann ag Easpáinneachaibh agus aithne na hEaspáinne ag Éireannchaibh*

74 Geoffrey Keating, *Foras feasa ar Éirinn*, ed. D. Comyn & P.S. Dinneen (4 vols, London, 1902–14), ii, pp 40–1. **75** Edward Grimston, *The generall historie of Spain ... written in French by Lewis de Mayerne ... translated into English, and continued unto these times by Edward Grimeston, Esquire* (London, 1612), sig. B iii. **76** For the major works of Gilla Cóemáin, see Peter J. Smith (ed.), *Three historical poems ascribed to Gilla Cóemáin: a critical edition of the work of an eleventh-century Irish scholar* (Münster, 2007).

sul rugadh Íoth mac Breoghain; ionnus da réir sin nach ó amharc aonoidh-
che d'fhagháil do mhullach thuir Breoghain fuair Íoth náid clan Bhreoghain
eolas ar Éirinn, acht ó chaidreamh imchian aimsire roimhe sin do bheith idir an
Easpáinn is Éirinn.[77]

For those thinking about a pilgrimage to Santiago, such stories provided a sense
that they were travelling through a well-known landscape and not uncharted, alien
territory.

ST JAMES IN IRELAND

If those interested in the secular history of Ireland could connect it with north-
west Spain, those concerned with the history of the Irish church also wove a
past that linked the two countries by bringing St James to Ireland. In the early
seventeenth century, an assertion that St James had visited Ireland personally featured in several historical narratives by Irish authors. For example, the idea of
St James as local evangelist in Ireland found supporters in the early seventeenth
century among the Irish Franciscan friars at St Anthony's College, Louvain. In a
book published in 1625, Irish Franciscan Robert Rochford commented, 'I doe not
deny that S. James the Great came long before S. Patricke to plant the Christian
Religion in Ireland, as Flavius Dexter an ancie[n]t Author living in the same age
with Ierom[e], Ioannes Gill, and Vincentius Bellovacensis teach.'[78] The archbishop
of Armagh, Peter Lombard, in his disquisition on Irish history, *De regno Hiberniae*
sanctorum insula commentarius, written in 1598–1600, likewise mentioned the legend that the Apostle James had come by sea from Spain and evangelized Ireland.[79]
The story was in circulation within Ireland, also, and was mentioned in 1627 in
Conall Mageoghegan's English translation of the Annals of Clonmacnoise.[80] This
idea persisted among later seventeenth-century writers (partly because authors
tended to copy one another). John Lynch's history of Irish bishops, *De praesulibus*
Hiberniae, written in 1672, included a prologue, which discussed the evidence that
the first bishops in Ireland were those appointed by St James who had preached
there with seven disciples, having sailed from Galicia, and had left bishops, pres-
byters and many deacons in Ireland. Richard Stanihurst's Life of St Patrick[81] and
Hugh Ward, OFM's Life of St Romuald[82] were among the published works Lynch
mentioned as sources.[83]

---

77 Geoffrey Keating, *Foras feasa ar Éirinn*, ii, p. 51.   78 Robert Rochford, *The Life of the glorious bishop*
S Patrick ... together with the Lives of the holy virgin S. Bridgit and of the glorious abbot Saint Columbe,
English Recusant Literature, 210 (St Omer, 1625; reprint, 1974), p. viii.   79 Peter Lombard, *De regno*
Hiberniae, ed. P.F. Moran (Dublin, 1868), p. 60. Lombard's work was first printed at Louvain in 1632
but had circulated in manuscript form prior to that.   80 *A.Clon*, p. 65.   81 Richard Stanihurst, *De*
vita Sancti Patricii (Antwerp, 1587).   82 Hugh Ward, *Sancti Rumoldi* (Louvain, 1662).   83 John
Lynch, *De praesulibus Hiberniae*, ed. J.F. O'Doherty (2 vols, Dublin, 1944), i, pp 15–16.

Protestant authors also accepted this idea. A mid-seventeenth-century manu-script history, entitled 'The church history of Ireland', intimated that St James could have had a role in the Christianization of Ireland:

> Some writers affirm that in a short time after the ascension of Our Saviour from earth to Heaven St James the Apostle and others travelling into the western parts did first instruct the Irish people in the Christian faith and religion, preaching the Gospel unto them; so that even then many amongst them were baptised and believed on [*sic*] the name of the Lord Jesus Christ; but not in such numbers as that it may be thought the country was generally converted.[84]

Roger Boyle, earl of Orrery, published *Poems on most of the festivals of the church* in 1681, which contained the idea that St James came to Ireland and Britain.[85] Similarly, a popular history of the kingdom of Ireland published in 1693 asserted:

> The Irish as some authors write were first converted to Christianity by St James the Apostle about this time though [they] themselves say that Palladius was first sent from Pope Celestine to preach the gospel to them and after him the renowned St Patrick.[86]

This story, generally attributed by early modern writers to Flavius Dexter (Flavio Destro), was a Spanish invention but taken up with enthusiasm by others. Flavius Dexter was a fictitious author invented by Jerónimo Román de la Higuera, SJ, who created a series of 'ancient' chronicles as part of his invention of an appropri-ate past for Catholic Spain in the late sixteenth century.[87] His fabricated history included narratives of the exploits of Spain's patron saint in other lands. This notion of St James as evangelizer in Ireland echoed the much earlier claim that St James had evangelized in Galicia. In Spain, where the presence of the relics of St James had a long history, the idea that James had personally evangelized in Spain during his lifetime was a later development in the cult, mentioned by the twelfth-century author of the *Codex Calixtinus*, from where it found its way into James of Voragine's *Legenda aurea* in the thirteenth century. However, while it circulated as a miracle story, the idea did not find favour with medieval historians. It was only in the Renaissance era that the story emerged as part of the Spanish historical nar-rative, as an element of an international trend towards emphasizing the antiquity of national Christian traditions. In the early sixteenth century, the story attracted the attention of Marineus Siculus, a royal historian, and was incorporated into his

---

84 British Library, Sloane MS 1449, p. 1 (= fol. 4). 85 Boyle, *Poems*, p. 61. 86 R. B[urton], *The history of the kingdom of Ireland* (London, 1693), p. 8. 87 Diarmaid MacCulloch, *Reformation: Europe's house divided, 1490–1700* (London, 2003), pp 421–2; T.D. Kendrick, *St James in Spain* (London, 1960), pp 116–27.

overview of Spanish heritage, *De rebus Hispaniae memorabilius* (1530).[88] An early seventeenth-century debate on the issue was addressed in Antonio Caracciolo's *Biga illustrium controversiarum: de S. Iacobi Apostoli accessu in Hispaniam* (1618).

In a parallel scenario, seventeenth-century Irish Franciscans were familiar with a tradition that St Francis had come from Santiago de Compostela to Ireland in 1214 to establish a friary. It appears that this was a misinterpretation of a statement in a history of the order published at Rome in 1587, which had merely stated that a follower of Francis had come from Santiago to Ireland, without specifying a date. Given the involvement of Irish Franciscans in Spanish diplomacy in the early seventeenth century, the suggestion that the Irish Franciscans owed their origins to Spanish links was an appealing one.[89] The idea of St James having evangelized in Ireland was equally attractive, and no more far-fetched than the *Leabhar Gabhála* legend of the peopling of Ireland from Spain, still popular with historians of Ireland in the seventeenth-century.

MATERIAL CULTURE OF PILGRIMAGE

Sermons, romantic tales and history all played their parts in shaping knowledge of and interest in the pilgrimage to Santiago in the Middle Ages. However, equally powerful were the personal stories and reminiscences of those who had returned from the pilgrimage, stories given tangible expression by the souvenirs that they brought back with them. The scallop shell was the most evocative souvenir. Scallop shells were to be found in abundance on the Galician coast, and were on sale to pilgrims near the cathedral in Santiago. It was an appropriate emblem of the shrine of the fisherman Apostle, James. Shells were trimmed and perforated, so that they could be worn by the pilgrim or attached to a satchel. The earliest documentary reference comes from Aymeri Picaud, who recorded them on sale in the twelfth century in a courtyard not far from the fountain of St James near the north entrance of the cathedral, in front of the medieval Benedictine monastery of San Martin Pinario.[90] The twelfth-century *Codex Calixtinus* explicitly stated that the shell, as a symbol of good works, would help save the pilgrim on judgment day.[91] This belief underpinned the tradition of pilgrims choosing to be buried with their shell. One of the earliest European burials in which a perforated scallop shell has

---

88 Katherine Elliot Van Liere, 'Renaissance chroniclers and the Apostolic origins of Spanish Christianity' in K. Van Liere, S. Dichfield & H. Louthan (eds), *Sacred history: uses of the Christian past in the Renaissance world* (Oxford, 2012), pp 121–44. 89 Cotter, *The Friars Minor in Ireland*, p. 12; Brendan Jennings, 'Brussels MS 3947: Donatus Moneyus, de Provincia Hiberniae S. Francisci', *Analecta Hibernica*, 6 (1934), 12–138, at 15; Brendan Jennings, 'Brevis synopsis provinciae Hiberniae FF Minorum', *Analecta Hibernica*, 6 (1934), 139–91, at 143, 181; Gregory Cleary, 'Saint Francis and Ireland', *Studies: an Irish Quarterly Review*, 15:60 (1926), 542–56. 90 Paula Gerson, et al. (eds), *The pilgrim's guide: a critical edition, ii: the text* (London, 1998), pp 73, 205 note 63. 91 *Liber Sancti Iacobi Codex Calixtinus* (3 vols, Santiago, 1944), i, p. 17, cited in Xunta de Galicia, *Compostela and Europe*, p. 58.

been recorded was found in Schleswig and dates from the late eleventh or early twelfth century.[92] Another was discovered associated with a burial that predates 1120 during an excavation of the central nave of Santiago cathedral itself.[93] In England, a particularly complete late medieval pilgrim burial, dressed in pilgrim attire, but with a cockle shell rather than scallop shell, was excavated in Worcester in 1986.[94] In Ireland, some returned pilgrims were likewise buried with their scallop shell souvenirs, or other manufactured mementos of the Santiago pilgrimage, though precise dating of such burials has not always proved feasible.[95] The scallop shell came to be used as part of the iconography associated with St James on statues, woodcuts and funeral monuments. Irish depictions of St James on funeral monuments for the period 1200 to 1600 – though rarely linked to the pilgrimage – have been recorded by John Hunt. Most of them depicted St James with a pilgrim's hat bearing a scallop shell, though in a few instances the shell was omitted.[96] These images on Irish funeral monuments generally occur in the context of other Apostles, and cannot usually be directly associated with the pilgrimage. However, each church or chapel in Ireland that was dedicated to St James would have had a statue or other image of their local patron saint, but unfortunately no such statues of St James survive from medieval Irish churches.[97]

Many occurrences of scallop-shell designs in art and architecture have no connection to St James or the pilgrimage to Santiago de Compostela.[98] The scallop shell was widely used in the art of the classical world. In the fourth century, a scallop-shell design was used to decorate the shrine of the tomb of Christ in Jerusalem, and its use there may have been the inspiration for its subsequent use in other Christian settings. Thus, baptismal fonts using a scallop shell design were widespread in medieval Europe; a twelfth-century Irish example is found at St Audoen's church in Dublin.[99] The scallop shell was not associated with St James the Apostle in the eastern Mediterranean.[100] Perforated scallop shells have been recovered from the seventh- to ninth-century monastic site at Illaunloughan island, Co. Kerry.

92 Gerson, et al. (eds), *The pilgrim's guide: a critical edition, ii: the text*, p. 205 note 63. 93 Xunta de Galicia, *Compostela and Europe*, p. 58. 94 Helen Lubin, *The Worcester pilgrim* (Worcester, 1990), pp 11–15; Anja Greve, 'Pilgrims and fashion: the functions of pilgrims' garments' in S. Blick & R. Tekippe (eds), *Art and architecture of late medieval pilgrimage in northern Europe and the British Isles: texts* (Leiden, 2005), pp 3–27, at p. 14. 95 See below, pp 87–8. 96 For his summary list, see John Hunt, *Irish medieval figure sculpture, 1200–1600: a study of Irish tombs* (2 vols, Dublin & London, 1974), i, p. 250; see also Stalley, 'Maritime pilgrimage from Ireland and its artistic repercussions', pp 255–75. 97 For a selection of Continental examples of such statues, see the collection in the cathedral museum, Santiago de Compostela. An indication of the former popularity of such images throughout Europe can be gauged from the many examples that survive from Brittany. These are recorded and illustrated in Jean Roudier, *Saint Jacques en Bretagne: culte et patrimoine* (Ploudalmézeau, 2005). 98 Ian Cox (ed.), *The scallop: studies of a shell and its influences on mankind* (London, 1957). 99 Mary McMahon, *St Audoen's church, Cornmarket, Dublin: archaeology and architecture* (Dublin, 2006), pp 88–9. 100 Jenny White Marshall & Claire Walsh, *Illaunloughan island: an early medieval monastery in Co. Kerry* (Bray, 2005), pp 95–6.

Scallop shells occur naturally on the island, and those found in the relic shrine there have been radio-carbon dated to 665–1048, so it is very unlikely they have a link with the pilgrimage to Santiago de Compostela, which was only in its formative state at the end of that date range.[101]

Archaeological excavations in Ireland in recent years have uncovered some instances where individuals were buried with a scallop shell, the traditional souvenir of the Santiago pilgrimage. The first such find to be documented in Ireland was the result of archaeological excavations by Miriam Clyne at Tuam, Co. Galway, in 1986, in the grounds of the medieval St Mary's cathedral. Two pilgrim burials, identified by scallop shells, were discovered. One male, aged about 45, was buried with a shell positioned near the hip, suggesting that he had been buried along with a satchel bearing the shell. The other Tuam burial had been disturbed and two associated shells were fragmentary when found.[102]

There have been similar finds in other parts of Ireland. In September 1986 two perforated scallop shells were found in disturbed topsoil in the burial ground at Lionsden, in the parish of Castlerickard, Co. Meath; the context of the burials has been lost, but was probably medieval.[103] A curious example of a burial was found in 1994 in excavations at the Dominican priory of St Mary Magdalene in Drogheda, Co. Louth. This was a female skeleton with an oyster-shell pendant around the neck, perhaps a deliberate imitation of a scallop-shell burial, in the same way that the Worcester pilgrim used a cockle shell. The woman had been buried in a mortar-lined grave within the south transept.[104] A sherd of Spanish Merida-type pottery found in the context of this burial established that the burial could not be earlier than the fifteenth century. The prominent burial place suggests the woman may have been a patron of the priory;[105] it also indicates that burials at the priory were not confined to members of the Dominican community. Other similar burials with perforated scallop shells have been found at Mullingar, Co. Westmeath, in 1996;[106] possibly the Augustinian friary at Galway in 1998;[107] at Claregalway friary on the river Clare 10 km north-east of Galway city;[108] at the site of the former priory of the Holy Cross in Tralee, Co. Kerry in 2000;[109] at the substantial medieval settlement

101 White Marshall & Walsh, *Illaunloughan island*, pp 89–96.   102 Burials 38 and 32, as reported in Miriam Clyne, 'Excavation at St Mary's cathedral, Tuam, Co. Galway', *JGAHS*, 41 (1987–8), 90–103 (includes illustrations).   103 meathheritage.com/index.php/archives/item/meo2604-lionsden-burial-ground, accessed 4 Mar. 2018.   104 See Donald Murphy, 'Archaeological excavations at the Magdalene Tower, Drogheda, County Louth', *JLAHS*, 24:1 (1997), 75–128, at 97–101.   105 Murphy, 'Archaeological excavations at the Magdalene Tower, Drogheda, County Louth', 101.   106 *Westmeath Examiner*, 21 Oct. 2000; *Irish Times*, 30 Oct. 1996.   107 Dagmar Ó Riain-Raedel, 'The Irish medieval pilgrimage to Santiago de Compostela', *History Ireland*, 6:3 (1998), 17–21, at 17.   108 Jim Higgins & Aisling Parsons, *St Mary's cathedral (Church of Ireland) Tuam: an architectural, archaeological and historical guide* (Tuam, 1995), p. vii.   109 See Michael Connolly, 'Medieval Tralee uncovered', *Kerry Magazine*, 15 (2005), 18–22, at 21. One of the seven burials excavated from the area within the abbey car park identified as the cloister had a perforated scallop shell in a position that suggests the person was buried with their scrip with shell attached.

at Ardreigh, overlooking the River Barrow south of Athy, Co. Kildare, *c.*2003;[110] at the site of a medieval church at Ballyhanna on the outskirts of Ballyshannon, Co. Donegal, excavated in 2003–4,[111] and in two separate burials in a cemetery close to Thomas Street, Dublin, in 2016–18.[112] All of these archaeological discoveries are relatively recent, and it has been suggested that in earlier decades perforated scallop shells may have been uncovered in Irish excavations without their significance being recognized and thus went unrecorded.[113]

The excavation of the cemetery at Ballyhanna revealed a female buried with a scallop shell, suggesting she had been on pilgrimage to Santiago. The cemetery at Ballyhanna was in use from the late eighth to the early seventeenth century, and an accurate date for the scallop shell burial has not yet been established. Nevertheless, the shell associated with a burial is clearly suggestive of a pilgrimage link between Galicia and Donegal or Fermanagh. The adjacent settlements of Assaroe and Ballyshannon in south-west Donegal, at the mouth of the River Erne, were the location of a significant trading port in west Ulster that could have facilitated pilgrim traffic in the late medieval period. The harbour at Assaroe saw general trade, with imports of wine, beer and cloth, and exports of fish, salt-meat and hides.[114] Assaroe harbour was the backdrop for a military encounter recorded in the Annals of Connacht in 1420, with one of the protagonists (Niall Ó Domhnaill) swimming out to a merchant ship to make his escape.[115] Passing reference to the wine trade there is found in the Annals of the Four Masters for the year 1310, when twenty tuns of wine were washed ashore.[116] Indeed, repeated mentions of wine consumption in a poem relating to Tomás Óg Mág Uidhir clearly suggest that fifteenth-century Fermanagh had an established Continental wine trade, perhaps with northern Spain, and that 'sweet red wine-feasts are their delight' (*fleadha millse dearga a ndeoch*), as they enjoyed the profits of fisheries and other trading links with the Continent.[117] Such references also hint of the wealth enjoyed by

110 At Ardreigh, an Anglo-Norman borough, a perforated scallop shell was found in the neck/shoulder area of a male skeleton, one of 1,060 late medieval burials excavated at the site. Colm Moloney, Louise Baker, Jonathan Millar & Damian Shiels, *Guide to the excavations at Ardreigh, County Kildare* (Dublin, 2016), pp 34–5, www.rubiconheritage.com/wp-content/uploads/2016/01/guide-to-the-excavations-at-Ardreigh-Co.-Kildare.pdf, accessed 5 Apr. 2018. See also caminoways.com/the-journey-of-a-medieval-camino-pilgrim, accessed 22 Oct. 2014.   111 C.J. McKenzie, E.M. Murphy & C.J. Donnelly (eds), *The science of a lost medieval Gaelic graveyard: the Ballyhanna research project*. TII Heritage, 2 (Dublin, 2015), p. 37.   112 Paul Duffy, unpublished lecture to Friends of Medieval Dublin seminar, 19 May 2018.   113 Victor Buckley, personal communication, Mar. 2016.
114 McKenzie, Murphy & Donnelly (eds), *The science of a lost medieval Gaelic graveyard*, p. 37. For Ireland's main medieval trading ports, see Timothy O'Neill, 'Map 12: Irish ports in the later Middle Ages' in Cosgrove (ed.), *NHI*, ii: *medieval Ireland*, p. 499; Wendy Childs & Timothy O'Neill, 'Overseas trade' in ibid., p. 505; for archaeological evidence of Iberian pottery in use throughout late medieval Ireland, see Rosanne Meenan, 'A survey of late medieval and early post-medieval Iberian pottery from Ireland' in D. Gaimster & M. Redknap (eds), *Everyday and exotic pottery from Europe, c.650–1900* (Oxford, 1992), pp 186–93.   115 *A.Conn*, pp 450–3.   116 *AFM*, iii, p. 497.   117 McKenna (ed.), *Aithdioghluim dána*, poem 28, stanzas 5 & 37; Simms, 'Medieval Fermanagh', pp 77–103, at p. 97.

the elite in fifteenth-century Ulster lordships, a factor that may have contributed to their enthusiasm for overseas travel, while these commercial links also created channels for the flow of information about foreign places. The increasing wealth of Europe's Atlantic seaboard in the fifteenth century, not least through increased income from fisheries and general trade, meant a shift in Europe's focus towards the Atlantic rim,[118] a phenomenon that coincided with the heyday of the Santiago pilgrimage.

Such shell burials were not restricted to coastal areas or trading ports. There were newspaper reports of burials uncovered at Mullingar, Co. Westmeath, in autumn 1996 during excavations at the probable site of St Mary's priory for Augustinian canons regular in the town. The priory of St Mary was known as the *Domus Dei de Mollingare*, a name that implies a hospital. A list of the property of the priory compiled in 1571, a generation after the buildings had been taken over for secular use, included a building called 'the Spittle' that may have catered for pilgrims as well as locals.[119] Two of the thirty-five excavated burials had scallop shells associated with them, suggesting that some of those buried in the friary had been pilgrims and had probably made the journey to Santiago de Compostela.[120] The burials are thought to date from the late thirteenth or early fourteenth century. The shells found at Mullingar were perforated so that they could be threaded and worn. One of them was reported to have been buried with another bone relic also.[121] Since these shells and relics were easily portable objects they might have been used as gifts. We cannot be absolutely certain that their discovery in conjunction with burials in medieval cemeteries confirms that the person had made the journey to Santiago, but it seems very likely. The Mullingar finds may indicate the active involvement of Augustinian canons in ministering to the needs of Irish pilgrims.

That individuals were buried with scallop shells indicates that such trinkets were more than just souvenirs. While the shells would have evoked memories of the pilgrimage that had been undertaken, they were also treasured as something that would give protection to the owners for the rest of their lives and even beyond the grave.[122] Scallop shells symbolized the redemptive power of pilgrimage. Those who had gained the relevant indulgence following great personal effort might well want the tangible evidence of their 'ticket to Heaven' to be buried with them, particularly if those shells had been blessed or had been placed near the relics of St James by the pilgrim when in Santiago. The rituals associated with such pilgrim burials may have inspired others to undertake similar journeys.

118 Michael Bennett, 'Late medieval Ireland in a wider world' in B. Smith (ed.), *The Cambridge history of Ireland, i, 600–1550* (Cambridge, 2018), pp 329–52, at p. 349.   119 Gwynn & Hadcock, *Medieval religious houses*, p. 189.   120 Nugent, 'Medieval pilgrim's tokens and other souvenirs', pp 38, 43, based on information provided by Michael Gibbons. *Irish Times*, 30 Oct. 1996; *Westmeath Examiner*, 8 July 2000. A full report of the excavations at Mullingar has not yet been published.   121 Nugent, 'Medieval pilgrim's tokens and other souvenirs', p. 43.   122 Stalley, 'Sailing to Santiago', p. 411.

IMAGES OF ST JAMES IN IRELAND

Shrines, sermons and souvenirs all melded in a multi-media experience of pilgrimage from which emerged an image of the saint and his powers. Images are notoriously difficult to recover, but among John Hunt's collection of artefacts, now in the Hunt Museum, Limerick, there is a small jet carving of St James, possibly of French origin.[123] Such items were popular upmarket souvenirs of the Santiago pilgrimage by the fifteenth century, and the one in the Hunt Museum adopts the standard fifteenth-century French iconography of St James as pilgrim.[124]

The original story linking St James to Galicia does not reflect the idea of St James as pilgrim, and the image of St James in the early copies of the *Liber Sancti Jacobi*, or the statue of St James in the medieval Irish monastery at Regensburg, for example, are among those that pre-date this artistic tradition.[125] However, it seems that the emergence of French confraternities from the fourteenth century gave rise to a new iconographic trend, depicting St James as pilgrim (fig. 3.2). When such confraternities undertook pilgrimages to Santiago, one member of the group may have dressed as St James.[126] The fourteenth-century statue of St James in the parish church of Santiago at A Coruña is an intermediate representation, depicting a pilgrim St James but without his hat (fig. 3.3). This polychrome statue, now near the main entrance, was formerly in a more prominent position near the altar, where it would have been venerated by pilgrims from Britain and Ireland if they disembarked in the port of A Coruña.

A medieval Irish reliquary known as the *Domnach Airgid* may also contain a depiction of St James as pilgrim (fig. 3.4).[127] This appears to be the earliest surviving representation of St James in Ireland and the only example on metalwork.[128] The reliquary was probably created to protect valuable relics obtained on pilgrimage. Cormac Bourke suggests this may be the same shrine mentioned in the tenth-century *Tripartite Life of Patrick*[129] and also described in a Latin Life of Mac Cairthinn:

---

123 *The Hunt Museum essential guide* (London, 2002), p. 170. This object has no known medieval Irish association. **124** Stalley, 'Sailing to Santiago', p. 411, fig. **125** Stones, et al. (eds), *Pilgrim's guide to Santiago de Compostela: i: the manuscripts*, plates 48 & 53 reproduce images of St James from two different copies of the text. Ó Riain-Raedel, 'The Irish medieval pilgrimage to Santiago de Compostela', 21, includes an image of this statue of St James at Regensburg. **126** John Cherry, 'The depiction of St James Compostela on seals' in S. Blick (ed.), *Beyond pilgrim souvenirs and secular badges: essays in honour of Brian Spencer* (Oxford, 2007), pp 37–47, at pp 37–8. **127** The *Domnach Airgid* reliquary is in the National Museum of Ireland. Illustrated in Raghnall Ó Floinn, *Irish shrines and reliquaries of the Middle Ages* (Dublin, 1994), p. 28; see also E.C. Rae, 'The Rice monument in Waterford cathedral', *Proc. RIA*, 69C (1970), 1–14, at 5. **128** Stalley, 'Maritime pilgrimage from Ireland and its artistic repercussions', p. 268. **129** Kathleen Mulchrone (ed.), *Bethu Phátraic: the tripartite Life of Patrick* (Dublin, 1939).

3.2 Typical late medieval French iconography of St James as pilgrim, at Luxeuil, France, from Margaret Stokes, *Three months in the forests of France* (1895), p. 72.

3.3 Medieval statue of St James, in parish church of Santiago at A Coruña.

A shrine in which relics of the holy Apostles, and of St Mary's hair, and of the holy cross of the Lord, and of his tomb, and other relics are contained.

scrinum, in quo de sanctorum apostolorum reliquiis et de sancte Marie capillis et sancta cruce Domini et sepulcro eius et aliis sanctis reliquiis continentur.[130]

Such contents would link the shrine with the Holy Land rather than Santiago. The figure of James (if correctly identified) on the *Domnach Airgid* reliquary shows him with a hat and holding palms as symbol of pilgrimage. The palm was originally used to symbolize the pilgrimage to Jerusalem but its use came to be extended to represent pilgrimage in general. The original reliquary has been dated to the eighth century, but it was reworked in the fourteenth century, by which time it would not have been unusual to depict St James as a pilgrim.

Elsewhere in Western Europe, images of James the Great prior to the thirteenth century depict a man with a dark beard holding a book or scroll or a sword (symbol of his martyrdom). After the thirteenth century the iconography of James as pilgrim came to be widely used outside Spain. The inclusion of an image of St James as pilgrim on the reworked *Domnach Airgid* reliquary, which is associated with the diocese of Clogher, would suggest some devotion to the saint in south Ulster by the fourteenth century. The forename James came into use in the south Ulster diocese of Clogher in the fifteenth century and named pilgrims from the diocese will be discussed below.[131]

The most public images of St James that survive from late medieval Ireland were those carved on funeral monuments. Identifiable by his pilgrim hat and purse or scrip, most of the surviving examples are from Kilkenny, Tipperary and Waterford, the heartland of the Anglo-Norman colony. As will be discussed later, James Rice's tomb in Waterford cathedral can be associated with the Santiago pilgrimage, as can the image of St James on a wall tomb in the Franciscan friary at Kilconnell, Co. Galway (fig. 5.1), but most other carved representations of St James that survive from medieval Ireland occur in a more generic context of representations of the Apostles, without any implied link to pilgrimage.

CONCLUSION

While the evidence comes from rather miscellaneous sources, and while the cult of St James did not rival that of local Irish saints such as Patrick, Brigid or Colum Cille, there was familiarity both in Anglo-Irish and Gaelic Ireland with stories involving St James the Great, such that a journey to his shrine was an aspiration for many. The Iberian peninsula, and Galicia in particular, was known through trade

---

130 Cited in Cormac Bourke, 'The *Domnach Airgid* in 2006', *Clogher Record*, 19:1 (2006), 31–42, at 32. 131 See pp 131–40.

3.4 St James on *Domnach Airgid* shrine, reworked in the fourteenth century. Sketch by Margaret Stokes (RIA, MS MSA/2/1/3).

links and through the origin legend of the sons of Míl, and stories of Charlemagne. In addition, the idea of pilgrimage was well embedded locally and there was an interest in relics and indulgences and in the various means through which salvation might be pursued, including the invocation of apostolic intercessors. The preconditions were there for men and women to consider embarking on a pilgrimage to Santiago from late medieval Ireland and, when the indulgence business reached its height in the later Middle Ages, the Irish joined many like-minded men and women from other parts of Europe in their journey towards the sacred. The cult was evident in Anglo-Norman regions in the thirteenth century, but became more popular in Gaelic parts of Ireland in the fifteenth century, and these two strands of the pilgrimage from Ireland will now be considered in turn.

4

The pilgrim experience: the Anglo-Norman phase

There were two distinct strands in the history of the medieval Irish pilgrimage to Santiago de Compostela. The first phase was dominated by Anglo-Norman influence, for which the earliest documentary evidence dates from the thirteenth century. It was only in the fifteenth century that pilgrims from Gaelic parts of Ireland showed an interest in going on pilgrimage to Santiago. Indeed, the very earliest pilgrims travelling from Ireland to Santiago who can be traced in documentary sources were Anglo-Norman officials from England whose careers brought them to Ireland, such as Fulk de Sandford and William de Vescy. The fragmentary evidence suggests that the cult of St James was one of the cultural influences that Anglo-Norman settlers brought to Ireland.

The distinction between the Anglo-Norman and Gaelic strands of devotion to James the Great can be discerned, for instance, in church dedications, where St James was associated with many parish churches in Anglo-Norman regions of the south and east, but not in Gaelic areas.[1] Within families, too, James was in use as a forename in elite Anglo-Irish families from the thirteenth century but was only adopted much later in Gaelic regions. What could be some of the earliest evidence in Ireland for the Santiago pilgrimage comes from excavations at the impressive Anglo-Norman castle at Trim, Co. Meath, which revealed two small objects pressed into scallop-shell shapes. These were found in a probable twelfth-century context, at a location where large numbers of horseshoes and arrowheads were also found. It is conjectured they might have been used on horse harnesses or on human clothing, although they do not have any apparent means of attachment. However, given the early date, it is uncertain whether they should be seen as merely a decorative motif or as associated with pilgrimage to Santiago.[2]

READING ABBEY

At least some of the Anglo-Norman enthusiasm for the cult of St James the Great in Ireland may well have originated not with Santiago de Compostela but with Anglo-Norman settlers who knew about the shrine of the hand of St James at Reading Abbey in southern England. The hand, which was reputed to have worked many miracles, had been given to the abbey at Reading by King Henry I about the year 1133. When the English and Welsh episcopate authorized indulgences for a

---

1 See appendix 2. 2 See Alan R. Hayden, *Trim Castle, Co. Meath: excavations, 1995–8* (Dublin, 2011), pp 334, 336.

pilgrimage to the shrine in 1155, Reading became the most popular pilgrimage destination in England until the canonization of Thomas Becket in 1173 gave rise to an alternative pilgrimage to Canterbury.[3] The shrine at Reading served primarily as a local healing shrine and many stories were recorded of cures attributed to the intercession of St James. Among them was a story of an accident that occurred on the 1185 expedition to Ireland of King Henry II's son, John, and this may be evidence of the earliest connection between Anglo-Norman settlers in Ireland and Reading. The story illustrates both the efficacy of visiting the shrine of St James at Reading and also the risks of neglecting to fulfil vows. It gives an inkling of the mindset that encouraged pilgrimage to shrines associated with James the Apostle in the twelfth and thirteenth centuries:

> As the king's son, John, was setting out for Ireland, one of the young men going with him broke his arm, I know not how. And when after a long time it failed to heal in response to physicians and plasters, he vowed to go to Reading and there fulfil his vow to St James, if he might be healed by his merits and recover his health. And his arm was immediately healed and became sound. In due course this young man came to England, but he neglected to perform to St James the vows which he had pronounced with his own lips and was shortly afterwards punished by an event of similar misfortune. This time his other arm was broken and he began inwardly to reflect on what he had suffered and the vows which he had made and not fulfilled. Remorsefully, therefore, he admitted the fault of his transgression, penitently had a wax arm with a hand made, and hurried to Reading. And so, when he had fulfilled his vow, his broken and fractured arm was healed and made completely sound. From this case one can see how much it pays to keep one's word and how dangerous it is to dissemble a vow.[4]

At Reading Abbey, the cult of St James was actively promoted. The feast of St James was celebrated on 25 July and the octave following, and there was a further celebration on a feast of the translation of the relics of St James on 30 December. The community also celebrated the feast of St James the Less on 8 May, probably just as an excuse for another Jacobean feast day.[5] In the early thirteenth century the abbey actively promoted its indulgences and the bishops of many Irish dioceses were active participants in the process of encouraging pilgrims to avail of those indulgences. These included the dioceses of Achonry, Annaghdown, Ardfert,

3 Brian Kemp, 'The hand of St James at Reading Abbey', *Reading Medieval Studies*, 16 (1990), 3–22, at pp 8–11.   4 Brian Kemp, 'The miracles of the hand of St James', *Berkshire Archaeological Journal*, 65 (1970), 1–19, at 16–17.   5 Nigel Morgan, 'The calendar and litany of Reading Abbey', *Reading Medieval Studies*, 42 (2016), 89–102; the relic of the hand of St James was later preserved at the church of St Peter, Marlow-on-Thames. See W.J. Gaffney, *The early history of St Peter's church, Marlow, 1846–1912* ([Marlow], 1974).

Armagh, Clonmacnoise, Dublin, Elphin, Emly, Ferns, Kildare, Kilmacduagh, Leighlin, Limerick, Lismore, Tuam and Waterford. These were areas that had come under Anglo-Norman influence. Noticeable absences were the Gaelic-Irish-dominated dioceses of Ardagh, Clogher, Clonfert, Connor, Down, Killala and Raphoe. Some of the Reading Abbey indulgences related specifically to the feast of St James, but most did not, indicating that it was a shrine that might be visited on any feast day during the year.[6] On the Monday before 1 January 1388 a group of Irish people who claimed to be pilgrims came to the notice of the authorities in Ailesbury, just over 40 km north of Reading. They may well have been visiting Reading for the 30 December feast day there, as otherwise it would be an unusual time of year for Irish visitors to travel there.[7]

IRELAND AND SANTIAGO

For some devotees of St James, a visit to Reading Abbey was not enough, and elite pilgrims from England and Anglo-Ireland were drawn to Santiago de Compostela, a pilgrimage destination that was growing in importance in the thirteenth century. A somewhat eccentric travel guide to the pilgrimage route across northern Spain, partly attributed to the French monk Aymeri Picaud, had been compiled in the twelfth century. It proved an influential source of information about the shrine in Galicia and multiple copies of the work circulated in manuscript within Spain, encouraging devotion to St James and the Santiago pilgrimage. However, no copy can be associated with Ireland, and indeed the section containing the pilgrim's guide appears to have had very limited circulation outside Spain.[8]

The pilgrims from Anglo-Ireland from the thirteenth century onwards included bishops and prominent members of religious orders, along with nobles and gentry, some of whom made more than one pilgrimage. A third category was townsmen, whose familiarity with the practicalities of overseas trade undoubtedly helped with the logistics of planning a long pilgrimage.[9]

Although relatively few named pilgrims to Santiago can be identified from thirteenth-century Ireland, those we know of fit a similar profile to those who went from England. Among the earliest named pilgrims from Ireland recorded

---

6 B.R. Kemp (ed.), *Reading Abbey cartularies: British Library manuscripts: Egerton 3031, Harley 1708 and Cotton Vespasian E XXV, 1*, Camden 4th ser., 31 (London, 1986), pp 174–9. 7 Petition of Thomas Woodstock and others [1388], TNA, SC 8/148/7385. 8 Stones, et al. (eds), *The pilgrim's guide*, p. 11. For discussion of earliest surviving medieval manuscript of the 'Codex Calixtinus', which contains much of the evidence for the origins and early history of the Santiago pilgrimage, see Alison Stones, 'Codex Calixtinus' in Xunta de Galicia (ed.), *Compostela and Europe*, pp 374–5. The earliest manuscript dates from the mid-twelfth century and is now in the Santiago cathedral archive (Archivo de la Catedral de Santiago, MS 1). Three early fourteenth-century copies survive, in the British Library, Salamanca University, and the Vatican Library. See Alison Stones, 'Codex Calixtinus Vaticanus' in Xunta de Galicia (ed.), *Compostela and Europe*, p. 376. 9 Storrs, *Jacobean pilgrims from England*, pp 44–5.

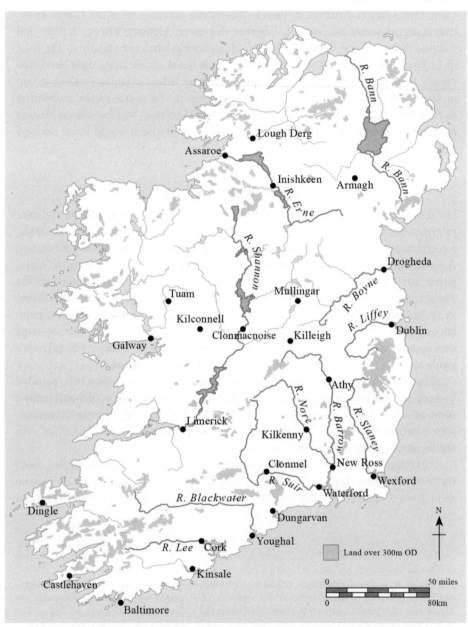

4.1 Ports of departure from Ireland and principal places mentioned in the text.

in documentary sources was Richard de Burgh of Clonmel, who applied for and received protection to go on pilgrimage to Santiago in autumn 1222, just over a decade after the rebuilt Romanesque basilica was consecrated in the Galician city.[10] Others who planned to go on the 1222 pilgrimage included the archbishop of York and a handful of other Englishmen. De Burgh was lord of the manor of Clonmel beside the River Suir, then a centre of Anglo-Norman colonization. Clonmel's development as a commercial centre owed much to his initiative as lord of the manor. In 1225 he obtained a grant of a yearly seven-day fair in the town.[11] Clonmel had trading links via Waterford to Bristol and other English ports, and such networks may have helped create awareness of the feasibility of overseas pilgrimage.[12] Arrangements had to be made for the conduct of affairs in Clonmel in de Burgh's absence on pilgrimage to Santiago, and it is for that pragmatic reason that the fact of his pilgrimage was officially recorded. In October 1222 a legal case in which he was defendant was postponed until such time as he returned from his journey.[13]

Richard de Burgh had departed Ireland for Santiago sometime after October 1222 and was back in England in June 1223 when he hired a ship at the king's expense to cross the Irish Sea. It appears he had completed his journey to Santiago, via England, within a period of eight months.[14] (He may well have combined the pilgrimage with business while passing through England in each direction.) Brian Tate has estimated that the land route from Paris to Santiago and back could take more than six months;[15] it would have been longer still for pilgrims starting further north, or indeed from Ireland before the direct sea route became possible. Those who hired horses or mules on mainland Europe could have made the journey in rather less time, and this may well have been the norm for wealthy pilgrims with a long distance to travel.

Later in the thirteenth century we know of other prominent Anglo-Normans who made the pilgrimage from Dublin to Santiago. The archbishop of Dublin, Fulk de Sandford (d. 1271), who had previously served as chancellor of St Paul's cathedral in London, was granted safe conduct in England for his journey to and from Santiago in 1267, suggesting that he was part of an English pilgrimage group. Sandford was no stranger to foreign travel as he had spent time in Rome on at least two occasions (in 1256 and 1259) on ecclesiastical business.[16] His pilgrimage to Santiago took place just four years before he died, suggesting that it may have been undertaken at a time when he was becoming increasingly concerned about the need to minimize the torments of Purgatory.

---

10 *Cal. Carew MSS: Book of Howth*, p. 414; David Beresford, 'Burgh, Richard de' in *DIB*; document 1054, dated 2 Oct. 1222 in *Cal. doc. Ire., 1171–1251*, p. 162; Vázquez de Parga, et al., *Las peregrinaciones a Santiago de Compostela*, iii, pp 109–10; Barral Iglesias & Yzquierdo Perrín, *Santiago cathedral: a guide to its art treasures* (3rd ed., Leon, 2009), pp 53–4.   11 William P. Burke, *History of Clonmel* (Clonmel, 1907; 3rd ed., 2010), p. 12.   12 Childs & O'Neill, 'Overseas trade', p. 518.   13 *Cal. doc. Ire., 1171–1251*, p. 162.   14 *Cal. doc. Ire., 1171–1251*, pp 133, 170.   15 Tate, *Pilgrimages to St James of Compostella from the British Isles*, p. 10.   16 *Cal. patent rolls, 1266–72*, p. 53; Ronan Mackay, 'Sandford, Fulk de' in *DIB*.

William de Vescy (d. 1297), who became lord of Kildare, was a wealthy, elite pilgrim who embarked on his pilgrimage from Ireland. His mother was co-heiress of the vast estates of William Marshal in Ireland and Britain. He received letters of protection to go on pilgrimage to Santiago in 1276. Six other named pilgrims feature in English administrative records as having been granted permission to go to Santiago in the same year, including another member of the Vescy family, and thus William may well have joined a family group from England.[17] Some fourteen years later, in 1290, William de Vescy became justiciar of Ireland.[18] He had gone on pilgrimage to Santiago when he was a relatively young man, about 30 years old. For others of the Anglo-Norman colony the pilgrimage was their final journey: it was recorded at the assizes held at Naas, Co. Kildare, in 1308 that William le Paumer, brother of Roger le Paumer, had died while on pilgrimage to the shrine of St James.[19]

The thirteenth century marked a phase of expansion of the English and pre-sumably the Anglo-Irish pilgrimage to Santiago. At that time, an overland route through France was necessary and would generally encompass other major shrines along the way.[20] Among the places that might be visited on the journey south were Chartres, Tours, Poitiers and perhaps Toulouse, Conques and Moissac. These were the kind of routes followed by the pilgrims from Anglo-Norman Ireland, who would probably have assembled initially at a port on the south coast of England before crossing to the Continent. It was a lengthy undertaking even for those who hired horses and mules for transport. Unfortunately, none of those who com-menced their journey in Ireland have left a record of the route they followed.

An estimate of the maximum length of time international pilgrimages were expected to take is seen in evidence from Hereford, close to the English/Welsh border. When those associated with the Hereford cathedral community were given leave to go on overseas pilgrimage, *c*.1250, the time allotted was seven weeks for a return journey to the shrine of St Denis in Paris, sixteen weeks for either Rome or Santiago and twelve months for Jerusalem.[21] Such pilgrimages, if mostly overland, would have had to be accomplished with the assistance of horse or mule to meet the Hereford deadlines. Similarly, the stages described in Aymery Picaud's well-known medieval guide to the Camino Francés were calculated for horsemen, the entire overland journey across Spain from Jaca in the Pyrenees to Santiago being

17 Appendix ii, to the *Forty-fifth annual report of the deputy keeper of the public records* (London, 1885), p. 346; Storrs, *Jacobean pilgrims from England*, p. 160.   **18** Ronan Mackay, 'Vescy (Vesci), William de' in *DIB*. For the de Vescy family, see K.J. Stringer, 'Nobility and identity in medieval Britain and Ireland: the de Vescy family' in B. Smith (ed.), *Britain and Ireland, 900–1300: insular responses to medi-eval European change* (Cambridge, 1999), pp 199–239.   **19** *Calendar of justiciary rolls, I–VII years of Edward VII*, ed. H. Wood, A.E. Langman and M. Griffith (Dublin, 1956), p. 83. English Inquisition evidence suggests most pilgrims to Santiago were in the 25–34 age group, with very few aged over 44 (Diana Webb, *Pilgrimage in medieval England* (London, 2000), p. 189).   **20** Storrs, *Jacobean pilgrims from England*, pp 23, 44–5, 158.   **21** Ibid., p. 66.

described as a thirteen-day journey.[22] For pilgrims travelling in this way, the logistics of the journey would have included provisioning for the animals as well as the people, with mules being the easier animal to care for.[23] Numbers of pilgrims to Santiago from Anglo-Ireland in these centuries were probably low, and in terms of the personnel who travelled and the likely routes they took, the phenomenon was essentially an extension of an English pilgrimage experience rather than a distinct Irish one.[24]

PILGRIM INFRASTRUCTURE IN IRELAND

While the names of some pilgrims from England who went to Santiago can be recovered from official sources, sometimes ten or more people per year, we have only a relatively small number of named pilgrims starting their journey from Ireland in the thirteenth and early fourteenth centuries, all of them Anglo-Norman. Yet, the existence of an infrastructure to provide hospitality to pilgrims at some ports hints of a larger movement of people than is evident from these incidental references to high-profile pilgrims found in official sources. There may have been pilgrim hostels at Drogheda, Dublin, Waterford and elsewhere on the Irish coast by the thirteenth century. The existence of such places, or even the evidence of plans to provide such facilities, points to a perceived demand from pilgrims, though not all would have been destined for Santiago. In Dublin, it has been suggested that St Stephen's church and leper hospital, located at the site of the later Mercer's hospital, may have been an assembly point for pilgrims going overseas.[25] It was situated about 600 metres south-west of All Saints priory, now the site of Trinity College, Dublin.[26] Another proposal for a pilgrim hostel at Dublin was drawn up by Henry de Londres, archbishop of Dublin, in 1216 or 1217, after his return from the Fourth Lateran Council in Rome. In line with his experience at the council, the archbishop clearly wished to promote the Santiago pilgrimage, which he may have seen as a modernizing initiative, aligning Ireland with European trends in devotion, including pilgrimage. Moreover, the Santiago pilgrimage was expanding,

22 Gerson, et al. (eds), *The pilgrim's guide to Santiago de Compostela*, ii, p.13; Starkie, *Road to Santiago*, p. 180; see also Colin Smith, 'The geography and history of Iberia in the *Liber Sancti Jacobi*' in M. Dunn & L.K. Davidson (eds), *The pilgrimage to Compostela in the Middle Ages: a book of essays* (New York, 1996), pp 23–41.   23 Storrs, *Jacobean pilgrims from England*, pp 69–71.   24 For the English pilgrimage, see Tate, *Pilgrimages to St James of Compostella from the British Isles*; D.W. Lomax, 'The first English pilgrims to Santiago de Compostella' in H. Mayr-Harting & R.I. Moore (eds), *Studies in medieval history presented to R.H.C. Davis* (London, 1985), pp 165–75; Storrs includes some pilgrims from Ireland in her lists of English pilgrims in the thirteenth and fourteenth centuries (Storrs, *Jacobean pilgrims from England*, pp 159–69).   25 Dermot Neilis' report on the urban medieval graveyard at 1–5 Stephen Street Upper, Dublin (2000:0287). www.excavations.ie/report/2000/ Dublin/0005110, accessed 20 Feb. 2018.   26 The medieval St Stephen's hospital is marked 'H2' on H.B. Clarke's map, 'Medieval Dublin, c.840–c.1540' in his *Dublin, part 1, to 1610*, Irish Historic Towns Atlas, 11 (Dublin, 2002).

following the completion of the Romanesque cathedral *c.*1210, and the promotion of the site in other ways. The proposal also coincided with the fifth Crusade, launched in 1215, when Jerusalem was again inaccessible to Christian pilgrims, and Santiago was perceived as an appropriate alternative shrine. It was also just a few years before the first jubilee year at Canterbury, in 1220, which would have been expected to attract pilgrims from Ireland. According to Archbishop Alen's Register, a sixteenth-century compilation of medieval sources, funding was designated by the archbishop in 1216 or 1217 for a Dublin hostel of St James.[27] The funds were to be diverted from the Gaelic diocese of Glendalough, which was to be suppressed and absorbed into the diocese of Dublin, a proposal that was not implemented.[28] The priory of All Saints was to be given the responsibility of establishing the hostel, which was to be erected near the seashore to cater for the poor and for pilgrims. It was to be built beside All Saints priory, close to the long stone known as the 'stein', on the south bank of the River Liffey.[29]

John Speed's map of Dublin in 1610, if accurate, shows an inlet that would have formed a natural harbour immediately north of All Saints priory, which could have been an initial point of departure for pilgrims.[30] This landing place was in the area now occupied by Townsend Street and Fleet Street.[31] Excavations at Townsend Street/Luke Street in Dublin in 1998 revealed no medieval occupation levels; oak timber structures that post-date 1656 were found, designed to reclaim land and protect the highway from the sea.[32] The lack of archaeological evidence is reinforced by the absence of contemporary or later documentary or cartographic sources for the hostel proposed in 1216, suggesting that it may not have been built.[33]

Even if that proposed hostel was not built by All Saints priory, there was abundant accommodation in Dublin for pilgrims since the eleven religious houses in the town could have offered shelter to those awaiting departure. All religious

27 Charles McNeill (ed.), *Calendar of Archbishop Alen's Register, c.1172–1534* (Dublin, 1950), pp 55–6.   28 Myles Ronan, 'Union of the dioceses of Glendaloch and Dublin in 1216', *JRSAI*, 60 (1930), 56–72.   29 If built, it would have been near the site of the present Pearse Street Garda station. Richard Hayes, 'Ireland's links with Compostella', *Studies: an Irish Quarterly Review*, 37:147 (1948), 326–32, at 326–7. Richard Butler (ed.), *Registrum Prioratus Omnium Sanctorum juxta Dublin* (Dublin, 1845), introduction, p. x (citing *Alen's Register*).   30 I am grateful to Howard Clarke for this observation (personal communication, June 2018).   31 See Clarke, *Dublin, part 1, to 1610*, Irish Historic Towns Atlas, map of 'Medieval Dublin, *c.*840–*c.*1540', where the long stone is marked 'K3'.   32 'Townsend Street/Luke Street, Dublin', www.excavations.ie/report/1998/ Dublin/0003365, accessed 1 Nov. 2017.   33 Clarke, *Dublin, part 1, to 1610*, Irish Historic Towns Atlas, p. 28, topographical information section 19: health. The medieval pilgrim hospital was deliberately omitted from the map of 'Medieval Dublin, *c.*840–*c.*1540' compiled by Howard Clarke because of the absence of documentary or archaeological evidence that might identify the site (Clarke, *Dublin, part 1, to 1610*, Irish Historic Towns Atlas, map 4). It is important not to confuse the proposed 1216 pilgrim hostel with another hospital built almost four centuries later. The building marked as no. 10 and labelled 'The hospitall' on John Speed's map of Dublin was Carey's hospital, newly built *c.*1602 towards the end of the Nine Years War (1594–1603) to provide for maimed soldiers and the poor. That seventeenth-century military hospital had no link to any medieval pilgrim hostel.

houses were expected to provide hospitality to poor pilgrims and other travellers.[34] Merchants as well as pilgrims availed of accommodation in monastic houses, and Santiago de Compostela was only one of very many possible destinations for those who stayed in religious houses in places like Dublin, Waterford and Drogheda prior to boarding a ship. Both local and foreign merchants would have stayed at the guesthouses attached to medieval friaries, and conducted business from there.[35] Indeed, the international networks of these religious orders gave merchants a network of contacts in other countries, and these interactions were a channel for foreign news and information about far distant places.

In Dublin, the Augustinian priory of All Saints, founded in 1166, was just metres away from the shore and it provided accommodation for visitors.[36] Those who lodged there at different times included members of the royal administration, but pilgrims would also have been welcomed there. Similarly, the wealthy abbey of St Thomas, founded in 1192 to the west of the walled city of Dublin, included hospitality to pilgrims among its many other roles.[37] The nearby parish church of St James had been founded just a few years earlier, c.1190, while the parish church of St Catherine was built in the early thirteenth century, replacing an earlier church of St Thomas.[38] John Smyth, a seventeenth-century observer, asserted that the cemetery of St Catherine's had been used by the abbey of St Thomas for the burial of strangers, meaning people from outside the local parish, which might explain the presence of pilgrim burials there.[39] The two separate burials with scallop shells recently found on a site that was part of the medieval abbey of St Thomas the Martyr could have been lay pilgrims passing through Dublin rather than monks from the abbey. Still on the south side of the Liffey, the cathedral of Christ Church, with its multitude of relics, would have attracted pilgrims, including those travelling to or from Santiago, and the Augustinian canons there might also have offered their usual hospitality to visitors.[40] On the north bank of the River Liffey, the Cistercian St Mary's abbey may have fulfilled similar functions.

Well to the north of Dublin, at the mouth of the River Boyne, there was a pilgrim hostel at Drogheda. It provided shelter and accommodation for intending pilgrims and other travellers.[41] Excavations undertaken prior to road building in the early 1980s in an area between St James's Street and the River Boyne in

34 Gwynn & Hadcock, *Medieval religious houses*, pp 344–5.   **35** Colmán Ó Clabaigh, *The friars in Ireland, 1224–1540* (Dublin, 2012), pp 114–16.   **36** Butler (ed.), *Registrum Prioratus Omnium Sanctorum*, pp xxv–xxvi.   **37** Clarke, *Dublin, part 1, to 1610*, Irish Historic Towns Atlas, p. 19; Gwynn & Hadcock, *Medieval religious houses*, p. 172.   **38** Clarke, *Dublin, part 1, to 1610*, Irish Historic Towns Atlas, p. 18.   **39** H.F. Berry, 'Notes of a statement dated 1634, regarding St Thomas's Court and St Katherine's churchyard, Dublin', *JRSAI*, 37:4 (1907), 393–6, at 396; see also Áine Foley, *The abbey of St Thomas the Martyr, Dublin* (Dublin, 2017), p. 19.   **40** See above, p. 24.   **41** John Bradley, 'The topography and layout of medieval Drogheda', *JLAHS*, 19:2 (1978), 98–127, at 108–9; Gwynn & Hadcock, *Medieval religious houses*, p. 349; Anthony Cogan, *The diocese of Meath, ancient and modern* (3 vols, Dublin 1862–70), i, p. 180; John d'Alton, *The history of Drogheda* (2 vols, Dublin, 1844), i, pp 135–6.

Drogheda revealed the remains of a building that might plausibly have been the pilgrim hostel, though there is uncertainty about this identification.[42] Part of the town wall was also uncovered in the same excavation. The remnants of the medieval building uncovered at Drogheda included three parallel stone walls, 2.60m high, with several windows and an internal doorway.[43] The available archaeological evidence allowed the building to be dated to the early thirteenth century.[44] More recent excavations at a site immediately to the east of the medieval town wall in Drogheda have uncovered evidence for a thirteenth- to fifteenth-century religious house or other high-status structure. This has been tentatively identified as a priory of St James that might also have acted as a pilgrim hostel.[45] The suggestions linking these discoveries with the pilgrimage remain very tentative; the archaeological evidence is inconclusive.

In thirteenth-century Waterford, another Anglo-Norman town, the Dominican community counted the care of pilgrims among their functions. The ruins of the thirteenth-century St Saviour's priory, founded in 1235, lie near Blackfriars Street. When surveyed in 1541, there was a particularly extensive complex of buildings there that appears to have been intended to accommodate visitors. The baron's hall had three upper rooms, the great hall also had upper rooms while the little hall had a kitchen and an upper room. All of these rooms could have been used to provide hospitality to pilgrims and other travellers.[46] Meanwhile, the Augustinian house on the seashore at Dungarvan, founded c.1290, housed a community that may also have looked after pilgrims and other travellers.[47] An emblem of St James is preserved on a stone carving taken from the former Augustinian chapel there.[48] Dungarvan was not, however, a deep-water port, suggesting that it did not serve as the final point of departure for Irish pilgrims about to sail directly to Santiago in the fifteenth century.

Waterford and Dungarvan were among the southern ports that had strong trading links across the Irish Sea.[49] They were potential points of departure for pilgrims from east Munster and south Leinster, particularly if they envisaged an onward sea voyage from the port of Bristol or elsewhere in south-west England. Other Irish ports that served as points of departure probably also had hostels

42 Stalley, 'Sailing to Santiago', 1988, note 9.   43 Kieran Campbell, 'The archaeology of medieval Drogheda', *Archaeology Ireland*, 1:2 (1987), 52–6; S.M. Youngs, J. Clark & T.B. Barry, 'Medieval Britain and Ireland in 1982', *Medieval Archaeology*, 27 (1983), 218–19.   44 Kieran Campbell, 'James Street, Drogheda, Co. Louth, E210, E249/E701' in www.heritagecouncil.ie/unpublished_excavations/section17.html#JamesStreet, accessed 28 Apr. 2017; S.M. Youngs, J. Clark & T.B. Barry, 'Medieval Britain and Ireland in 1983', *Medieval Archaeology*, 28 (1984), 256.   45 James Kyle, '2008:825 South Bank development, Marsh Road, Drogheda', accessed 1 Nov. 2017. No priory in Drogheda with a dedication to St James is listed in Gwynn & Hadcock, *Medieval religious houses*.   46 Ó Clabaigh, *The friars in Ireland*, pp 112–17; Newport B. White (ed.), *Extents of Irish monastic possessions, 1540–41* (Dublin, 1943), pp 351–2.   47 T.C. Butler, *Journey of an abbey, 1292–1972* (Dublin, [1973]), p. 6.   48 Dóirín Mhic Mhurchú, *Bealach na bó finne* (Dublin, 1994), plate [1], facing p. 106.   49 A.F. O'Brien, 'The development and evolution of the medieval borough and port of Dungarvan, Co. Waterford, c.1200 to c.1530', *JCHAS*, 92 (1987), 85–94.

attached to religious houses to accommodate pilgrims and other travellers while they waited to sail, but they remain to be positively identified.[50] No reference has been found in later documentation to hostels for pilgrims being established in Irish port towns, but other ports on the south and west coasts that facilitated pilgrim traffic included Wexford, New Ross, Youghal, Kinsale, Dingle, Limerick, Galway and Assaroe.

By the fifteenth century the land-bridge route through England was no longer necessary and pilgrims could sail directly from Ireland to the Iberian peninsula. Others may have continued to join pilgrim or merchant ships leaving from Bristol, Penzance, Plymouth, Dartmouth, Weymouth, Poole, Southampton, Dover or other southern English ports, some of them perhaps choosing to visit popular shrines at Reading and Canterbury while in England.[51] The Welsh port of Pembroke was also well located for ships heading south, and the route from Wexford to Pembroke was among the shortest possible sea crossings from Ireland. If no ship heading for Spain was to be found there, pilgrims could proceed by sea to Plymouth or other ports on the south coast of England that may have offered better prospects of finding a ship setting sail for Spain.

JOURNEYS WITHIN IRELAND TO THE COAST

There was also, of course, the journey within Ireland to reach the initial port of departure. Some may have used river transport for that element of the journey, or followed a riverbank. For south-midland pilgrims there was the convenient route through Co. Carlow served by the River Barrow and another through south Co. Kilkenny served by the River Nore, leading south to New Ross and Waterford.[52] The etching of a ship in the plaster of the medieval parish church of St Mary at New Ross may recall its pilgrim traffic.[53] Ocean-going vessels could be accommodated at New Ross, a river port developed by William Marshal, which capitalized on the transport networks of these two important rivers at the point where they merged.[54] The catchment area of these two rivers was second only to the Shannon. Although rapids and shallows made navigation difficult, the River Nore was navigable for smaller boats as far north as Inisteague and Thomastown, though not to the city of Kilkenny. The River Barrow was navigable as far north as Carlow and Athy. However, merchants operating in those mid-Leinster regions generally found the

50 See map of Drogheda's European trade routes in Bradley, 'Topography and layout of medieval Drogheda', 122; Stalley, 'Sailing to Santiago', *passim*. 51 Childs, 'The perils, or otherwise, of maritime pilgrimage', pp 123–43; for a list of ships and ship-owners licensed to carry pilgrims from England, 1235–1484, see Storrs, *Jacobean pilgrims from England*, pp 173–82. 52 Linda Doran, 'Lords of the river valleys: economic and military lordship in the Carlow corridor, c.1200–1350: European model in an Irish context' in L. Doran & J. Lyttleton (eds), *Lordship in medieval Ireland* (Dublin, 2007), pp 99–129. 53 Karl Brady & Chris Corlett, 'Holy ships: ships on plaster at medieval ecclesiastical sites in Ireland', *Archaeology Ireland*, 18:2 (2004), 28–31. 54 O'Sullivan & Breen, *Maritime Ireland*, pp 185–6.

overland journey to Dublin more economic than the southerly river route through New Ross.[55] Pilgrim journeys almost certainly mirrored the mercantile routeways.

There was a strong commercial rivalry between New Ross and Waterford. The latter port handled traffic from south Tipperary, the River Suir being navigable as far inland as Clonmel for small craft. Pilgrims taking that route could join a larger ship at Waterford for the onward journey, perhaps sailing first to Bristol. Another possible point of departure was Wexford, at the mouth of the River Slaney. It offered the closest safe harbour in Ireland for merchants or pilgrims destined for England, Wales or Western Europe, and had particularly close trading links with Bristol.[56] The fledgling Anglo-Norman colony in Ireland had worked hard to build and protect communications networks across the Irish Sea. Ports around the coast formed part of this infrastructure, including Galway, Limerick, north Kerry, Cork, Youghal, Waterford, New Ross, Wexford, Dublin, Drogheda, and the east Ulster ports of Strangford, Carrickfergus and Coleraine.[57] Each offered a potential point of initial departure from Ireland for pilgrims to the shrine of St James.

Pilgrims from north Leinster would usually have opted to sail from Dublin or Drogheda, the latter being the place where the River Boyne met the sea. Generally, though, Drogheda's routine shipping trade was local – across the Irish Sea – rather than to far distant places. While there were exceptions, it was well into the fifteenth century before Drogheda merchants regularly ventured as far as Brittany.[58] Among those that did so were William Preston, Richard Barton and John Fowler, who were licensed in 1435 to ship salt, iron and other goods from Brittany to Ireland.[59] This John Fowler is probably to be identified with John Fowling, who was mayor of Drogheda when he went on pilgrimage to Santiago in 1473. Pilgrims departing from Drogheda probably went via Bristol or Plymouth and continued their journey to Galicia along the sea routes used by pilgrims from the west of England.

Pilgrims from south Munster could have travelled along the river Blackwater from Lismore to reach the port of Youghal, or the River Lee to sail from Cork.[60] Others might have sailed from Kinsale, Baltimore, Castlehaven or from Dingle further west. In 1473, for example, a Galway merchant and goldsmith named Germyn Lynch was at Kinsale trying to repair a ship, the *Mary* of Leybourne, in preparation for a journey from there to Santiago for the jubilee year. The ship

55 L.M. Cullen, 'The port and the local economy' in T. Dunne (ed.), *New Ross. Rosponte. Ros Mhic Treoin: an anthology celebrating 800 years* (Wexford, 2007), pp 243–51.   56 Nicholas Furlong, 'Life in Wexford port, 1600–1800' in K. Whelan (ed.), *Wexford history and society* (Dublin, 1987), p. 150; for social and commercial links with Bristol in the sixteenth century, see Niall O'Brien, 'Wexford apprentices in sixteenth-century Bristol', *Journal of the Wexford Historical Society*, 23 (2011–12), 169–76.   57 O'Sullivan & Breen, *Maritime Ireland*, pp 159–98.   58 Cullen, 'The port and the local economy', p. 243; O'Neill, *Merchants and mariners*, pp 86–7.   59 E. Tresham (ed.), *Rotulorum patentium et clausorum cancellariae Hiberniae calendarium* (Dublin, 1828), no. 257, p. 68. For John Fowling (possibly the same person as John Fowler) as mayor in 1467 and 1471, see also d'Alton, *History of Drogheda*, i, p. 247.   60 O'Neill, 'Map 12: Irish ports in the later Middle Ages' in Cosgrove (ed.), *NHI*, ii: *medieval Ireland*, p. 499.

had been damaged on an earlier voyage from Portugal, and he was forced to borrow money for repairs from a variety of merchants in Limerick and Galway before he could depart from Kinsale. The financial consequences troubled him for some years afterwards. Lynch's voyage to Santiago was an opportunistic one for the jubilee year; he was next heard of on a fishing expedition heading for Iceland.[61]

Once potential pilgrims had reached the Irish coast, there was often a wait of unpredictable length for suitable winds before the ship could venture out to sea. Even in the seventeenth century a delay of several weeks for favourable winds before crossing the Irish Sea was not unusual.[62] Prior to the fifteenth century, ships used on the Irish Sea were generally cogs, used for cargo, though they might occasionally carry perhaps twenty passengers across the Irish Sea. Even when the quality of merchant ships capable of trading between Ireland and Iberia had improved, if no suitable ship destined for Spain was available at an Irish port then Irish pilgrims could opt to cross first to Bristol, Plymouth or elsewhere, and hope to pick up a Spain-bound vessel from there. On arrival at Bristol, some pilgrims may have availed of hospitality at the priory of St James just outside the walled city, or at other religious houses there.[63] Having reached an English port, there could still be significant delays. One experienced English pilgrim, the intrepid Margery Kempe, when travelling to Santiago in 1417, recorded waiting six weeks for a ship on her outward journey.[64] In contrast, she spent just fourteen days in Santiago, and claimed that the return journey took a mere five days by sea.[65] Ships usually sailed on the high seas in convoys including vessels of varying sizes. In some circumstances the smaller ships were better able to withstand adverse sea conditions.[66] Research by Constance Storrs on fourteenth- and fifteenth-century records of English shipping, and on licences awarded to ship owners to transport pilgrims, indicate that it was only in jubilee years that ships sailed specifically to transport pilgrims to and from Santiago. In other years far fewer pilgrims made the journey and they would have been accommodated on regular merchant ships alongside other cargo.[67]

While the sea route to A Coruña, followed by a short trek to Santiago, was much more feasible than travelling overland most of the way from the north coast of France, there is direct evidence of one individual taking the land route from

61 James F. Morrissey (ed.), *Statute rolls of the parliament of Ireland: twelfth and thirteenth to the twenty-first and twenty-second years of the reign of King Henry the Fourth* (Dublin, 1939), pp 571–7; Timothy O'Neill, 'A fifteenth-century entrepreneur: Germyn Lynch, fl. 1441–1483' in J. Bradley (ed.), *Settlement and society in medieval Ireland: studies presented to F.X. Martin* (Kilkenny, 1988), pp 412–18. **62** For the case of the earl of Clanricard and his family waiting twelve days at Dublin to sail to Holyhead in summer 1609, see Clanricard to Salisbury, 30 Aug. 1609, *Cal. S.P. Ire., 1608–11*, p. 281. **63** *St James priory: the story* (Bristol, c.2017). **64** S.B. Meech & H.E. Allen (eds), *The Book of Margery Kempe*, EETS, original ser., 212 (London, 1940), pp 106–7. **65** Ibid., p. 110; Goodman, *Margery Kempe and her world*, p. 158. **66** S.D. Goitein, 'The unity of the Mediterranean world in the "middle" Middle Ages', *Studia Islamica*, 12 (1960), 29–42, at 39. **67** Storrs, *Jacobean pilgrims from England*, pp 173–82.

Galicia to Ireland in the mid-fourteenth century before a direct sea journey was possible. The Hungarian pilgrim George Crissaphan, who kept a record of his journey, was no average pilgrim. Guided by St Michael the Archangel, he had walked from his Hungarian home to Santiago specifically as a penance, taking just one attendant with him, and expecting to experience real austerity. Not satisfied with reaching Santiago, he continued to Finisterre, setting off there with bread and water for five months. When he reached Finisterre he was disappointed that there were too many people about. Looking for real remoteness, he heard about St Patrick's Purgatory at the end of the world and set off to walk to Ireland, arriving at his destination at Lough Derg probably in the autumn of 1353.[68] Going on foot was part of his effort to maximize the penitential aspect of the path he had chosen. The story mentions more than once that he managed the long walk only with great difficulty.[69] That he was nonetheless an elite pilgrim is confirmed by his encounters with Richard FitzRalph, primate of Ireland, Edward III, king of England, and various local kings in the province of Ulster.[70]

Another Hungarian pilgrim, Laurence Rathold, similarly combined the Santiago and Lough Derg pilgrimages in 1408–9, but we do not know what route he took. While in Ireland, he also visited the relics of Patrick, Brigid and Colum Cille in Dublin.[71] He was not just a pilgrim: Rathold had also been a diplomat and he hoped to combine his Continental travels with some military adventure in various regions.[72] These Hungarian travellers who pursued exceptional journeys in search of extended adventure were not normal pilgrims and their experiences cannot be regarded as typical of those pilgrims who journeyed between Ireland and Santiago in the same century.

FIFTEENTH-CENTURY URBAN PILGRIMS

By the fifteenth century, Anglo-Irish townsmen (and some women) from a range of coastal towns were keen to embark on the pilgrimage to Santiago, some of them making the journey more than once. In 1473, John Fowling, mayor of Drogheda, vowed to go on pilgrimage to Santiago and arrangements were duly made to appoint a deputy to serve in his absence.[73] In addition to visiting Santiago during a 'year of grace', Fowling planned to visit the shrine of St 'Trynyan', among

---

68 A.B. Scott, 'Latin learning and literature in Ireland, 1169–1500' in D. Ó Cróinín (ed.), *NHI*, i: *prehistoric and early Ireland* (Oxford, 2005), pp 934–95, at p. 984; Katherine Walsh, *A fourteenth-century scholar and primate: Richard FitzRalph in Oxford, Avignon and Armagh* (Oxford, 1981), pp 308–10. The Latin narrative of his pilgrimage is printed in L.L. Hammerich (ed.), *Visiones Georgii* (Copenhagen, 1930). **69** Hammerich (ed.), *Visiones Georgii*, pp 89–91. **70** Ibid., pp 310–16; Aubrey Gwynn, 'Archbishop FitzRalph and George of Hungary', *Studies: an Irish Quarterly Review*, 24:96 (Dec. 1935), 558–72. **71** Webb, *Medieval European pilgrimage*, p. 119. **72** Brendan Smith (ed.), *The register of Nicholas Fleming, archbishop of Armagh, 1404–1416* (Dublin, 2003), pp 174–5; Haren & de Pontfarcy (eds), *The medieval pilgrimage to St Patrick's Purgatory*, pp 124–6. **73** Morrissey (ed.), *Statute rolls of the parliament of Ireland, 12–22, Ed. IV*, p. 53.

others, so that an extended period away from his official duties was envisaged.[74] Almost a century later, in 1562, one of Fowling's successors as mayor of Drogheda was similarly licensed to go on pilgrimage to Santiago, indicating that the link between Drogheda and the shrine of St James persisted into the Reformation era.[75] It seems that a town mayor and his associates going on an extended pilgrimage was not unusual. The strong trading links between the ports of Drogheda and Bristol are probably sufficient explanation for the viability of the pilgrimage for these Drogheda townsmen. Their motivation is not recorded, but they may have seen themselves as undertaking the pilgrimage on behalf of all the people of the town, interceding for them for some special cause. In the case of John Fowling in 1473 he had made a vow that he felt obliged to fulfil.

In a later jubilee year, 1484, Mayor James Rice of Waterford, together with the bailiffs of that town, went on pilgrimage to Santiago. They were already planning their departure in 1483.[76] These men felt compelled to undertake the journey, having made a vow to do so. The licence granted them by parliament noted the circumstances:

> the said mayor and bailiffs, long before they were elected to office, made a promise to go on pilgrimage to St James of Galicia in Spain; upon which, considering the premises, it is ordained and established by authority of this parliament that the said James, Patrick [Mulligan] and Philip [Bryan] and each of them may go on the said pilgrimage of St James of Galicia in Spain ... provided that ... each of them appoint such person and persons as their deputies to occupy their said offices in their absence as shall be admitted by the advice of the council and jurats of the same city.[77]

In the years since the previous jubilee, the mayor had had time to make elaborate preparations. Prior to his departure, Rice arranged to build a chantry chapel in Christ Church cathedral, Waterford. Construction commenced in March 1482 and it was dedicated to St Catherine and St James in December of the same year.[78] (His wife's name was Katherine, which helps explain the choice of dedication.) The construction work involved the removal of part of the side wall of the cathedral; that it was permitted at all is an indication of the wealth and influence of the mayor, and the support of the dean, John Collyn.[79] In the new chantry chapel,

---

74 Trinian was a variant form of Ninian, a fifth- or sixth-century saint whose burial place at Whithorn in south-west Scotland was a place of pilgrimage; there was also a thirteenth-century parish church of St Trinian on the Isle of Man. A.W. Moore, *A history of the Isle of Man* (2 vols, London, 1900), i, pp 66–7; Peter Hill, *Whithorn & St Ninian: the excavation of a monastic town, 1984–91* (Stroud, 1997), pp 1–4. 75 *Cal. Carew MSS, 1515–74*, p. 317. 76 Philomena Connolly (ed.), *Statute rolls of the Irish parliament, Richard III–Henry VII* (Dublin, 2002), pp 38–9. 77 Translated from French in ibid., p. 39. 78 Niall Byrne with Michael Byrne (ed. & trans.), *The register of St Saviour's chantry of Waterford* (Dublin, 2013), p. 70; Rae, 'The Rice monument', 1–14. 79 Eamonn McEneaney, 'Politics and the art of devotion in late fifteenth-century Waterford' in Moss, Ó Clabaigh & Ryan (eds), *Art and devotion*, pp 33–50, at p. 37.

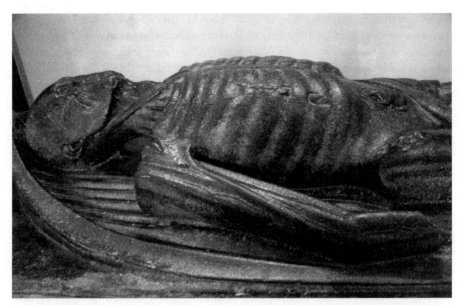

4.2 Late fifteenth-century tomb of Mayor James Rice in Waterford cathedral.

which was intended to serve as a place in which he would be remembered and prayed for after his death, Rice placed a large box tomb. It was such an imposing structure that others wished to emulate it, and while Rice was away on pilgrimage a law was enacted in Waterford forbidding others from digging up the cathedral floor to construct tombs.[80] The chantry chapel built in 1482 no longer survives, but James Rice's box tomb can still be seen, topped by a cadaver effigy being consumed by vermin, with an inscription that reminded passers-by of their own impending death:

> Here lies James Rice, formerly a citizen of this city and founder of this chapel, and Katherina Brown, his wife. You that stand here consider that what I am you will be, I was what you are. I beg you pray for me that when it is your fate to pass through the gate of death, our Christ who has come to redeem the lost lest the redeemed be damned, will have pity.[81]

St James as pilgrim was among the Apostles and saints depicted on a side panel of the mayor's funeral monument. Although the scallop shell and scrip are no longer

---

80 Eamonn McEneaney, *A history of Waterford and its mayors from the 12th to the 20th century* (Waterford, 1995), p. 89.   81 Translated from Latin in McEneaney, 'Politics and the art of devotion in late fifteenth-century Waterford' in Moss, Ó Clabaigh & Ryan (eds), *Art and devotion*, pp 33–50, at p. 36.

evident, a staff of the type associated with James is depicted, as is his hat, high-crowned with a small brim, which E.C. Rae explains is characteristic of figures of St James the Great found in Irish contexts.[82] The depiction of the Apostles on the tomb signified that they were being invoked as protectors of James Rice. Given the mayor's enthusiasm for the Santiago pilgrimage it is no surprise to find St James the Great included, although it is likely that he was simply depicted as an Apostle with his brethren.[83] In stylistic terms, the decorative details on James Rice's cadaver tomb echo similar work in south-west England, reminding us of the close links between Waterford and ports in Somerset and Devon.[84] The stonemasons who constructed such monuments were among those whose work involved travel, and whose movements would have facilitated the spread of information and ideas on many topics, perhaps including the cult of St James. The medieval cathedral at Waterford containing the chantry chapel erected for James Rice was demolished in 1773, and his tomb was left outside the new cathedral until sometime after 1824, when it was brought inside.[85] The survival of Rice's tomb offers a very rare instance in Ireland of a connection between an Irish pilgrim to Santiago and the iconography on his funeral monument.

The funeral monument and its associated chantry chapel of St Catherine and St James were not James Rice's only investments in Waterford cathedral. Earlier in his life he had also made significant contributions to St Saviour's chantry chapel in the same cathedral, in the form of gifts of property, and income from property. St Saviour's chantry chapel had been founded in 1468 by John Collyn (d. 1484), the English dean of the cathedral from 1441. Collyn actively promoted the chantry and in 1470 he obtained authorization from four cardinals permitting indulgences of 100 days to those who attended the chapel of St Saviour and contributed to its ornamentation and upkeep.[86] James Rice was among its most generous benefactors. The motivation for investing in a chantry chapel was to establish a fund to pay for chaplains to pray for the salvation of the soul of the patron or confraternity associated with it. In the case of St Saviour's chantry chapel, Collyn arranged that two or three chaplains would be paid – from the property income – to pray for the souls of benefactors, including Collyn himself, as well as William Lyncoll and his wife Beuflour Poer and their family. The Lyncoll family had contributed generously towards the gold ornamentation of the chapel. Collyn also arranged

---

82 Rae, 'The Rice monument', 5, & plate 5. The image of St James on the north panel is one of two tentatively identified as the Apostle Thomas in Hunt, *Irish medieval figure sculpture, i*, pp 234–5, but Rae's identification seems correct. A clearer representation of St James on a Munster tomb can be seen at Kilcooley abbey, Co. Tipperary, on the tomb of Piers Fitz James Oge Butler (www.gothicpast.com, accessed 22 Oct. 2014).   83 Rae, 'The Rice monument', 8.   84 Ibid., 13. For the English influences on late medieval Waterford, see Brendan Smith, 'Late medieval Ireland and the English connection: Waterford and Bristol, *ca.* 1360–1460', *Journal of British Studies*, 50:2 (2011), 546–65.   85 Roger Stalley, 'Reconstructions of the Gothic past: the lost cathedral of Waterford', *Irish Architectural and Decorative Studies*, 16 (2013), 94–131, at 114 and 128, note 90.   86 Byrne (ed.), *Register of St Saviour's chantry*, pp 43–4.

that the said chaplains shall pray specifically and by name for the souls of Peter Rice and of his wife Anne, for their son James Rice and for his wife Katherine, for the souls of William Roop and of Magine Burnam, for the brothers and sisters in general of the said chapel both living and dead, and for all others for whom we are obliged to pray.

I also regulate that the said chaplains shall officiate each day in the choir save those who will properly celebrate the Mass for the dead in their week on duty who must every day throughout that week recite the office of the dead with the nine lessons in the said chapel, and that each chaplain of my foundation shall be able to wear a vicar's habit in the choir.[87]

The personal possessions of the dean, including his vestments and books, are documented in the manuscript register of St Saviour's and, aside from books on Scripture and canon law, they also included a book on the sacraments and the *ars morendi*, the art of making a good death, 'which I have written with my own hand'. Collyn left that particular book to his personal chaplain. He also owned a copy of the *Summa confessorum* by John of Freiburg (d. 1314), which he left to the library of the chantry. This was a manual on penance for use by clergy.[88] That such books were part of his personal library would suggest that Dean Collyn had a particular interest in promoting the idea of a good death. Rice's own tomb, with its image of a cadaver within a shroud, likewise indicates his preoccupation with death.

Heightened concern with such matters had come to the fore in the mid fourteenth century when the outbreak of bubonic plague killed up to half the population of Europe in the years after 1348. Like Drogheda and Dublin, as a well-populated port with a strong overseas trade, Waterford could not escape the plague. Among the first recorded victims in the town was the prior of St Catherine's Augustinian priory, who died in June 1349, and the plague soon spread to other towns such as New Ross, Clonmel, Cork, Youghal and Cashel. Not long afterwards, other regions were affected and significant deaths from plague were also recorded in inland parts of north Connacht and south Ulster, including the territories of Moylurg and Breifne.[89] An intensification of piety was among the responses to the plague, in Ireland and elsewhere, and pilgrimage was one manifestation of that piety.[90] For the devout, one perceived consequence of the Black Death was the great increase in souls in Purgatory whose lives had been cut short, without the opportunity to repent of their sins, and who were reliant on those still living to intercede for them and to earn indulgences on their behalf.

---

87 Ibid., p. 49.   88 Michael Byrne, *Waterford 1470: Dean John Collyn and the chantry chapel of St Saviour* (Drogheda, 2013), pp 165–8, 178–9. Some of the extraordinarily elaborate liturgical vestments used by Dean Collyn survive and are displayed in Waterford Museum. See Eamonn McEneaney with Rosemary Ryan (eds), *Waterford treasures: a guide to the historical and archaeological treasures of Waterford city* (Waterford, 2004), pp 92–106.   89 Maria Kelly, *A history of the Black Death in Ireland* (London, 2001), pp 35–7.   90 Ibid., pp 46–62.

This increased concern about Purgatory was particularly noticeable on Europe's Atlantic fringe, from Galicia to Germany.[91]

In addition to their connection through St Saviour's, it seems that James Rice and Dean Collyn were personal friends. Rice was mentioned in Collyn's first will, drawn up in September 1468, being bequeathed 'a silver cup which has in it the likeness of a ship'.[92] This gesture of friendship could also be an indication of Rice's association with shipping, which may have been the origin of his considerable wealth. The survival of the manuscript register of St Saviour's chantry in Waterford is unique in Ireland. If a similar register were available for the chantry chapel of St Catherine and St James founded by James Rice in the same cathedral fourteen years later it would no doubt have recorded similar donations of property to be used to fund chaplains to pray for the patron's soul after his death. The spiritual context of these investments in chantry chapels, to intercede for souls in Purgatory, is paralleled by a belief in the efficacy of pilgrimage, as displayed by James Rice and his fellow members of Waterford corporation, on their repeated visits to Santiago to avail of the indulgences offered there.

Overseas travel was not unusual for the leading citizens of medieval Waterford. In 1477 the city officials ruled that given the frequency with which the mayor, bailiffs and recorder of the city travelled to England, Flanders, Portugal and other countries, as well as to other parts of Ireland, they should not be permitted to do so without licence from the mayor and council. The fine for flouting this rule was set at a substantial £5.[93] That such a regulation was needed suggests that foreign travel was a growing phenomenon for townsmen in the late fifteenth century. Galicia was not mentioned in this edict, suggesting that Santiago was not necessarily a routine destination, but rather a place to be visited in special circumstances. Even when people had made a vow to go to Santiago, they were likely to await a jubilee year before attempting to fulfil that vow. One such jubilee year was 1473. Roger Stalley has calculated that passengers who made the journey from New Ross across the Bay of Biscay on the ship named the *Mary* of London in 1473 probably paid an average of 7s. 6d. each to the ship's captain, the equivalent of several weeks' wages.[94] The relatively modest cost of the voyage put the Santiago pilgrimage within reach of more than just a wealthy elite. According to a source in the patent rolls, *quadringentos* (400) pilgrims had boarded the ship at New Ross, in Co. Wexford, bound for Santiago. Admittedly the 320-ton ship must have been very crowded if there were indeed 400 pilgrims on board. The ship was later attacked by three Waterford-based pirate ships on the return journey as it approached the port of Waterford.[95] Piracy off the south coast of Ireland was a known risk. The incident

91 MacCulloch, *Reformation*, p. 14. 92 Byrne (ed.), *Register of St Saviour's chantry*, p. 13. 93 Niall J. Byrne (ed.), *The great parchment book of Waterford: liber atiquissimus civitatis Waterfordiae* (Dublin, 2007), pp 94–5. 94 Stalley, 'Sailing to Santiago', p. 405 & p. 418 note 37. 95 *Cal. patent rolls, 1476–1485*, pp 78–9; the captain of the ship, Bartholomew Cowper of London, was still pursuing a case against the pirates five years later. The relevant Latin text outlining the total number of passengers is printed in Gearóid Mac Niocaill, *Na Buirgéisí, xii–xv aois* (2 vols, Baile Átha Cliath, 1964), ii, p. 534, note.

was evidently part of a long-standing rivalry between the merchants of New Ross and Waterford in the late medieval period. The *Mary* of London had probably made similar journeys from either England or Ireland to the Iberian peninsula and elsewhere at other times without attracting the same amount of adverse attention. These same years saw a marked increase in the number of licences granted to English ship owners to carry pilgrims to Santiago, and it is likely that some pilgrims from Ireland travelled on those ships operating out of English ports, but they cannot now be identified as Irish from the surviving documentation.

The 1483/4 journey for the jubilee year was Mayor Rice's second pilgrimage to Santiago. He had first gone to the shrine of St James some eleven years earlier, in a preceding jubilee year of 1473. On that occasion, too, he was holder of the office of mayor and required permission from the Irish parliament to appoint a deputy mayor prior to his departure.[96] The fact that both of these pilgrimages from Waterford coincided with occasions when James Rice was mayor indicates that he may have travelled as leader of a group of Waterford townsmen. Certainly in 1483/4 he was accompanied by Philip Bryan and Patrick Mulligan and it has been suggested that many others of the town council may have joined them.[97] Mayor Rice and his pilgrim companions from Waterford were doubtless among those who had been influenced by John Collyn's theological understanding of death and the afterlife. They would have been very aware of the need to take appropriate spiritual measures to reduce the length of time they and their relatives would have to spend in Purgatory. They would have regarded the pilgrimage to Santiago in a jubilee year as a particularly effective way of gaining the necessary indulgences.

There is some evidence from the Dublin Guild of Cooks and Vintners that fifteenth-century Dublin townsmen shared the interest of Waterford and Drogheda citizens in devotion to St James. Originally founded as the Guild of Cooks in 1444, their swearing-in day was the feast of St James. A new charter in 1565 combined the Guild of Cooks with the Society of Vintners, and they received a grant of arms c.1608. Their arms displayed three scallop shells.[98] Members of that guild may well have been among the Irish pilgrims to Santiago in the fifteenth century, although no records survive of any pilgrimages they made.

AN URBAN WOMAN PILGRIM

Townswomen, as well as townsmen, had the opportunity to pursue the spiritual benefits that could be obtained at major shrines. In Galway, another Anglo-Irish port with strong Spanish links, Margaret Athy, a devout and wealthy townswoman, went on pilgrimage to Santiago in the early years of the sixteenth century. She also

96 Morrissey (ed.), *Statute rolls of the parliament of Ireland,12–22, Ed. IV*, p. 55. On James Rice as pilgrim, see McEneaney, *Waterford and its mayors*, pp 86–96. 97 McEneaney, *Waterford and its mayors*, pp 86–7. 98 Mary Clark & Raymond Refaussé (eds), *Directory of historic Dublin guilds* (Dublin, 1993), p. 18 (includes illustration).

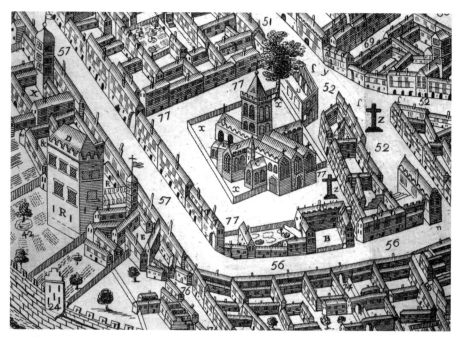

4.3 St Nicholas's collegiate church, Galway, with probable tower-house residence of Margaret Athy (from Hardiman, *History of Galway*, '1651' map).

intended to visit the Holy Land 'if her infirmity did not hinder her'.[99] The Athy family were wealthy merchants; their castle on Market Street in Galway, immediately north of St Nicholas's collegiate church, was one of the most prominent residential buildings in the early modern town.[100] Her husband, Stephen Lynch fitz Dominick, and her father-in-law, Dominick Dubh Lynch, each served as mayor of Galway on more than one occasion. The family were known for their philanthropy and in 1504 her husband founded St Nicholas's hospital, a 'poor men's house', which was located on the south side of the market place.[101]

Margaret Athy went on pilgrimage to Santiago some time after 1508–9, possibly in the jubilee year of 1512. Although the detail of her journey has not survived, her family's involvement in church affairs, and clear evidence for the cult of St James in Galway, which formed the context of her pilgrimage, can be recovered. It is

99 Paul Walsh, 'An account of the town of Galway', *JGAHS*, 44 (1992), 47–118, at 62. **100** John O'Connor, *The Galway Augustinians* (Dublin, 1979), p. 29. See '1651' map of Galway, castle denoted 'R', reproduced in Jacinta Prunty & Paul Walsh, *Galway/Gaillimh*, Irish Historic Towns Atlas, 28 (Dublin, 2016), map 12 and fig. 4.3 above. **101** James Hardiman, *The history of the town and county of the town of Galway* (Dublin, 1820), p. 77. The location was on present-day Shop Street (Prunty & Walsh, *Galway/Gaillimh*, Irish Historic Towns Atlas, p. 19).

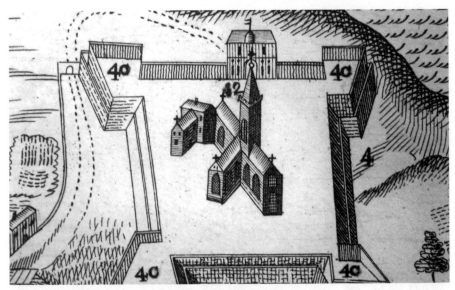

4.4 Augustinian friary at Forthill, Galway (from Hardiman, *History of Galway*, '1651' map).

clear that her pilgrimage was just one of many spiritually motivated investments by her immediate family, which had much in common with the range of investments in church and pilgrimage undertaken by James Rice in Waterford. Earlier, while her husband Stephen Lynch was away in Spain in 1508–9, apparently on business rather than on pilgrimage, Margaret had sponsored the building of a religious house for the Augustinian Order, on the elevated site close to the sea now occupied by Forthill cemetery.[102] A story was told of Stephen's surprise at seeing the building as he sailed into Galway, a surprise that increased when he heard that his wife had funded the initiative.[103] Stephen's will requested 'that mine and my wife Margaret Athyes dirges be celebrated in St Augustin's clay in the convent uppon the hill'. To pay for these prayers for Margaret and himself, Stephen bequeathed all his arable lands to the east of Galway to the Augustinian friary.[104] It is highly likely that Stephen Lynch and Margaret Athy were buried in the friary, and were prayed for at Masses there. It is tempting to speculate that some of the seven scallop shells

102 Paul Walsh, 'The foundation of the Augustinian friary at Galway: a review of the sources', *JGAHS*, 40 (1985–6), 72–80; F.X. Martin, 'The Irish Augustinian reform movement in the fifteenth century' in Watt, Morrall & Martin (eds), *Medieval studies presented to Aubrey Gwynn*, pp 230–64, at pp 257–8; Roderic O'Flaherty, *A chorographical description of west or h-Iar Connaught*, ed. James Hardiman (Dublin, 1846), p. 40; Prunty & Walsh, *Galway/Gaillimh*, Irish Historic Towns Atlas, p. 20. 103 Walsh, 'An account of the town of Galway', 61–2. 104 O'Connor, *The Galway Augustinians*, p. 138. The friary had been dissolved by 1578, and the buildings were demolished in 1645, two years after the fort had been slighted (ibid., pp 40–2).

discovered in 1998 in the cemetery on the site of the Augustinian friary at Galway could have a connection to Margaret Athy's pilgrimage to Santiago.[105]

Margaret Athy's father-in-law, Dominick Dubh Lynch, who died in August 1508, had been a very rich man, and a keen benefactor of the church. He was influential in securing collegiate status for St Nicholas's parish church in the town in 1485, which was dedicated to the patron saint of mariners, and 'bestowed upon it three stately houses of marble within the walls of the town', intended as residences for the warden and vicars. He also helped fund the building of the south aisle, making it the largest parish church in medieval Ireland.[106] In his will Dominick left generous bequests to the Franciscans at Galway and the Dominicans at both Athenry and Galway, as well as a smaller sum of money to every religious house in Ireland.[107] He also left explicit instructions to his son, Stephen, to build an altar dedicated to St James next to the column of the chapel of the Virgin Mary. The chapel of the Virgin Mary was in the south transept, and the pier at the entrance to the south transept still bears the arms of Stephen Lynch and Margaret Athy.[108] The Athy arms on the crest are thought to be a later modification of the original carving, probably added after the death of Dominick Lynch, and done in recognition of Margaret Athy's involvement along with her husband in the expansion of St Nicholas's.[109] The arms of Margaret Athy and her husband can also be seen on the external parapet on the south facade.[110] Despite these indications of Margaret's involvement, when Galway priest John Lynch wrote about the work a century later, he credited only Stephen Lynch, and did not mention her. He likewise credited only Stephen with the building of the 'Convent of the Hermits of St Augustin, on an eminence hard by the city'. Margaret was written out of the story.[111] Dominick Dubh had bequeathed property he owned in Galway and Athenry to fund two priests to pray every day for him and for his parents and his wife, one priest to be in the chapel of the Virgin Mary, where Dominick Dubh was to be buried, and one at the altar of St James.[112] The transept was extended *c.*1561 by Nicholas Lynch, son of Stephen and Margaret, continuing a family tradition of ecclesiastical

---

105 The discovery of scallop shells and human bone was made when a digger was used behind a 1960s wall on the site; the context of the finds was lost and it is not certain that the shells were associated with medieval burials. There was no licensed archaeological excavation. **106** James Hardiman, 'The pedigree of Doctor Dominick Lynch, regent of the Colledge of St Thomas of Aquin, in the city of Seville, AD 1674, from a coeval MS', *Miscellany of the Irish Archaeological Society*, i (1846), 44–90, at 49–50; H.J. Leask, 'The collegiate church of St Nicholas, Galway: a study of the structure', *JGAHS*, 17 (1936–7), 1–23. **107** Walsh, 'The foundation of the Augustinian friary', p. 80. **108** Jim Higgins & Susan Heringklee (eds), *Monuments of St Nicholas's collegiate church, Galway: a historical, genealogical and archaeological record* (Galway, 1992), pp 214–22; Adrian Martyn, *The tribes of Galway, 1124–1642* ([Galway], 2016), pp 126–8. **109** Paul Walsh, 'The medieval merchant's mark and its survival in Galway', *JGAHS*, 45 (1993), 1–28, at 17–19. **110** Ibid., 19. **111** John Lynch, *The portrait of a pious bishop, or the life and death of the most Rev. Francis Kirwan, bishop of Killala*, ed. C.P. Meehan (Dublin, 1884), pp 27–9. **112** Hardiman, 'Pedigree of Dominick Lynch', 76–81; Hardiman, *History of Galway*, p. 235, note d.

patronage.[113] Others of the Lynch family in Galway were also active church patrons at this time. Another town mayor, James Lynch fitz Stephen, a wealthy merchant with Spanish trading links, paid for stained glass windows in the church of St Nicholas in 1493, while one Stephen Lynch fitz James is credited in some sources with building a chapel of St James at Newcastle *c.*1510.[114]

The interest of Margaret Athy and her family in the cult of St James, and particularly in the pilgrimage to Santiago, was a reflection of a wider cult of the saint in Galway. There were at least three medieval churches and two holy wells dedicated to St James in Galway, which suggests a significant level of popular devotion to St James in the town. One chapel was at Ballybane, on the east side of this town.[115] One holy well was close to the medieval parish church of St James at Rahoon on the west side of the city. The well appears to have been a natural spring.[116] Another holy well was on the northern edge of the town in the Newcastle area (Distillery Road).[117] That well was close to the site chosen for the chapel erected *c.*1510 by Mayor Lynch.[118] It was located at a strategic point on the western end of a fording point on the River Corrib, known as the Terryland ford, which stretched from Terryland Castle on the east bank to the 'new castle' of the Lynch family on the west bank.[119] A late seventeenth-century plan of Galway and environs published in 1774 by J.N. Bellin shows the ford as an element of one of three routeways that converged on the site of the castle and its enclosed garden at Newcastle.[120] The '1651' pictorial map of Galway did not extend sufficiently far north to show the new castle or the *c.*1510 chapel, but a roadway leading northwards to the chapel of St James was mentioned in the key to the map.[121] Roderic O'Flaherty recorded in the late seventeenth century that the chapel of St James at Newcastle 'was wont to be visited on St James eve and day yearly by the people of Galway for devotion', indicating that it was still a notable feature in the environs of the town at that time and that the feast of St James was celebrated there in the late seventeenth century.[122]

---

113 Leask, 'The collegiate church', 2–23.   114 Hardiman, 'Pedigree of Dominick Lynch', 50; Walsh (ed.), 'An account of the town of Galway', 62, 92.   115 Jim Higgins, *St James' church and cemetery, Gleninagh Heights, Galway* (Galway, *c.*1996).   116 Paul Gosling, *Archaeological inventory of County Galway, vol. 1: West Galway* (Dublin, 1993), no. 608, p. 108 (the medieval parish church of St James in the old Rahoon cemetery was destroyed before 1938); ibid., no. 758, p. 131; Peadar O'Dowd, 'Holy wells of Galway city', *JGAHS*, 60 (2008), 136–53, at 148–9 (the well is now incorporated into the garden of a house in Cruachan Park, Galway).   117 Gosling, *Archaeological inventory of County Galway, i, West Galway*, no. 747, p. 129.   118 There is some confusion in historical sources between James Lynch fitz Stephen, mayor in 1510, and Stephen Lynch fitz James, mayor in 1509.   119 Paul Walsh, 'The topography of the town of Galway in the medieval and early modern periods' in G. Moran (ed.), *Galway, history and society: interdisciplinary essays on the history of an Irish county* (Dublin, 2006), pp 27–96, at pp 37–8. The Jacobean townhouse at Terryland was built on the site of an older castle that was in the possession of Dominic Lynch in 1574. J.P. Nolan, 'Galway castles and their owners in 1574', *JGAHS*, 1 (1901), 109–23, at 115; Billy Quinn, Linda G. Lynch & Declan Moore, 'Excavations at Terryland, Galway', *JGAHS*, 66 (2014), 46–55.   120 Prunty & Walsh, *Galway/Gaillimh*. Irish Historic Towns Atlas, map 18.   121 Ibid., map 12.   122 O'Flaherty, *Chorographical description of west or h-Iar Connaught*, p. 56. A modern church dedication to St James survives at Bushypark.

By the nineteenth century, Thomas O'Conor, a researcher working on behalf of the Ordnance Survey in 1838, observed that 'The chapel of Saint James remains as yet entire, in its walls and roof.' It measured approximately 9 metres x 4.5 metres and had a tall twin-light window. However, he went on to record that 'It stands within the concerns at the distillery of Burton Persse ... the chapel has been converted into a stall for feeding cows.' He also noted that 'Saint James's well was destroyed by a mill race made about 40 years ago by Messrs Henry and Robert Persse ... the well was about 50 or 60 yards to the south of the chapel.'[123] These distillery buildings, in turn, had been demolished by the 1940s and no remains of the chapel or the holy well are now visible at the site near Distillery Road, between the university's science buildings.[124] However, the sixteenth-century window and its rear arch from the chapel of St James were rescued from demolition in the 1940s and are preserved elsewhere within the university campus.[125]

The trading links between fifteenth-century Galway and the Spanish ports are well known,[126] and the prosperous merchant families in the town that can be linked with the pilgrimage are probably just part of a much larger pilgrim traffic through the port of Galway. Pilgrims could have utilized merchant ships to get to A Coruña or Vigo, or perhaps sailed on ships that were en route to places further south such as Lisbon. Pilgrims might spend just a few days in Santiago and at most a few weeks in Galicia before returning home again by sea. The discovery of scallop shells probably associated with burials on the site of the former Augustinian friary at Galway is therefore unsurprising. Elsewhere in the town, a funeral monument with a small image of St James with a scallop shell on a chain around his neck forms part of a finely carved (but probably seventeenth-century) funeral monument now preserved in the grounds of the Mercy Convent on Francis Street.[127] An earlier carved image of St James, from a fragmentary tomb, is in the cemetery of the nearby Franciscan friary, but without any known link to pilgrimage. The two fourteenth-century pilgrims buried at St Mary's cathedral in Tuam with their scallop shells[128] probably sailed from the port of Galway. Similarly, Friar David of the Dominican convent at Athenry, who was granted leave by the master general in 1520 to visit the shrine of St James in Galicia, probably also travelled through Galway on one of the many Spain-bound ships that frequented that port.[129]

123 Michael Herity (ed.), *Ordnance Survey letters, Galway* (Dublin, 2009), p. 85. 124 Richard Crumlish, 'Distillery Road, Galway, extension to Bank of Ireland', www.excavations.ie/report/2012/ Galway/0023213, accessed 1 Nov. 2017. 125 Paul Walsh, 'The chapel of St James at Newcastle, Galway', *JGAHS*, 42 (1989–90), 150–5. Walsh's article includes a drawing of the window and its arch. See also Jim Higgins, *The stone carving collection at National University of Ireland Galway*, Galway's Heritage in Stone, catalogue 3 (Galway, 2011). 126 M.D. O'Sullivan, *Old Galway: the history of a Norman colony in Ireland* (Cambridge, 1942), pp 42–7. 127 The Galway image is undated, and probably post-medieval. Jim Higgins, *The stone carving collection, Convent of Mercy, Francis St, Galway* (Galway, 1989), pp 14–15 & plate 4. 128 Miriam Clyne, 'Excavation at St Mary's cathedral, Tuam, Co. Galway', *JGAHS*, 41 (1987–8), 90–103. See above, p. 86. 129 Hugh Fenning, 'Irish material in the registers of the Dominican masters general (1360–1649)', *Archivum Fratrum Praedicatorum*, 39 (1969), 249–366, at 268 (no. 64), cited in Ó Clabaigh, *The friars in Ireland*, p. 198.

CHURCHES AND WELLS DEDICATED TO ST JAMES

While it is possible to trace the lives and worlds of some of the elite who went to Santiago from Ireland, it is more difficult to measure the impact of their experiences when they returned. One indication of this may be the spread of the cult of St James in Ireland. Naming practices and church dedications both provide measures of how the cult spread in the medieval period. The impressively comprehensive book of genealogies compiled by Dubhaltach Mac Fhirbhisigh in the mid-seventeenth century indicates that where versions of the name James did occur, three-quarters of instances were in families of Anglo-Norman descent, with instances occurring from the twelfth century onwards. James was used as a forename among the leaders of Anglo-Norman families such as the Butlers of Ormond from the fourteenth century and by leading members of the Fitzgeralds of Kildare and of Desmond from the fifteenth century.[130]

The majority of the medieval churches dedicated to St James in Ireland were in areas of Anglo-Norman influence. Most were in the province of Leinster. It is difficult to date the churches involved, since they may have been in existence for some time before they featured in extant documents. Connections between the pilgrimage to Santiago and churches dedicated to St James in Ireland are tenuous. In north Leinster, the church at Athboy in the diocese of Meath was dedicated to St James, and it featured in a range of early fifteenth-century documents.[131] Excavations on an adjacent site in 2008 revealed medieval pottery and a twelfth- or thirteenth-century dressed stone window fragment, possibly a remnant of the Carmelite friary, but nothing that might hint of a pilgrimage connection.[132] The parish church of St James at Athlumney in Meath was also of medieval origin.[133] In Co. Westmeath the rectory of St James at Newtown was recorded in 1515.[134] The rectory of Usk and the vacant rectory of Ballysonan in Kildare were also dedicated to St James, as indicated in sixteenth-century sources.[135] While these patronal dedications suggest an awareness of the cult of St James the Apostle, no clear link to the pilgrimage has been established.

---

130 For outline genealogies of the main lines of these families, see T.W. Moody, F.X. Martin & F.J. Byrne (eds), *NHI*, ix: *maps, genealogies, lists* (Oxford, 1984), pp 167–9. On naming practices within families, see Freya Verstraten, 'Naming practices among the Irish secular nobility in the high Middle Ages', *Ossory, Laois and Leinster*, 5 (2012), 187–211; Clodagh Tait, 'Namesakes and nicknames: naming practices in early modern Ireland, 1540–1700', *Continuity and Change*, 21:2 (2006), 313–40; Freya Verstraten Veach, 'Men's names among the Uí Mhórdha of Laoighis, *c*.1000–*c*.1500'. *Ossory, Laois and Leinster*, 5 (2012), 187–211.   131 *Cal. papal letters, vi: 1404–1415*, p. 111 (1406); Smith (ed.), *Register of Nicholas Fleming*, no. 200 (1411); no. 254 (1416); *Cal. papal letters, viii: 1427–1447*, pp 503, 512 (1434).   132 'Townparks, Athboy, Co. Meath', www.excavations.ie/report.2008/Meath/0019951, accessed 1 Nov. 2017.   133 Report by Thomas O'Conor (1836) in Michael Herity (ed.), *Ordnance Survey letters, Meath* (Dublin, 2001), p. 54.   134 *Cal. papal letters, xx, 1513–1521*, p. 216 (1515).   135 *Ir. Fiants, Eliz.*, 740 [Usk, 1565]. *Cal. papal letters, xvii, pt 1: 1495–1503*, p. 565 [Ballisonan, 1502].

A rectory and parish church of St James existed in Dublin city from the 1190s,[136] while some distance to the west of the city there was a chapel and well of St James in Palmerstown (barony of Uppercross) before 1540, and a fair was held there annually on the eve and day of the feast of St James.[137] The medieval parish of St James in Dublin city was part of the property of the abbey of St Thomas, the parish being formed at about same time as the adjoining one dedicated to another foreign saint with a significant Irish cult – St Catherine. These two parishes were located just outside the walled city. A recent study of the medieval streetscape found that the medieval church of St James on the site at James's Street was on a significant hill. The immediate area has since been levelled to some extent, but remnants of medieval structures survive just below the modern surface of James's Street.[138] Parts of a medieval roadway are among the discoveries in excavations of the graveyard adjoining the former St James's church in 2017. The roadway, which probably dates from the 1180s, was 20 metres wide and since it lay on natural subsoil it was created where there had been no road before.[139] The 'new' road is roughly coterminous with the building of the parish church. Closer to the city, the gate known as St James's gate appears to have been a street gate that would have been closed at night, and may have been built much later than the church. Its location does not indicate the line of the city wall, which was some distance further east. The earliest documentary reference to St James's gate is in a sixteenth-century narrative of events that had occurred in 1485, though it may have been constructed some time before that.[140]

On James's Street in Dublin, the obelisk fountain erected in 1790 at the former marketplace is said to mark the site of an ancient well of St James. Into the twentieth century there was a tradition of carrying coffins three times around the fountain before burial in the nearby cemetery, which was probably a continuation of an older tradition associated with a holy well.[141] The fountain, with its two water troughs, marked the location of the annual fair that was held on 25 July and following days in St James's Street, Dublin, with market stalls extending from there to St James's gate. The dates of fairs are of interest as they often reflect local cults

136 J.T. Gilbert (ed.), *Register of the abbey of St Thomas the Martyr* (London, 1889), p. 284; Foley, *Abbey of St Thomas the Martyr*. **137** *Fairs & markets rep.*; *Ir. Fiants, Eliz.*, no. 4012; N.B. White (ed.), *Extents of Irish monastic possessions, 1540–1541* (Dublin, 1943), p. 57; for evidence of a pre-Norman church at Palmerstown, see Máirín Ní Mharcaigh, 'The medieval parish churches of south-west County Dublin', *Proc. RIA*, 97C (1997), 245–96, at 254. **138** Antoine Giacometti, 'Thomas Street/ James Street quality bus corridor', www.excavations.ie/report/2014/Dublin/0023933, accessed 1 Nov. 2017. **139** Aisling Collins, 'St James's church and graveyard', www.excavations.ie/report/2017/ Dublin/0025382, accessed 1 Nov. 2017; Antoine Giacometti, 'The archaeology of medieval James's Street, Dublin', unpublished lecture to Friends of Medieval Dublin seminar, 21 May 2016. **140** *Cal. Carew MSS: Book of Howth*, p. 176; Clarke, *Dublin, part 1, to 1610*, Irish Historic Towns Atlas, p. 22; The later history of the pre-nineteenth-century church on this site is outlined in Maurice Dufficy, 'The story of St James's church, James's Street, Dublin', *Dublin Historical Record*, 29:2 (1976), 66–9, but his chronology is misleading. **141** Jim Cooke, 'The obelisks of Greater Dublin', *Dublin Historical Record*, 56:2 (2003), 146–60, at 152.

because when people gathered to worship they would also celebrate and spend, creating a ready seasonal market for goods. For that reason the dates of fairs often reflect devotion to particular saints. By the late sixteenth century the six-day fair had ceased to function but was recorded by historian Richard Stanihurst in 1577. He explained that the fair was suppressed because local merchants suffered a decline in business because so many foreign traders came from England, France and Flanders for it. Even in Stanihurst's day, the event was remembered, 'for a memorial of this notable faire a few cottages, bouthes, and alepoles are yerely pitcht at S. James his gate'.[142]

A group of early stone crosses at Rathdown in south Co. Dublin include one close to an ancient roadway through the townland of Jamestown, near Stepaside, where it is at the head of St James's well. While the cross and well may have been associated with a very early church, the townland name of 'Jamestown' does not appear in documents before 1547, and thus the dedication to St James is probably not original.[143] The church of Kilmokevogue in the diocese of Ossory, to judge from the place-name, presumably had an original dedication to St Mochaomhóg, but by the Middle Ages it was dedicated to St James, possibly as a result of a lay patron's pilgrimage to Santiago.[144] This was one of several churches dedicated to St James recorded in the diocese of Ossory in a late medieval list.[145] Similarly in Kilbeggan, Co. Westmeath, the parish church had a dedication to St James by the time of the Ordnance Survey in the nineteenth century, but on the place-name evidence the original dedication was probably to St Beagán, whose feast day was on 24 July.[146] In south Kildare, the parish of Castledermot was dedicated to St James. In Co. Carlow, a small rectangular oratory dedicated to St James was part of a more extensive ecclesiastical site at St Mullins. The chapel measured just 2.1 metres by 2.5 metres.[147] In Kilkenny city, there was a medieval chapel of St James, which was demolished in the mid-fourteenth century by Richard Ledred, who reused the stone for his bishop's palace. The adjoining cemetery has recently been excavated, but no evidence of pilgrim burials has been reported.[148]

Several medieval church dedications to St James existed in the diocese of Ferns. The cemetery near Ballyhack Castle in the old parish of St James is on the site of a former church of St James,[149] and one of the two annual fairs at Ballyhack was

142 Richard Stanyhurst's 'Description of Irelande' in *Holinshed's Irish chronicle*, p. 45; for a slightly later account by James Ware, see Robert Ware's notes on Dublin churches, BL, Add. MS 4813, fol. 40v (NLI, microfilm P 17).   143 P.J. O'Reilly, 'The Christian sepulchral *leacs* and freestanding crosses of the Dublin half-barony of Rathdown', *JRSAI*, 31:2 (1901), 134–61, at 252–4.   144 William Carrigan, *The history and antiquities of the diocese of Ossory* (4 vols, Dublin, 1905), iv, pp 92–3.   145 P.F. Moran, *Spicilegium Ossoriense, first series* (Dublin, 1874), pp 9–10: Mallardstown in Kells deanery, 'Killokighan' in Iverk deanery, and 'Kilmahenock' (Kilmokevoge, now Glenmore parish).   146 Ó Riain, *Dictionary of Irish saints*, pp 92–3.   147 J.F.M. Ffrench, 'St Mullins, Co. Carlow', *JRSAI*, 22 (1892), 377–88, at 382–4; Brindley & Kilfeather, *Archaeological inventory of County Carlow*, no. 603.   148 'St James's Green, Kilkenny', www.excavations.ie/report/2012/Kilkenny/0023397, accessed 1 Nov. 2017.   149 The church at Ballyhack is shown on Francis Jobson's map of Waterford estuary, 1591, printed in Damien McLellan, 'Reclaiming an Irish "Way of St James"', *History Ireland*, 24:3 (2016), 16–19, at 16.

held on the feast of St James.[150] Some distance to the east of Dunbrody there was a medieval church of St James at Horetown,[151] a place known for its Carmelite religious house. Arthur's Bay to the south was formerly named after St James, an indication that it might have been a place of departure on pilgrimage.[152] North of Dunbrody there is another church of St James at Horeswood.[153] At Tomhaggard, a well of St James had a pattern day on 25 July into modern times.[154] This concentration of dedications suggests a local cult of St James in that south-east region of Ireland, and it is certainly likely that some Santiago pilgrims were drawn from this area. It should not be assumed, however, that this was a normal point of departure on the pilgrimage for people from distant parts of Ireland who had easier access to other ports.[155] Pilgrims from other parts of Ireland would have used the ports of departure most accessible to them, the normal ports utilized by merchants in their neighbourhoods. At the same time, the importance of the rivers Barrow, Nore and Suir as conduits drawing pilgrims as well as merchandise from inland parts of south Leinster to the south coast should not be underestimated.

In east Munster, the parish church at Stradbally, on the Co. Waterford coast east of Dungarvan, is dedicated to St James. It is located beside a small thirteenth-century ecclesiastical site affiliated with the Anglo-Norman Augustinian House at Kells, Co. Kilkenny, excavated in 2001.[156] It is another instance of an apparent Augustinian link with the Santiago pilgrimage from Ireland. Further west, the rectory of Dangandonovan in the diocese of Cloyne was associated with St James in the late twelfth century.[157] Elsewhere in Co. Cork, the parishes of Durrus, Mallow and Ringrone have modern churches dedicated to St James. Perhaps surprisingly, Cork, with its large Anglo-Norman community and trading links with Europe, does not retain much evidence of the cult of St James. However, in 1582, Edmund White directed in his will that he be buried where his ancestors lay at St James's chapel in Christ Church (Holy Trinity), one of two churches within the medieval walled city of Cork. He also bequeathed money for candles and to pay for work on the fabric of the building.[158] The Whites were a major Cork merchant family and the dedication is clearly an old one. Indeed, the Whites may well have founded the chantry chapel of St James in which they were buried.

On the coast of south-west Ireland the parish of St James in Dingle, Co. Kerry, had established medieval trade links with Spain, and the church dedication to St

150 P.H. Hore, *History of the town and county of Wexford* (6 vols, London, 1900–11), ii, pp 241–5, 250. **151** 'Horetown, Co. Wexford, Medieval church of St James', www.excavations.ie/report/2008/Wexford/0020296, accessed 1 Nov. 2017. **152** McLellan, 'Reclaiming an Irish "Way of St James"', 17. **153** Ibid., 18 (map). **154** Michael J. Moore, *Archaeological inventory of County Wexford* (Dublin, 1996), no. 1309. **155** McLellan, 'Reclaiming an Irish "Way of St James"', overstates the case for the significance of this route for pilgrims from Dublin and environs. **156** 'Rectory field, Stradballymore, Co. Waterford', www.excavations.ie/report/2001/Waterford/00007182, accessed 1 Nov. 2017. **157** Paul Mac Cotter, *A history of the medieval diocese of Cloyne* (Dublin, 2013), p. 169. **158** Richard Caulfield (ed.), 'Original documents relating to the county and city of Cork', *Gentlemen's Magazine*, ser. 3, vol. 12 (June 1862), 713–14.

James (recorded only from the early nineteenth century) is accepted as indicating a link with the medieval pilgrimage, though there is no clear documentary or archaeological evidence.[159] However, in 1756 the antiquary Charles Smith noted that 'several Spanish merchants resided at Dingle, before Queen Elizabeth's time, who traded with the natives for fish and other kinds of provision', and his writings may have influenced later popular tradition.[160] In 1841 an Ordnance Survey researcher reported that the church was 'said to have been formerly built at the charge of the Spaniards', but that 'most of the old structure is gone to ruin'.[161] The parish church in the coastal parish of Ballyheigue in north Kerry was also dedicated to St James.[162] These parishes lay in that part of Kerry that had come under Anglo-Norman influence by 1210,[163] as did Ardfert. At the site of the medieval cathedral of Ardfert, Co. Kerry, excavations overseen by Fionnbarr Moore uncovered the remains of two individuals in a stone-lined grave in the nave. A decorated pilgrim badge, with a figure of St James attached, was found in the north wall of the grave. Dating from the fourteenth or fifteenth century, and probably originating in Santiago, the small gilded figure of St James, approx 2 cm in height, depicted the saint with pilgrim attire.[164] Two inland parish churches in Co. Tipperary were also dedicated to St James: Borrisoleigh (Two Mile Borris)[165] and Peppardstown, again located in a region that had seen Anglo-Norman settlement.[166]

The Trinitarian House at Adare in mid-Co. Limerick, founded *c.*1226, was dedicated to St James, and that house also maintained a hospital. The saint's feast day would have been celebrated there and in the thirteenth century Geoffrey de Marisco had a licence to hold an annual fair at Adare on the eight days following the feast of St James the Great.[167] A little distance to the west, Nantinan parish in the same county was also dedicated to St James, and there was a holy well of St James at Ardgoul North within that parish.[168] In modern times an annual fair was still held in Nantinan on the feast of St James, and patterns were held on 25 July at the holy wells at Nantinan, Tervoe and Ballymacave.[169] In St Mary's cathedral in

159 Isabel Bennett, 'Some aspects of the connections between Dingle and Spain', *CSJ Bulletin*, 59 (May 1997), 34–40; Pádraig Ó Fiannachta, 'Oilithireacht ón Daingean go Santiago de Compostella', *Irisleabhar Mha Nuad* (2007), 167–90.   160 Charles Smith, *The ancient and present state of the county of Kerry* (Dublin, 1756; reprint Cork, 1979), p. 101.   161 'The parish of Dingle' [7 Aug. 1841] in M. O'Flanagan (ed.), *Letters containing information relative to the antiquities of the county of Kerry ... Ordnance Survey, 1841* (typescript, Bray, 1935), p. 49.   162 E.A. Brandon, *To whom we dedicate* (Dundalk, 1954).   163 F.J. Byrne, 'Map 2. Anglo-Norman Ireland and its neighbours' in Cosgrove (ed.), *NHI*, ii: *medieval Ireland*, p. 133.   164 Fionnbarr Moore, *Ardfert cathedral: summary of excavation results* (Dublin, 2007). On the proliferation of pilgrim badges at shrines throughout Europe, see Sumption, *Pilgrimage*, pp 174–5; see also Cherry, 'The depiction of St James Compostela on seals', pp 37–47.   165 *Cal. papal letters, xx: 1513–1521*, p. 174; *Cal. papal letters, xix: 1503–1513*, p. 205.   166 *Cal. papal letters, xx: 1513–1521*, p. 466.   167 *Cal. papal letters, xvii, pt 2: 1492–1503*, p. 65. *Cal. papal letters, xviii: 1503–1513*, p. 422; Gwynn & Hadcock, *Medieval religious houses*, p. 217.   168 Maurice Lenihan, *Limerick: its history and antiquities* (Dublin, 1866), p. 563; Caoimhín Ó Danachair, 'The holy wells of Co. Limerick', *JRSAI*, 85 (1955), 193–217, at 198.   169 Ó Danachair, 'The holy wells of Co. Limerick', 193–217. A fourth holy well dedicated to St James was located at Ballinlough, Co. Limerick, but no pattern seems to have been associated with it.

Limerick, a fourteenth-century side chapel in the south transept was dedicated to St James. It had been funded in the 1360s by Thomas Balbeyne, a wealthy citizen of Limerick who was originally from Bristol, and by Richard Bultingfort, whose family were probably from Hertfordshire.[170] However, from at least 1291 there was a fair in the city on St James's Day,[171] suggesting that a cult may have been established by then.

Given the Anglo-Norman origins of the cult in Ireland, it is unsurprising that church dedications to St James are far less common in Connacht and west Ulster and are mostly confined to the immediate hinterland of the town of Galway. The vicarage at Claregalway was recorded in 1480 as being dedicated to St James, and the discovery of a scallop-shell burial suggests that at least one person was inspired by the cult to go on pilgrimage. Finds of scallop-shell burials at Tuam, Co. Galway, confirm the influence of the pilgrimage in this region. The medieval parish church at Rahoon, to the west of Galway city, and two chapels at Ballybane and Newcastle to the east and north of the city, respectively, were also dedicated to St James.[172]

In east Ulster, the area of strongest Anglo-Norman influence in the province, the medieval chapel of Drumnakill in Co. Antrim[173] and the parish of Rathmullan in the diocese of Down are among the few recorded medieval dedications to St James.[174] The latter was in lay patronage by the 1490s and had long been vacant.

In short, the distribution of known medieval church dedications to St James throughout the island reflects the extent of Anglo-Norman colonization. The evidence indicates that when parishes were formed in the twelfth century, the cult of St James was popular in Anglo-Norman regions but not in areas that remained under Gaelic influence. Over time, those cultural distinctions diminished, and by the fifteenth century the Anglo-Norman element of the pilgrimage to Santiago from Ireland came to be surpassed by an upsurge of pilgrims from Gaelic backgrounds.

CONCLUSION

Opportunity as well as motive was important in determining who could participate in overseas pilgrimage. The earliest known pilgrims from Ireland to Santiago were senior ecclesiasatics and government officials, people of Anglo-Norman backgrounds whose careers involved mobility and overseas travel in the thirteenth century. By the fifteenth century, urban dwellers in Anglo-Irish port towns such as Drogheda, Galway and Waterford had relatively easy access to merchant ships that

170 T.J. Westropp, 'St Mary's cathedral, Limerick: its plan and growth [part 1]', *JRSAI*, 28 (1898), 35–48, at 38, 40. **171** *Fairs & markets rep.*, p. 93. **172** Walsh, 'An account of the town of Galway', 47–118; Hardiman, *History of Galway*, p. 234. **173** William Reeves, *Ecclesiastical antiquities of Down, Connor, and Dromore* (Dublin, 1847), pp 282–3; James O'Laverty, *An historical account of the diocese of Down and Connor* (5 vols, Dublin, 1878–95), iv, pp 486–9. **174** 'Ramaylyn', *Cal. papal letters, xvi: 1492–1498*, p. 437.

could be used by pilgrims as well as for trade. Those urban pilgrims to Santiago who can be identified by name were generally part of the wealthy elite of coastal towns, often connected with civic office. They were people with the necessary wealth and social networks to make overseas travel feasible. It is possible that the stories of these named pilgrims are not typical of the wider phenomenon of pilgrimage from Anglo-Ireland associated with the cult of St James, since their elite status is what ensured that information about them has survived. It is interesting nonetheless that a 'typical' pilgrim seems to emerge from the available evidence. Margaret Athy of Galway, John Fowling of Drogheda and James Rice of Waterford almost certainly never met, and they lived very different lives in different parts of Ireland, but the social, cultural, economic and religious backgrounds of their families were very similar, such that the circumstances of their lives seem to have favoured their becoming pilgrims to Santiago.

5

The pilgrim experience: the Gaelic Irish phase

The second major strand of the medieval Santiago pilgrimage from Ireland can be termed the Gaelic Irish phase, and the heyday for this category of pilgrims going to the shrine of St James in Galicia was in the fifteenth century. The primary explanation for the increased interest in overseas pilgrimage in the century before the Reformation was the pursuit of indulgences. That Santiago de Compostela was favoured over Rome by pilgrims from Ireland can only be partly explained in geographical terms. It was certainly more easily accessible by sea. Its greatest attraction, however, was the frequency with which jubilee years, in which especially generous indulgences could be gained, occurred at the shrine of St James – every six, five, six, and eleven years – as compared with every fifty years at Rome (approximately every twenty-five years from 1400). Occurring four times in every twenty-eight-year cycle, numerous jubilee years at Santiago would be celebrated in the average adult lifetime; in contrast, given low life-expectancy, a jubilee year in Rome might not occur at a time in a medieval person's life when it was feasible to go there.

The evidence for fifteenth-century Gaelic pilgrims comes from a range of sources, some of which are more informative than those for the earlier Anglo-Norman phase. At various dates from the 1420s to the 1480s in particular we can glimpse evidence of pilgrimages to Santiago undertaken by Gaelic lords and ladies from many parts of Ireland. Among the families represented in the records are Mág Uidhir of Fermanagh; Mac Diarmada and Ó hUiginn from north Connacht; Ó Fearghail from Longford; and Ó Cearbhaill, Ó Conchobhair Fáilghe and Mac Eochagáin from the midlands. Also represented, more than once, was the family of Ó Drisceoil from west Cork, a renowned seafaring family with something of a reputation for piracy. Individual pilgrim stories can be reconstructed, but, as with the Anglo-Norman pilgrims, there is still the caveat that these were wealthy, high status individuals within their communities, whose spiritual adventures often merited attention for secular reasons. In these cases, evidence generally comes from the medieval Irish annals, in contexts where the shrine at Santiago and the pious intentions of those who went there were often peripheral to the political interests of the chroniclers.

CULT AND ICONOGRAPHY OF ST JAMES IN GAELIC AREAS

It is clear that the pilgrimage to Santiago became popular among the Gaelic elite in the fifteenth century. As already mentioned, one indicator of the cult of St

James within Ireland is the use of the forename James/Séamus. Among Gaelic families, one of the few regions in which the forename Séamus/James attained some popularity was in Oirghialla (an area of south Ulster encompassing much of Fermanagh, Monaghan and Armagh). Here, the family of Mág Uidhir visited Santiago and adopted the name in the fifteenth century, but not earlier than that. Otherwise, the population group known as the Uí Fhiachrach in east Galway and north Connacht also occasionally used the forename James, whereas among Gaelic families elsewhere in the country instances of the name remained extremely rare into the seventeenth century and beyond.[1]

As has been seen, most medieval parish church dedications to St James were in those parts of Ireland that had experienced Anglo-Norman colonization. Elsewhere, the parish church of Laragh, in mid-Co. Cavan, had a dedication to St James recorded in the nineteenth century, as did the parish of Kilgefin, in east Co. Roscommon, but these may not have been of medieval origin. At the time of the Ordnance Survey, in the 1830s, the local informant in Laragh did not know the date of the feast of St James, and confirmed that there was no holy well in the parish. John O'Donovan noted that St James's well in Kilgefin parish was still venerated, but he did not think the church dedication to St James was original.[2] The most obvious explanation for the scarcity of such dedications in Gaelic regions is that parishes had been formed, and patronal dedications established, long before Santiago de Compostela began to attract pilgrims from Gaelic regions of Ulster and Connacht in the fifteenth century, and that the cult in those areas was never sufficiently strong to warrant changes in parish dedications.

How Gaelic Irish people imagined the saint whose cult they followed in the fifteenth century is difficult to reconstruct. Little visual evidence has survived. Few examples survive of medieval tombstones in Gaelicized areas incorporating an image of St James. One exception is the canopied wall tomb in the Franciscan friary in a Gaelicized area at Kilconnell, Co. Galway, dated to the second half of the fifteenth century, which situates an image of St James as pilgrim among a slightly unusual selection of Continental saints instead of the usual Apostles.[3] He appears, as Roger Stalley comments, 'a cheerful, amiable saint', in the style of the early sixteenth-century Ormond school in Kilkenny.[4] St James is depicted

1 This analysis is based on the data in Ó Muraíle's 'Index of personal names', which comprises volume 5 of Nollaig Ó Muraíle (ed.), *Leabhar mór na ngenealach: the great book of Irish genealogies, compiled (1645–66) by Dubhaltach Mac Fhirbhisigh* (5 vols, Dublin, 2003). Mac Fhirbhisigh's genealogical compilation did not confine itself to families with Gaelic surnames. 2 For John O'Donovan's letter regarding Laragh (8 June 1836), see Michael Herity (ed.), *Ordnance Survey letters, Londonderry, Fermanagh, Armagh-Monaghan, Louth, Cavan-Leitrim* (Dublin, 2012), pp 369–70; for O'Donovan's letter regarding Kilgefin (30 July 1837), see Michael Herity (ed.), *Ordnance Survey letters, Roscommon* (Dublin, 2010), pp 32–3. 3 Hunt, *Irish medieval figure sculpture*, i, pp 150–1; ii, plates 257–8; Rachel Moss, 'Permanent expressions of piety: the secular and the sacred in late medieval stone sculpture' in Moss, Ó Clabaigh & Ryan (eds), *Art and devotion*, pp 72–97, at pp 86–9; Stalley, 'Maritime pilgrimage from Ireland and its artistic repercussions', p. 257. 4 Stalley, 'Maritime pilgrimage from Ireland and its artistic repercussions', p. 274; www.gothicpast.com/items/show/3837, accessed 22 Oct. 2014.

5.1 St James on wall tomb at Kilconnell friary, Co. Galway.

among a miscellany that includes St Louis of Toulouse and possibly St Denis (or St Dominic),[5] alongside more conventional figures such as John the Evangelist, John the Baptist and Catherine of Alexandria.[6] The inclusion of St Louis among those represented on the tomb might suggest a pilgrimage to Toulouse, and if the attribution to St Denis is correct it would point to a Paris connection. The abbey of St Denis claimed to have the arm of St James, making it an appealing intermediate shrine for a Santiago-bound pilgrim.[7] This suggests a more extensive pilgrim experience than the direct sea journey from Galway to a Galician port would have allowed. The figure of St James on the Kilconnell tomb includes four carved shells, and he is wearing a pilgrim hat, tunic and bag (fig. 5.1). This kind of tunic was common in the iconography of St James elsewhere in Europe by the fifteenth century.[8] The identity of the person for whom this tomb was erected is not known, but it is likely to have been a leading member of the Ó Ceallaigh family of Uí Mhaine, who may well have been on pilgrimage to Santiago and other overseas shrines. It may also be significant that in 1616 a grant of a fair at Kilconnell on the feast of St James was made to the earl of Clanricard.[9] This is likely to be a reaffirmation of an older fixture and may indicate an older parochial dedication to St James.

There are few earlier signs of artistic influence in Gaelic and Gaelicized Ireland as a result of the pilgrimage. It has been suggested that the scalloped design found on a twelfth-century church doorway at Dysert O'Dea in Co. Clare could be one such example. The design is very rare in Ireland, but is found on the facade of the south transept of the cathedral at Santiago and on other churches in northern Spain.[10] However, since the Santiago pilgrimage from Gaelic areas only became popular in the fifteenth century, we should probably not expect to find artistic influences associated with that pilgrimage in east Clare as early as the twelfth century. As already discussed, not all scallop-shell designs have a Santiago connection.[11] In terms of artistic influences on medieval Ireland, France was more

5 Colmán Ó Clabaigh observes that 'St Denis' may be misidentified and that the person represented may be St Dominic. See Colmán Ó Clabaigh, 'The mendicant friars in the medieval diocese of Clonfert', *JGAHS*, 59 (2007), 25–36, at 33. 6 For the cult of Catherine of Alexandria in Ireland, see Arthur Spears, *The cult of Saint Catherine of Alexandria in Ireland* (Rathmullan, 2006); the earliest evidence for her cult in Ireland is in the *Martyrology of Gorman*, which dates from 1166. See John Hennig, 'Studies in the Latin texts of the *Martyrology of Tallaght*, of *Félire Oengusso* and of *Félire húi Gormáin*', *Proc. RIA*, 69C:4 (1970), 45–112; two different Irish versions of her Life are found in a Cavan manuscript of the late fifteenth century (BL, Egerton MS 1781), and an early sixteenth-century Donegal manuscript (*Leabhar Chlainne Suibhne*). 7 Sumption, *Pilgrimage*, p. 154. 8 Stalley, 'Sailing to Santiago', p. 414. See also fig. 3.2 above. 9 *Fairs & markets rep.* The grant was awarded at a time when Richard Burke, fourth earl of Clanricard, was actively extending his influence in east Co. Galway, including the lands around Kilconnell (Bernadette Cunningham (ed.), 'Clanricard letters: letters and papers, 1605–1673, preserved in the National Library of Ireland, manuscript 3111', *JGAHS*, 48 (1996), 162–208.) 10 Garton, 'The influence of pilgrimage on artistic traditions in medieval Ireland', p. 183. 11 On the local pilgrimage context of Dysert O'Dea in the twelfth and thirteenth centuries, see Peter Harbison, 'An ancient pilgrimage "relic-road" in north Clare', *The Other Clare*, 24 (2000), 55–9.

important than Spain,[12] and the pilgrim traffic was less regular and probably less important than the regular commercial trade between Ireland and the Continental ports on the Atlantic seaboard.

MÁG UIDHIR

Although there is scant iconographic and ecclesiastical evidence, some individuals from Gaelic parts of fifteenth-century Ireland were keen to seek the intercession and protection of St James through pilgrimage to Santiago. Members of one of the leading Gaelic kin groups of west Ulster, the family of Mág Uidhir of Fermanagh, were among the high-profile pilgrims who made the journey in the early fifteenth century. By that time the family had achieved ecclesiastical as well as political prominence in Fermanagh through strategic intermarriages with the main ecclesiastical family of Mac Cathmhaoil. They retained ecclesiastical control of the diocese of Clogher for much of the fifteenth century.[13] We hear of the overseas pilgrimage of two leading secular members of the family, Aodh Mág Uidhir and his nephew Tomás Óg Mág Uidhir, in 1428 because their journey ended in tragedy. The Annals of Ulster and the Annals of the Four Masters record that Aodh, son of Pilib Mág Uidhir, died at Kinsale on 11 August 1428 having just returned from Santiago.

> Hugh the Hospitable, son of Philip Maguire, the most famous and illustrious man of his time for hospitality, died at Kinsale, the first night after his arrival in Ireland, after performing the pilgrimage of St James, on the third of the Ides of August, and after rigid penance for his sins. Thomas Og Maguire, who was along with him, conveyed his body to Cork, where he was interred.

> *Aodh an Einigh mac Pilib Meg Uidhir fer ro badh mó clú 7 oirdearcus einigh dá mbaoí hi comhaimsir fris decc hi ccind Sáile an chéd oidche táinic i nErinn iar ndenamh turais S. Sem an treas idus augusti iar naithrighe diocra ina pheacthaibh. Tomás ócc Mag Uidhir baoí ina farradh do thabhairt a chuirp lais co Corcaigh, 7 a adhnacal innte.*[14]

For the professional historians who compiled the annals, the death of a man who could have been expected to succeed to the lordship of Mág Uidhir of Fermanagh was an event worth recording. The landing point at a port on the south coast of Ireland was a long way from home. We do not know whether the returning pilgrims

12 Stalley, 'Maritime pilgrimage from Ireland and its artistic repercussions', p. 274.   13 S. Ó Dufaigh, 'The Mac Cathmhaoils of Clogher', *Clogher Record*, 2:1 (1957), 25–49; Lanigan Wood, 'Ecclesiastical sites in County Fermanagh', pp 657–8.   14 *AFM*, iv, pp 872–3; a similar account is found in *AU*, iii, pp 104–5.

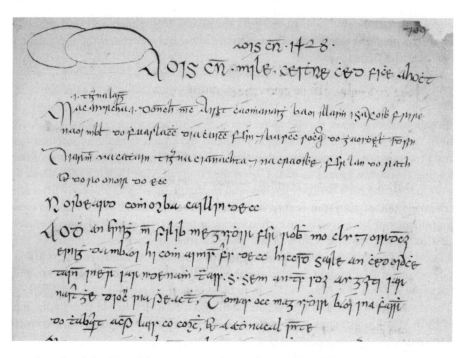

5.2 Annals of the Four Masters entry for 1428 recording pilgrimage of Aodh and Tomás Óg Mág Uidhir. © RIA.

had been forced by bad weather to make landfall at Kinsale, or whether that had been their intended point of return. The event was mentioned in the annals so as to explain why Aodh Mág Uidhir was buried in Cork rather than in his rightful burial place alongside his family in Fermanagh. Other members of his family were buried at the house of the Augustinian canons at Lisgoole just south of Enniskillen. Nor do we know the cause of his death, but disease or the poor quality of food and drink available on the voyage might have contributed. This journey was made in the height of summer and those travelling from Ireland may have been unaware that food could not be preserved as long in the warmer temperatures in Spain. It is likely that the uncle and nephew had travelled as part of a larger group, but no detail of the other pilgrims is recorded.

The annalist was aware, at least, that the Santiago pilgrimage had allowed Aodh Mág Uidhir to perform 'rigid penance for his sins'.[15] A poet, Maoil Eachlainn Ó hUiginn, composed a long poem lamenting the death of his pilgrim friend, Aodh Mág Uidhir. The poet travelled to Cork to visit the burial place more usually reserved for the elite of the Mac Carthaigh family. His poem, *Leaba charad i gCorcaigh* ('A friend's grave is in Cork'), focuses on the poet's personal sorrow,

15 *AFM*, iv, p. 873.

and the burial of his friend at a place far distant from Ulster.[16] It is unlikely that the poet had accompanied Aodh Mág Uidhir to Spain as he scarcely refers to the pilgrimage. Instead he expresses regret that no one stopped his friend from going to Santiago. The poet was aware, however, of the pilgrimage having been made in a jubilee year: 'The year of graces is an omen of sorrow. Sad is his death this year' (*bliadhain na ngrás tuar tuirrse, truagh a bhás an bhliadhainse*) (stanza 18).

In their poetry of praise or lament, it was common for poets to allude to earlier personalities or events relevant to their theme. In this 1428 lament, the poet cites an eleventh-century pilgrimage by Donnchadh son of Brian (Bóramha), whose pilgrimage had been to Rome rather than Santiago:

> How long he spent wayfaring is not told there, but Cashel's king went to the east to the relics of Paul and Peter.
> The king of Ireland's son on turning back after his pilgrimage died on the way. It was a grave matter not to rescue him.
> Aodh's death at which women and youths weep is similar since he fell having come from the east, save that Donnchadh's body remained in exile.

> *Ní hé aithristear ann sin*
> *an fad do bhí sé ar slighidh,*
> *Rí Caisil, acht do-chóidh soir*
> *go taisibh Póil is Peadair.*
> *Mac ríogh Éireann tar a ais*
> *ar n-iompódh d'éis a thurais*
> *fuair bás agus sé ar slighidh,*
> *fa cás gan é d'fhóiridhin.*
> *Cosmhail is oidhidh Aodha*
> *fá nguilid mná is macaomha*
> *mar torchair ar dtocht anoir*
> *acht corp Donnchaidh 'na dheóraidh.*[17]

The poet recalled that Donnchadh had died on pilgrimage and was buried overseas. The burial in an unfamiliar place, as well as the pilgrimage, was what made the much earlier event relevant in the mind of the fifteenth-century poet.

Another elegy, *Fada ó chéile clann Philib* ('Philip's family are far apart'), composed in or after 1430, also lamented the far distant burial place of the pilgrim Aodh Mág Uidhir. This later poem, on the brothers Aodh and Tomás Mór Mág Uidhir, contemplated the spiritual purpose of the pilgrimage that Aodh had

---

16 P.A. Breatnach, 'Ar bhás Aodha an Einigh Mhéig Uidhir, AD 1428', *Éigse*, 21 (1986), 37–52.   17 Ibid., stanzas 22–4.

undertaken. The poet claimed that the two brothers would share equally in the spiritual benefits to be derived from Tomás Mór's bequest to the church and from Aodh's pilgrimage to Compostela.[18] There may have been an element of poetic licence here, but it gives an insight into contemporary views on both pilgrimage and church patronage. Both were seen as ways of storing up treasure in Heaven.

The branch of the Mág Uidhir family to which the two named Santiago pilgrims from 1428 belonged were the most powerful lords in Fermanagh through the fourteenth and much of the fifteenth century. At the time of the 1428 pilgrimage, Tomás Mór Mág Uidhir had successfully retained the title of Mág Uidhir for thirty-three years, dominating eastern Fermanagh, while the pilgrim Aodh, as *tánaiste*, controlled western Fermanagh and Lower Lough Erne.[19] Tomás Mór was brother to Aodh, and father of Tomás Óg, the younger pilgrim. Tomás Mór had come to power in 1395, in succession to his own father, Pilib, who had held that position for thirty-two years, from 1363 to 1395.

That stability of leadership within the Mág Uidhir lordship continued into the next generation, with Tomás Óg succeeding his father in 1430 and retaining power for forty-one years, only withdrawing from that position in 1471, nine years before his death as a very elderly man in 1480. Political control was maintained at a price, usually with Uí Néill support, and it is clear from the annals that Tomás Óg's leadership was maintained by force and was sometimes contested internally by those who believed themselves worthy leaders of the Fermanagh lordship.

The violence that was an intrinsic part of such Gaelic polities was something that had affected the 1428 Fermanagh pilgrims personally. Eight or more years prior to their Santiago pilgrimage the younger man, Tomás Óg Mág Uidhir, had killed his cousin, Domhnall Carrach Mág Uidhir, in single combat.[20] The cousin who died was son of the older pilgrim, Aodh Mág Uidhir. The killing had occurred in the context of a typical power struggle within a Gaelic lordship involving the sons of Tomás Mór and their uncle Aodh and his sons, all of whom would have had a legitimate claim to succeed Tomás Mór. For one of the pilgrims, at least, the pursuit of forgiveness for this killing may have been a primary motivation in undertaking a challenging overseas pilgrimage, although the sources do not say that this was the case. Indeed, it may be that his military exploits were accepted as routine, and that is certainly how they were presented in the Annals of Ulster. The chronicler chose to portray these military exploits in a positive light, and no element of criticism or judgment was implied in the account of the killing of Domhall Carrach Mág Uidhir.[21]

---

18 Simms, 'Medieval Fermanagh', p. 95. See '*Fada ó chéile clann Philib*' in Damian Mc Manus & Eoghan Ó Raghallaigh (eds), *A bardic miscellany: five hundred bardic poems from manuscripts in Irish and British libraries* (Dublin, 2010), pp 299–302, poem 226.   19 Simms, 'Medieval Fermanagh', p. 93.   20 *AU*, iii, p. 83.   21 The annals of Ulster for this period were mostly compiled by members of the Mág Maghnusa family (fig 5.3), who were kinsmen and vassals of the leading Mág Uidhir lords (Simms, 'Medieval Fermanagh', p. 94).

Mág Uidhir genealogy (extract)

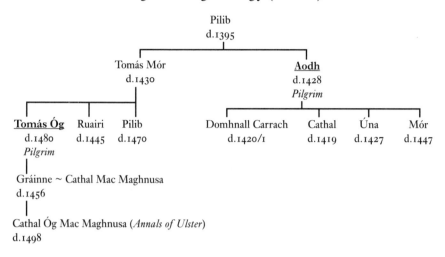

5.3 Mág Uidhir genealogy.

On the journeys to and from Santiago, Aodh and Tomás Óg Mág Uidhir were probably accompanied by servants and followers. On another occasion, when going to meet a political opponent, these men considered six horsemen and sixty footmen to be 'a few people' (*becan daine*) in their entourage,[22] a necessary precaution in the violent world of fifteenth-century Fermanagh. In 1428 they knew that they were both contenders to succeed Tomás Mór, but they understood that any further rivalry among themselves would have weakened their position in Ulster, where it was necessary to defend their territory from ambitious neighbouring lords including Ó Ruairc, Ó Domhnaill and Ó Néill. At a personal level, at the time of their pilgrimage the older man, Aodh, was mourning the death of one of his daughters, Úna, who had died in 1427.[23] He would also have been remembering his son Cathal, who had died in 1419, and his son Domhnall Carrach, who had died in single combat with Tomás Óg in 1419/20.[24]

The death of Aodh Mág Uidhir on the homeward journey meant that the 1428 Santiago pilgrimage had major political implications since the *tánaiste*, the heir apparent to the Fermanagh lordship, had died. The surviving pilgrim, the young Tomás Óg, wasted no time in asserting his authority against Aodh's sons as soon as he got home to Fermanagh, expelling them from their territory and seizing their castle.[25] Pilgrimage or no pilgrimage, political aspirations were still of paramount

22 *AU*, 1457, iii, p. 193.   23 *AU*, 1427, iii, p. 103.   24 *AU*, iii, p. 83.   25 *AU*, iii, pp 222–6; *AFM*, iv, pp 872–4; see also Simms, 'Medieval Fermanagh', p. 93.

importance to him. The real significance of the death of Aodh in 1428 was seen two years later, following the death of the head of the lordship, Tomás Mór Mág Uidhir, in 1430. The annalists recorded that Tomás Óg was then installed as the next Mág Uidhir 'by the will of God and by the laity and clergy and elders and yeomen and hospitallers of Fermanagh' (*do thoil Dé 7 le tuathaibh Fer-Manach 7 le ceallaibh 7 le sruithibh 7 le hollamnaibh 7 le brugadhaibh 7 le biatachaibh co haen-tadhach*).[26] He was now the clear successor to his father as head of the lordship. Fermanagh, under his control, was a violent place and the viciousness of the military encounters that he led from his stronghold are not in doubt. In one successful foray against the Uí Ruairc the triumphant Fermanagh raiding party returned with sixteen heads, which they displayed on the palisade of their residence for all the men of Ireland to see.[27]

Undaunted by the death of his uncle at the end of the 1428 pilgrimage, and despite his political and military responsibilities in his Fermanagh lordship, Tomás Óg Mág Uidhir made further pilgrimages later in his life. In the Roman jubilee year of 1450 – a year when plenary indulgences leading to full remission of sins could be earned by pilgrims to Rome – he travelled to the see of Peter. Rome was beyond the range of normal shipping routes from medieval Ireland, and Tomás Óg may have made part of his journey overland, crossing to France and eventually joining the Via Francigena through Turin and Siena, which pilgrims from France might have taken, but no record survives of the route he took.

Tomás Óg's pilgrimage to Rome in 1450–1 caused concern among the learned class, who feared the permanent loss of a generous patron. The annalists noted:

> And a year of the Indulgences [was] it in Rome: to wit, the Golden Door was opened in Rome. Mág Uidhir went to Rome this year, namely, King of Fir Manach; that is Thomas, son of Thomas, son of Philip of the [battle]-axe. And mournful were the [learned] companies and poets and clerics of Ireland after him ... And a month before Lammas he left his own residence to go on the pilgrimage.

> *Ocus bliadhain na n-Gras isin Roim hi; idon, an Dorus Ordha d'fhoslugadh isin Roim. Mag Uidhir do dhul cum na Roma in bliadhain si, idon, ri Fer Manach, idon, Tomas, mac Tomais, mic Pilib na tuaidhe. Ocus ba bronach damha 7 filedha 7 lucht uird Erenn i n-a diaigh ... Ocus mí re Lughnusadh do fhagaibh re a baile fein do dul ar in turus sin.*[28]

They were right to be concerned for his welfare. The same annalists recorded the death in Rome of Muircertach Ua Flannagáin, who died of the plague in 1450, and

---

26 *AU*, iii, pp 110–11.   27 *AU*, iii, pp 192–3.   28 *AU*, iii, pp 164–7. Lammas Day was 1 August.

of Andrias Ua Droma, who had just returned from Rome when he died at the age of 55.[29] Tomás Óg Mág Uidhir's return in 1451 was widely welcomed by those of the Gaelic learned class who hoped for his patronage and had perhaps come to rely on it:

> Mag Uidhir, namely Thomas junior, son of Thomas, came from Rome in the beginning of this year. And joyful indeed were the Foreigners and Gaidhil of Ireland and the [learned] companies and pilgrims likewise through his coming [back] into Ireland.

> *Mag Uidhir do thoighecht o'n Roim i tosac na bliadhna sa, .i. Tomas og, mac Tomais. Ocus ba failigh imorro Gaill 7 Gaidhil Erenn 7 dama 7 deoraidh archena tria n-a toighecht a n-Erinn.*[30]

The annals record that Tomás Óg made a second pilgrimage to Santiago, though the year was not specified. However, we do know that on one of his pilgrimages to Santiago undertaken before the year 1439 he feared he would not survive. On the return journey, we are told, he was so close to death that he swore if he survived he would take a vow of poverty for the rest of his life. (This may have been on the occasion of the 1428 pilgrimage that had cost the life of his uncle.) Such a solemn vow, though made in time of crisis, was binding and could cause difficulties later. In this case, his family was not willing to accept his opting out of his worldly responsibilities. This gave rise to Tomás Óg's 1439 petition to receive an ecclesiastical dispensation from his oath. The petition is preserved in the Vatican Archives and records that:

> he was placed in grievous danger of death and vowed to Almighty God that in the event that he should be delivered from this danger he would no longer be of the world but would remain in some hospital as a poor man living on alms, though his vow was not solemnised otherwise than in the foregoing, nor was the consent requested for this of his lawful wife and children, who were on the contrary dissentient and opposed.[31]

In May 1439 the papal dispensation from his vow was granted 'so that he may remain in the world with his wife and children'.[32] Tomás Óg Mág Uidhir had clearly taken his vow very seriously and went to the trouble of requesting a formal ecclesiastical dispensation. A man who took that much care to settle his conscience in this officially prescribed way was also a man who would be attracted by the promise of indulgences attached to particular pilgrimages. It is noteworthy that

29 *AU*, iii, pp 167, 171.   30 *AU*, iii, pp 170–1.   31 Michael J. Haren, 'The religious outlook of a Gaelic lord: a new light on Thomas Óg Maguire', *Irish Historical Studies*, 25:98 (1986), 195–7, at 196.   32 Ibid., 196.

the year 1428, when he first went to Santiago, was a jubilee year there when special indulgences allowing remission of time in Purgatory could be earned. Likewise his Rome pilgrimage was in a Roman holy year, when similar indulgences could be gained. We do not know the date of his second Santiago pilgrimage, but it was almost certainly undertaken in a jubilee year there.

A man such as Tomás Óg Mág Uidhir who made so many challenging overseas pilgrimages might be expected to be a generous supporter of the church at home, as James Rice was in Waterford and the Lynch/Athy family were in Galway. This had been the case with his father, Tomás Mór, whom the Annals of Ulster portrayed on his death in 1430 as

> a man that frequently set up oratories and churches and monasteries and holy crosses and images of Mary, and established peace amongst clergy and laity and defended his territory against its neighbours ... And elders and seniors of state and church venerated and honoured him for the excellence wherewith he administered his sovereignty and his princedom. And he died after victory of Penance and Unction.

> *Fer do cumdaigh reiglesa 7 tempaill 7 mainistreacha 7 crocha naemdha 7 dealba Muire co meinic 7 tuc sith a ceallaibh 7 a tuathaibh 7 do chosain a crich ar a comursannaigh ... Ocus ro badar sruithi 7 senoraigh tuatha 7 eclusa 'ga adhradh 7 'ga onorughadh ar a fhebhus ro fhollamhnaigh fein a righi 7 a fhlaithus. Ocus a eg iar m-buaidh Ongtha 7 aithrighi.*[33]

Allowing for the conventional pieties of the annalist,[34] it emerges that Tomás Mór was a man who pursued temporal advancement while also attempting to store up credit for the next life through ecclesiastical patronage. His successor, the pilgrim Tomás Óg Mág Uidhir, was also an ecclesiastical patron in Fermanagh, and several parish churches in the region were restored during his lifetime. In 1447 Tomás Óg paid for a French roof and other improvements for the parish church at Aghalurcher, 'for the good of his own soul',[35] while St Mary's Augustinian priory on Devenish Island was rebuilt on an older ecclesiastical site in the 1440s, probably with Mág Uidhir patronage.[36]

At about the same time, the parish church at Inishkeen, Co. Fermanagh, was a beneficiary of a patron who had a devotion to St James. While we cannot definitively link it to any specific Mág Uidhir pilgrimage to the shrine of St James, a

---

33 *AU*, iii, pp 110–11.   34 The annalist, Cathal Óg Mac Maghnusa, was his great grandson. Cathal Óg was son of Gráinne, daughter of Tomás Óg Mág Uidhir, the pilgrim. See editor's notes in Aubrey Gwynn, *Cathal Óg Mac Maghnusa and the Annals of Ulster*, ed. N. Ó Muraíle (Enniskillen, 1998), p. 14, note 83.   35 *AU*, iii, p. 159.   36 Lanigan Wood, 'Ecclesiastical sites in County Fermanagh', pp 659–61; see also Katharine Simms, 'The medieval kingdom of Lough Erne', *Clogher Record*, 9:2 (1977), 126–41.

5.4 Fifteenth-century stone carving of an angel and a stone boat from Inishkeen church, Co. Fermanagh. © Northern Ireland Environment Agency.

fifteenth-century stone carving from a gothic window at Inishkeen parish church recalls the story of the origins of the Santiago shrine. The small carved fragment depicts a scallop shell, long the symbol of the Santiago pilgrimage. Alongside the shell there is a carving of an angel in a stone boat, the angel identifiable by two large wings (fig. 5.4).[37]

This image recalls the legend of St James's body being guarded by angels as it was miraculously transported in a stone boat from Judaea to the coast of Galicia

---

37 Lanigan Wood, 'Ecclesiastical sites in County Fermanagh', p. 660, plate 176. The stone carving is now preserved in Enniskillen Castle museum.

after his martyrdom. As seen earlier the story was widely known in the fifteenth century, and a version was available in Irish translation as part of a narrative of the exploits of Charlemagne in Spain.[38] The same legend was elaborately depicted in an English alabaster altarpiece given to the cathedral in Santiago in 1456 and could well have been seen there by pilgrims from Fermanagh.[39] However, there is no evidence to link that particular altarpiece with the Inishkeen carving. Rather, both artefacts, roughly contemporary but with very different provenance, simply recall the same well-known story.

Tomás Óg Mág Uidhir had a connection to Inishkeen, because it was there, on an island in Lough Erne, that his uncle had killed his kinsmen, the sons of Art Mág Uidhir, in 1420.[40] It is possible that the gothic window that contained this stone carving might have been sponsored by Tomás Óg Mág Uidhir, whom the annals of Ulster inform us was

> A man that was of the greatest charity and piety and hospitality that was in his own time and a man that defended his territory against its neigh-bours and a man that made churches and monasteries and Mass chalices and was in Rome and twice at the city of St James [of Compostela] on pilgrimage.

> *Fer do bo mo deirc 7 crabadh 7 eineach do bi i n-a aimsir fein 7 fer do cosain a crich ar a comarsannaibh 7 fer do cumdaigh teampaill 7 mainistreacha 7 coiligh-aiffrind 7 do bi 'sa Roim ag a oilithri 7 fo dho a cathair Sang Sem.*[41]

If Tomás Óg was not personally associated with the commemorative window at Inishkeen, then it was probably sponsored by another returned Santiago pilgrim.

WOMEN PILGRIMS FROM GAELIC IRELAND

By the mid fifteenth century, it was not unusual for elite women from Gaelic Ireland to undertake lengthy pilgrimages.[42] One of the best-known instances was the journey to Santiago undertaken by Mairgréag an Einigh Ní Chearbhaill with a large entourage in the jubilee year of 1445. Mairgréag was a prominent person in the Gaelic world of the Irish midlands, and an independent-minded woman. The daughter of Tadhg Ailbhe Ó Cearbhaill, lord of Éile (Ely O Carroll), who had died in 1407, she married An Calbhach Ó Conchobhair Fáilghe, who succeeded his father, Murchadh, as head of the neighbouring lordship in 1421. Murchadh had been head of the lordship of Ó Conchobhair Fáilghe for thirty-seven years,

38 Hyde (ed.). *Gabhaltais Shearluis Mhóir.* See above pp 74–6.   39 Now in the cathedral museum, Santiago.   40 *AU*, iii, p. 83.   41 *AU*, iii, pp 268–9.   42 For comparable women in England, see S.S. Morrison, *Women pilgrims in late medieval England: private piety as public performance* (London, 2000).

and his son, An Calbhach, enjoyed a reign of more than thirty years from *c.*1425 until shortly before his death in 1458. Their principal residence was located on the west side of Croghan hill in east Co. Offaly.[43] The marriage between An Calbhach and Mairgréag was almost certainly part of a political strategy to help consolidate Gaelic power within the region, on the frontier zone with the English Pale. Both families were patrons of the arts and of the church, and Mairgréag's father-in-law, Murchadh Ó Conchobhair Fáilghe, had been the founder of the Franciscan friary at Killeigh, Co. Offaly, in 1394.[44] That friary became the family's burial place.

The cemetery at Killeigh is one of the locations in which a burial with a possible fifteenth-century Spanish link has been uncovered. A cross, described as of fifteenth-century Spanish type, was found there associated with an upright female skeleton in a hollow space in a wall.[45] The suggestion that the upright burial with the Spanish cross might be that of Mairgréag Ní Chearbhaill has been made by at least one modern author.[46] It may equally be that the cross was a souvenir of one of the fifteenth-century pilgrims who travelled to Santiago with Mairgréag in 1445, or subsequently with her husband An Calbhach Ó Conchobhair Fáilghe in 1451, or someone who received the Spanish cross as a gift, or inherited it from a parent. We know, for example, that one of Mairgréag Ní Chearbhaill's daughters, Finola, spent forty-six years of widowhood in retirement at the convent of the Augustinian canonesses at Killeigh, Co. Offaly, before her death in 1493.[47] Having been twice widowed, Finola, 'the fairest and most famous woman in all Ireland, besides her own mother', entered the convent in 1447, 'renouncing all worldly vanities and terrestrial glorious pomps'.[48] The Annals of the Four Masters recorded that Finola 'deported herself chastely, honourably, piously and religiously [and] died on the 25th of July' (*go hionnraic, onorach, craibhdhech, caonduthrachtach* [&] *décc an 25 Iul.*)[49] There may have been an implied significance in the reference to Finola's death having occurred on the feast of St James.

Mairgréag Ní Chearbhaill belonged to a generation for whom the horror of the Black Death was still remembered within many families. Her father's first wife, Joan Butler, had died of the plague in 1383, along with many others.[50] In this context, we can hear the spontaneous prayer of one young law student, who was a member of the hereditary legal family who provided legal services in the lordship

43 John Feehan, *Cruachán Éile in Uíbh Fhailí; Croghan, County Offaly, Ireland* ([Tullamore], 2011), p. 51.   44 Elizabeth FitzPatrick, 'Mairgréag an-Einigh Ó Cearbhaill: "the best of the women of the Gaedhil"', *JKAS*, 18 (1992–3), 20–38, at p. 26; *AFM*, s.a. 1394.   45 T.U. S[adlier], 'Metal cross from Killeigh', *JKAS*, 9 (1918–21), 85–6; FitzPatrick, 'Mairgréag an-Einigh Ó Cearbhaill', 32.   46 Caimin O'Brien, *Stories from a sacred landscape: Croghan Hill to Clonmacnoise* (Tullamore, 2006), pp 54–5.   47 FitzPatrick, 'Mairgréag an-Einigh Ó Cearbhaill', 35; *AFM*, iv, pp 1202–3.   48 *A.Lecan*, 1447.   49 *AFM*, iv, pp 1202–3.   50 FitzPatrick, 'Mairgréag an-Einigh Ó Cearbhaill', 22–3.

of Ely O'Carroll.[51] He added this note to a manuscript he was copying in December 1350, at the height of the plague:

> And I myself am full twenty-one years old, that is Aedh, son of Concubhar Mac Aodhagáin, and let everyone who shall read this utter a prayer of mercy for my soul; Christmas Eve tonight and under the safeguard of the King of Heaven and earth who is here tonight I place myself, and may Heaven be the end of my life and may He put this great Plague past me and past my friends and may we be once more in joy and happiness. Amen, Pater Noster.[52]

This consciousness of death as an ever-present reality for young and old was among the influences that shaped attitudes to Purgatory and the afterlife, and may have nurtured Mairgréag's particular interest in the acquisition of indulgences through pilgrimage.

In 1441, a few years before either of them went to Santiago, Mairgréag Ní Chearbhaill with her husband applied to the papacy for a plenary remission of their sins, and this indulgence was granted to them, no doubt in return for a substantial sum of money, and on condition that they repented and confessed their sins on their deathbed to a confessor of their choice.[53] This indicates that the pursuit of indulgences at significant points in their lives was important to them.

Earlier, Mairgréag an Einigh (an epithet that alludes to her generous hospitality) had been prominent in works of charity. She adopted two orphans for the good of her soul, taking pity on them in a summer of great hunger.[54] Her obituary also recalled an occasion in 1433, a year of famine, when she invited large numbers of people to a feast at Killeigh, Co. Offaly:

> bestowing both meate and moneys with all other manner of guifts, wherinto gathered to [receive] gifts the matter of two thousand and seauen hundred persons, besides gamsters and poore men, as it was recorded in a Roll to that purpose ... so that the aforesaid number of 2700 was listed in that Roll with the arts of Dan or poetry, musick and Antiquitie ... we never saw, nor heard neither the like of that day, nor comparable to its glory and solace.[55]

---

51 Kelly, *Guide to early Irish law*, pp 226, 253.   52 Cited in translation in Kelly, *History of the Black Death in Ireland*, p. 47.   53 *Cal. papal letters, ix, 1431–1447*, p. 241. Many similar indulgences were granted to individual clergy, nuns, lay persons, and to married couples in England in the same year, and to a handful of clergy and laity in Ireland (ibid., pp 233–6). For an earlier surge in such petitions around 1350, when a jubilee year at Rome coincided with heightened concern over the Black Death, see Kelly, *History of the Black Death in Ireland*, pp 59–60.   54 Cormac Ó Cléirigh, 'The O'Connor lordship of Offaly, 1395–1513', *Proc. RIA*, 96C4 (1996), 87–102, at 93; *A.Lecan*, p. 228.   55 *A.Lecan*, pp 227–8.

She hosted a second large feast, 'nothing inferior to the first day', at the recently captured castle at Rathangan, Co. Kildare, at harvest time in the same year.[56] She was also known for her independence of action, exchanging hostages in what might be considered a humanitarian gesture in 1445, without consulting her husband, An Calbhach, whose warring actions had resulted in the hostage-taking.[57] Mairgréag appears to have travelled at about the same time as – or as part of – a large group of other lords and followers. The Annals of Lecan record that in the year 1445

> Many of the Irish of Ireland went towards the Citty of S. James ye Apostle to Spaine in the Summer about Tomaltach Mac Diarmoda King of Magh-luirg, and about Margarett, O'Caroles daughter of Calwaghs wife, and with Mageochagan the Duke of Kenel-fiacha mac-Neill, and about O'Edriskeol oge, and many more noble and ignoble persons.

The use of the words 'about' and 'with' in this summary account (a seventeenth-century translation) suggests that each of the named elite pilgrims had their own group of followers with them. Thus, for example, Mairgréag's sister, Isabell (d. 1454), was married to Mac Eochagáin,[58] another named pilgrim, and it is possible that Isabell was among the unnamed pilgrims in the midlands group who travelled to Santiago in 1445. The same chronicler records their return:

> Mac-Dermoda, Margarett, and Mageochagan returned safe and sound from Spaine to their owne houses in Ireland after receuing the Indulgences at S. James. But O-Edriskeoil died on sea coming from Spaine, and Gerott, the sons son of Thomas one of the Momonian Geraldines died in Spaine, and Evilin daughter to Edmond Fitz Thomas O'ffeargail mother to the sons of Piers Dalton died in Spaine also.[59]

It is unlikely that these pilgrims all travelled as part of one planned group. Ó Drisceoil Óg, from west Cork, died at sea, and was probably not part of the midlands group.[60] He had probably sailed from Baltimore or Castlehaven, Co. Cork, as it would have been logical for pilgrims from west Cork to sail directly from the south-west coast. The death of Ó Drisceoil Óg at sea on the way home from Santiago in 1445 is a reminder of the risks of the journey. A generation later, in 1472, Finghín Ó Drisceoil Mór and his son Tadhg both died on their return from Santiago, a journey they made despite the fact that their relative had died at sea on an earlier pilgrimage.[61] In another recorded tragedy the Annals of the Four Masters mentioned that historian Domhnall son of Tadhg Ó Fiaich drowned at sea in 1507, during the return voyage from Spain. He was part of the entourage of James Barry, Lord Barrymore, who also died

56 Ibid., p. 228. 57 Ibid., p. 212. 58 Ibid., p. 236. 59 Ibid., p. 211. 60 Ibid., p. 211. 61 *A. LCé*, pp 172–3.

on the homeward journey of the same pilgrimage. The 1507 pilgrimage from south Cork had been a large one, with many of his chief followers having accompanied Lord Barrymore. None of them returned and they were never heard of again.[62]

In Mairgréag Ní Chearbhaill's case, the motivation that led to overseas pilgrimage was also reflected in other aspects of her life. Her obituary in 1451 recorded that she was involved in building roads, bridges and churches and 'all manner of things profittable to serve God, and her soule'.[63] In a further allusion to pilgrimage, the annalist prayed that 'God's blessing, the blessings of all saints, and every one, blessing from Jerusalem to Inis Glaaire be on her going to heauen'.[64] Just one night after she died, her son Félim died after a long illness, probably leprosy. Félim Ó Conchobhair Fáilghe had been expected to succeed his father as leader of the lordship, and his death left it in a weakened position.[65] The year that Mairgréag and her son died, 1451, was another jubilee year at Santiago and her husband, An Calbhach Ó Conchobhair Fáilghe, followed her example as a pilgrim. The Annals of Lecan record that 'Calwagh O-conner went to the Civity of S. James in Spaine, and returned in health, after receuing indulgences in his sinns, and afterwards marryed he O'Kelly's daughter Catherine, O-Madadhan's relict or widow.'[66] An Calbhach made the journey to Santiago just seven years before his own death, which occurred 'after completion of his full age', as the annalists recorded. That he went in a jubilee year indicates that the pursuit of a special indulgence must be counted among his motives for tackling the pilgrimage when he was quite old. Like Aodh and Tomás Óg Mág Uidhir in Fermanagh, the aggressive style of military leadership that allowed him to maintain his position as an influential Gaelic chief in the Irish midlands involved the forceful collection of exactions from neighbouring lordships. Although he was leader of a lordship of modest size, he was generally successful in defending his territory from more powerful forces and regularly raided the English in Kildare and Meath.[67] His obituary in the Annals of the Four Masters affirmed his political achievements as well as his generosity, but made no mention of his Santiago pilgrimage:

> O'Conor Faly, Calvagh More, son of Murrough-na-madhmann, Lord of all Offaly, a man who never refused the countenance of man, and who had won more wealth from his English and Irish enemies than any lord in Leinster, died; and Con O'Conor, his son, was elected in his place, before his father was buried in [the monastery of] Killeigh.

62 *AFM*, v, pp 1292–3.   63 *A.Lecan*, p. 228.   64 Ibid. Inishglora, a small island off the coast of Belmullet, Co. Mayo, was associated with Christian pilgrimage, and the phrase conveyed the concept of the full span of the known world. Michael Gibbons & Myles Gibbons, 'Inishglora: "the western threshold between land and wave"' in J. Higgins (ed.), *Recent explorations and discoveries in Irish heritage* (Galway, 2017), pp 24–40.   65 *AFM*, iv, p. 973; *A.Conn*, p. 493.   66 *A.Lecan*, p. 230.   67 Art Cosgrove, 'Anglo-Ireland and the Yorkist cause, 1447–60' in Cosgrove (ed.), *NHI*, ii, p. 571.

Ó Conchobhair Failbhe, An Calbhach Mór mac Murchaidh na Madhmann, tighearna ua bFailghe uile, fear nár dhiúlt re drech nduine tighearna (do Laighnibh) ar mó fuair do chomthaibh ó Ghallaibh, 7 o Ghaoidhealaibh nó bítír ina aghaidh do écc, 7 Conn Ó Conchobhair a mac fein do óirdneadh ina ionad riasiú ro hadhnaiceadh esium i ccill Achaidh.[68]

OTHER MIDLAND PILGRIMS

In 1458, the same year that Ó Conchobhair Fáilghe died, the annalists recorded the death of another elite pilgrim from Gaelic Ireland, Tomaltach Mac Diarmada, lord of Moylurg, who had been to Santiago in 1445. The annalists described him as a general patron of the learned of Ireland, one who had shown great generosity and hospitality to his followers and was renowned for his almsgiving. His obituary did not mention his overseas pilgrimage, but recorded that he was buried in the abbey of Boyle, Co. Roscommon, alongside his son, Cathal, who had died two weeks earlier.[69] Tomaltach an Einigh Mac Diarmada had been a generous patron of poets during his long reign as lord of Moylurg from 1421 to 1458, and several poems addressed to him survive. *Dá mhac rugadh do rígh Connact* ('Two sons were born to the king of Connachta'), composed by Tuathal Ó hUiginn, may have been performed as an inauguration ode. It alluded to the potential claim of the lord of Moylurg over a more extensive territory in Connacht, but advised that he be content with his Moylurg lordship.[70]

In the tradition of bardic poetry, *Tosach féile fairsinge* ('The start of hospitality is wealth') alluded to the patron's ancestry and his lordly achievements, and made particular mention of his hospitality and his generosity to poets.[71] His epithet 'Tomaltach an Einigh' also referred to his reputation for hospitality. It is noteworthy that the same epithet was assigned to some other identifiable pilgrims also (Aodh an Einigh Mág Uidhir and Mairgréag an Einigh Ní Chearbhaill), perhaps indicative of their considerable wealth and high status in society as much as their personal character. Poets were anxious to retain a good relationship with such patrons, and one poem by Tuathal Ó hUiginn was concerned with preserving his professional status as *ollamh* to Mac Diarmada.[72] Another poem described Tomaltach as 'firm friend of churches and of crosses' (*lánchara ceall agus cros*), before describing his castle on an elevated site above Loch Cé where feasts fit for a king were held, and wine flowed plentifully. His military demeanour was also described, along with details of his armour, a reminder of his active enforcement of his lordly status as well as of his lordly lifestyle.[73] There is no doubt that he was

68 *AFM*, iv, pp 1000–1. **69** *AFM*, iv, pp 1001–3. **70** McKenna (ed.), *Aithdioghluim dána*, poem 31. **71** Lambert McKenna (ed.), *Dioghluim dána* (Dublin, 1938), poem 120; translated by McKenna in *Irish Monthly*, 49:571 (1921), 26–9. **72** McKenna (ed.), *Aithdioghluim dána*, poem 32. **73** *Lámh aoinfhir fhoirfeas i nÉirinn* ('The hand of one man in Ireland will succour'), W.J. Watson (ed.), *Scottish verse from the Book of the dean of Lismore*, Scottish Gaelic Texts Society, 1 (Edinburgh, 1937), poem 6, pp 32–45.

a wealthy, high-status pilgrim. The number of followers that accompanied him on pilgrimage cannot be ascertained.

While the nature of the documentary sources is such that it is elite individuals that are named, there are several passing references to a larger movement of pilgrims from Ireland. In an entry for the jubilee year of 1445, the Annals of Lecan mentioned that 'many more noble and ignoble persons', in addition to the prominent leaders named, had gone on pilgrimage to Santiago in that year.[74] They could have chosen any of a variety of routes. If we assume that those who accompanied Mairgréag Ní Chearbhaill commenced their journey in the vicinity of Killeigh, south of Tullamore, their initial route might have taken them southwards to Athy, 40 km away, from where they could have travelled southwards along the river Barrow to New Ross or Waterford. From there, they could have sailed on a larger ship directly to Spain. If they opted instead to follow an established trade route across the Irish midlands, then they could have begun their pilgrimage by travelling to Dublin, a journey of about 100 km. Killeigh was a significant ecclesiastical settlement and was close to a major east–west communication route. If horses and wheeled vehicles were used for the journey, they would have reached Dublin within two days, though given the strained political relations with the English of the Pale, careful planning and a show of military protection may have been needed.[75] They might have followed the line of the old *Slíghe Mór*, eventually arriving in Dublin near the Cornmarket. It is uncertain whether that route went through Kilmainham and followed the high ground along James's Street and Thomas Street.[76] Those arriving in Dublin from the west would have entered the walled city through Newgate, while those arriving from the south would have used St Nicholas's gate.[77] Pilgrims could, however, have visited the parish church of St James, outside the walls, on the west side of the city. In Dublin, potential pilgrims were also likely to take time to pray before the large relic collection at Christ Church cathedral and they would probably have sought guest accommodation in a religious house while they waited for a suitable ship to sail. Mairgréag Ní Chearbhaill's entourage in 1445 may have been joined by pilgrims from other parts of the midlands and east who were also intent on travelling to Santiago. When they eventually boarded a ship they were probably in the company of up to 100 pilgrims hoping to sail directly to A Coruña. It is not possible to estimate how many pilgrims

---

74 *A.Lecan*, p. 211.   75 The annals record a war between Ó Conchobhair Fáilghe and the English of Meath in 1446 (*AFM*, iv, p. 947). In 1452, an attack on travellers on a routeway is specifically recorded when a convoy of English fish merchants being escorted from Athlone via Trim to Dublin was attacked and killed by Fearghal Óg Mac Eochagáin (*A.Lecan*, pp 234–5).   76 Hermann Geissel, *A road on the long ridge: in search of the ancient highway on the Esker Riada* (Newbridge, 2006), pp 9–13.   77 Clarke, *Dublin, part 1, to 1610*, Irish Historic Towns Atlas, p.21; these gates are marked E7 and E15 on Clarke's 'Medieval Dublin, *c.*840–*c.*1540' map.

might have sailed from Ireland in 1445, but the number may have been in the hundreds.

In the jubilee year of 1456, an English pilgrim and diarist William Wey reported that he had seen Irish ships docked at the port of A Coruña, an important destination on the north coast of Galicia for those using the maritime route from Britain and from Ireland. In addition to the Irish ships, he also observed thirty-two English vessels there,[78] some of which may also have carried Irish pilgrims. Storrs has identified eighteen ships from England licensed to carry pilgrims to Santiago in 1456. The number of pilgrims carried ranged from 20 to 100 on each ship, originating in ports such as Dartmouth, Plymouth, Lynn, Southampton, Weymouth and Winchelsea, transporting in total approximately 1,000 pilgrims from England.[79] If William Wey did not exaggerate the numbers he saw, then perhaps more than 1,500 pilgrims from England and Ireland combined may have travelled in 1456. The Annals of Lecan mentioned the jubilee year at Santiago in that year, 1456, and again in 1462 where they observed 'This was the yeare of grace, many of the Irish repayred on pilgrimage towards S. James in Spaine.'[80] Similarly, the Annals of Connacht observed the departure of multiple Irish pilgrims for Santiago in the jubilee year of 1462, but without naming them: 'This was a year of Indulgence, many people going to St James's' (*Bliadain na nGras in bliadain-so, 7 moran do dol co San Sem inti*).[81]

CONCLUSION

The boom in pilgrimage to Santiago from Gaelic Ireland in the fifteenth century was the outcome of a variety of devotional, ecclesiastical and economic developments that created the desire for overseas pilgrimage at a time when information about such places circulated more freely than before and infrastructural improvements in transport made such journeys much more feasible. It was not the attraction of a long voyage, however, that appealed to these Irish pilgrims, it was the belief that the plenary indulgence they could gain by visiting the shrine of St James would make their journey to the next life considerably more pleasant.

The fifteenth century marked the high point in the medieval pilgrimage from Gaelic Ireland to Santiago. Those who travelled appear to have done so in jubilee years when special indulgences could be obtained. In this way the pilgrims from Ireland were of one mind with English pilgrims in the same century; the evidence of licences granted to ship owners in England suggests that the pilgrim trade from there was only commercially viable in jubilee years. Indeed, some pilgrims from Gaelic Ireland may have found themselves in the same boat as pilgrims from different backgrounds as they made their way by sea across the Bay of Biscay. Part of the experience of pilgrimage was encountering other pilgrims on the way, enduring

78 Davey, *William Wey: an English pilgrim*, p. 25.   79 Storrs, *Jacobean pilgrims from England*, p. 181.   80 *A.Lecan*, p. 249.   81 *A.Conn*, pp 512–13.

the hardships of the journey together, as they made their journeys in pursuit of indulgences, in repentance for past sins, and in the hope of securing a less painful journey through Purgatory as they negotiated the long, uncertain road towards eternal salvation.

Late medieval pilgrims from Ireland did not go entirely unnoticed in Spain. In about 1474 García Alonso de Torres, chronicler to Ferdinand of Aragon, was prompted to mention Ireland in the context of its pilgrims.

> In this kingdom of Ireland (or Hibernia as others call it), the king of England is lord. It is an island and some say that it lies outside the seven climates and that the inhabitants live long ... There is no bread on that island but livestock is abundant. The people are simple, exceedingly handsome and good-looking and many of them frequent the jubilee pilgrimages to Santiago.[82]

Pilgrims returning with stories of their adventures, and displaying their souvenirs, may have encouraged others to plan a similar journey in a subsequent jubilee year. The risks and hardships of the sea voyage and the overland journeys to and from the shipping ports did not deter pilgrims from following the examples of others who had made the journey. Returning pilgrims recounted their adventures, the sights, sounds and smells of a foreign country, the food and drink, and the splendour of the city of Santiago and of the Romanesque cathedral that had been designed to impress all who went there. Some returned pilgrims might also have communicated their sense of freedom at being temporarily outside the confines of the local community in which they spent most of the remainder of their lives. Perhaps their experience of an early form of spiritual tourism had also given them a sense of the irrelevance of material possessions and a sense of the equality of all humans in the face of the power of nature as they made their way across the Bay of Biscay. The extended pilgrimage to Santiago had certainly given them spiritual experiences beyond the liturgical norms of medieval Christian devotion. The framework of indulgences for such pilgrimages that had been constructed and promoted by ecclesiastical authorities may have had the effect of promoting a greater sense of piety and an interest in investing in ecclesiastical structures at home. There are clear indications in the extant evidence that some wealthy pilgrims were encouraged to be active patrons of the church at home, as another form of investment in their salvation. Their enthusiasm for pilgrimage might also have found expression

---

82 Cited in Óscar Recio Morales, *Ireland and the Spanish empire, 1600–1825* (Dublin, 2010), p. 35. Gerald of Wales (*c.*1147–*c.*1223) had commented somewhat similarly that Ireland had plentiful harvests, but grain 'can scarcely be reaped in the harvest because of unceasing rain' (John J. O'Meara (trans.), *The first version of the Topography of Ireland by Giraldus Cambrensis* (Dundalk, 1951), pp 14–15).

in the support of local and regional pilgrimages in their own localities, as may have occurred in Fermanagh.

Pilgrims from medieval Ireland have left only the barest traces in the written record, but those who successfully completed the pilgrimage to Santiago cannot have been unaffected by the experience. We know that some of those who returned home valued their scallop-shell souvenirs so much that they chose to be buried with them. These were a tangible reminder of their rare journey to such a sacred place. Such pilgrims would have truly believed that the initiative they had taken by going on pilgrimage and gaining plenary indulgences had brought them a step closer to paradise.

6

Decline of the medieval pilgrimage and modern revival

The medieval pilgrim journey was a multi-dimensional experience. It was embarked on as a religious undertaking rather than a cultural expedition, though the boundary between the two experiences could often be permeable. Pilgrims usually travelled within groups bound by kinship or other local loyalties and, like modern-day pilgrims to Marian shrines at Lourdes or Fatima, would have had relatively little contact with the local population while visiting the shrine.[1] At the same time the pilgrimage was undoubtedly an adventure; indeed it was one that some people chose to repeat, even after having achieved their goal on a previous visit. The souvenirs they brought home to Ireland were trinkets and do not point to significant cultural or artistic influence, but they appear to have been treated as being akin to relics or as visible proof of their pilgrimage so that some wished to be buried with them. There was little that was distinctively Irish about Irish involvement in the medieval pilgrimage to Santiago, either in terms of the motivations of pilgrims or their experiences on the route. Rather, the phenomenon of the Santiago pilgrimage, from the twelfth to the sixteenth century, provides evidence of the degree to which communities in medieval Ireland were in tune with English and Continental trends in terms of the practice of piety, as in many other aspects of their lives.[2]

THE DECLINE OF THE MEDIEVAL PILGRIMAGE IN CONTEXT

The heyday of the pilgrimage to Santiago lasted from the twelfth to the early sixteenth centuries, after which it went into steep decline. In European terms, there are some obvious explanations for the decline of the pilgrimage. Wider religious shifts emphasized scepticism towards the whole idea of extended pilgrimages in pursuit of indulgences. Martin Luther (d. 1546), a leading advocate for reform, dismissed the notion that pilgrimage offered a route to salvation. The veneration of St James of Compostela was among the devotions he came to regard as idolatrous.[3]

1 Síle de Cléir, *Popular Catholicism in 20th-century Ireland: locality, identity and culture* (London, 2017), pp 58–62. 2 See, for instance, Jan Van Herwaarden, *Between Saint James and Erasmus: studies in late-medieval religious life: devotion and pilgrimage in the Netherlands* (Leiden, 2003), pp 125–205; Henderson, *Pre-Reformation pilgrims from Scotland to Santiago de Compostela*; Storrs, *Jacobean pilgrims from England*. 3 For the development of Luther's thinking on indulgences, see MacCulloch,

The influential Dutch humanist writer Desiderius Erasmus (d. 1536) also criti-
cized both the cult of relics and the idea of extended pilgrimage to distant locations,
particularly where the pilgrim had responsibilities at home. In a work in dialogue
form that debated issues relating to pilgrimage, Erasmus argued the case against
having relics as the focus of pilgrimage. He objected to the tactile nature of such
devotional practices, with people literally grasping at the sacred.[4] He mocked the
idea of pilgrims returning from Santiago laden with shells and pilgrim badges. The
stay-at-home questioner asks the wandering pilgrim: 'But what's this fancy outfit?
You're ringed with scallop shells, choked with tin and leaden images on every side,
decked out with straw necklaces, and you have snake eggs [a rosary] on your arms',
to which the answer was 'I've been on a visit to St James of Compostela and, on
my way back, to the famous Virgin by the sea [at Walsingham], in England.'[5] In
general, throughout Europe, the era of the sixteenth-century Reformation saw a
marked reduction in pilgrimages to Santiago and other major Christian pilgrim
destinations, including Jerusalem.[6] Later, the wars of religion in the seventeenth
century affected travel, further discouraging potential pilgrims from undertaking
long journeys far from their homelands.

THE IRISH IN GALICIA IN THE SEVENTEENTH CENTURY

Ireland was not isolated from these trends. In addition to this, links between Ireland
and Spain were reshaped in the sixteenth and seventeenth centuries. Pilgrimage
endured, but at a lesser level.[7] In 1580, the chancellor of the cathedral in Limerick,
Nicholas Fagan, having been in Rome, decided to walk to Santiago, and appears
to have been supported by the archbishop of Toledo in his effort to do so.[8] In the
same year, Margery Barnwall, a Catholic noblewoman living as a nun, was arrested
in Dublin by the civil authorities, but was helped to escape on a ship bound for
St Malo. After further adversity and miraculous escapes, she and her maidservant
went on pilgrimage to Santiago and other places in thanksgiving. The maid died in
Spain, but Margaret continued on pilgrimage to Rome before eventually returning to Ireland.[9] Thomas Field, SJ, of Limerick, having studied at Paris, Douai
and Louvain, joined the Jesuits at Rome in 1574 at the age of 25. He received

Reformation, pp 121–6.   **4** MacCulloch, *Reformation*, pp 101–2.   **5** Erasmus. *Ten colloquies*, ed.
and trans. C.R. Thompson (New York, 1986), pp 56–91, at p. 57.   **6** Colin Morris, *The sepulchre
of Christ and the medieval West: from the beginning to 1600* (Oxford, 2005), pp 363–83.   **7** Thomas
O'Connor, *Irish voices from the Spanish Inquisition: migrants, converts and brokers in early modern Iberia*
(Basingstoke, 2016), pp 17–119; R.A. Stradling, *The Spanish monarchy and Irish mercenaries: the Wild
Geese in Spain, 1618–68* (Dublin, 1994).   **8** Enrique García Hernán, *Ireland and Spain in the reign
of Philip II* (Dublin, 2009), p. 178.   **9** For Margery Barnwall's story, in Latin, as told by Revd John
Howling, see P.F. Moran (ed.), *Spicilegium Ossoriense, being a collection of original letters and papers
illustrative of the Irish church* (1st ser., Dublin, 1874), pp 106–9; for a summary in English, see Edmund
Hogan, *Distinguished Irishmen of the sixteenth century* (London, 1894), pp 34–7.

permission to go to Brazil, but first he begged his way on foot to Santiago and from there to Lisbon.[10]

Hardly surprisingly, given its reputation, Santiago became a favoured location for some Irish Catholic clergy who could not exercise their mission in Ireland. Peter Power, bishop of Ferns, was appointed bishop of Santiago in 1582 and died there in 1587. Thomas Strong, OFM, who was appointed bishop of Ossory in 1582, lived most of his adult life on the Continent. He was able to visit Rome in 1582, was in Lisbon in 1583, and returned to Ireland for a short time in 1583–4, but found it impossible to function as a Catholic bishop at home. He left Ireland permanently, serving as auxiliary bishop of Santiago in the 1580s and 1590s, and advising the Spanish king on the loyalty or otherwise of those Irish who were resident in Galicia. In 1599 he was granted Spanish citizenship (because he had served in the 1588 Armada), and this new status allowed him to claim an income from the see of Santiago. He died in Santiago in January 1602, aged 55, and was buried in the cloister of the cathedral. A fellow Waterford man, Cistercian author Malachy Hartry, who likewise lived for many years on the Continent, recorded in 1640 that he had seen Bishop Strong's marble tomb in the cathedral cloister with the arms of the Strong family carved on it.[11] The bishop's nephew, Thomas White, SJ (1556–1622), of Clonmel, was active in establishing an Irish college at Salamanca in 1592. White was also involved in founding the Irish colleges at Lisbon, Santiago and Seville, which functioned mainly as seminaries, and he served for a time as rector of the Irish College at Santiago de Compostela.[12]

By the late sixteenth century, as the Irish were drawn into Anglo-Spanish hostilities, most famously in the ill-fated Spanish Armada expedition of 1588, the Spanish monarchy was keen to attract skilled Irish seamen to places such as Ferrol, A Coruña and elsewhere on the north coast. Some soldiers and their families who migrated from Ireland settled in A Coruña and elsewhere in Galicia; others moved on to serve in Spanish armies in other regions.[13] Other Irish people were political exiles or economic migrants.[14] As a result of the more permanent movement of people from Ireland to Galicia in the late sixteenth and early seventeenth centuries, the pilgrim story becomes diluted with other endeavours.

Irish people known to have been in Santiago cannot be assumed to be pilgrims, although it seems that the pilgrimage continued in tandem with these other business links with north-west Spain. Henry Dillon, for instance, hoped to go to northern Spain in 1572 on a political mission. Having failed to find a suitable ship

---

10 Pádraig Ó Maidín, 'A mission to Brazil', *Cork Examiner*, 6 Oct. 1969.   11 Carrigan, *Diocese of Ossory*, i, pp 74–5; Denis Murphy (ed.), *Triumphalia chronologica Monasterii Sanctae Crucis in Hibernia* (Dublin, 1891), pp 84–5.   12 Terry Clavin, 'White, Thomas' in *DIB*; García Hernán, *Ireland and Spain in the reign of Philip II*, p. 125.   13 Ciaran O'Scea, 'The devotional world of the Irish Catholic exile in early modern Galicia, 1598–1666' in T. O'Connor (ed.), *The Irish in Europe, 1580–1815* (Dublin, 2001), pp 27–48; Ciaran O'Scea, *Surviving Kinsale: Irish emigration and identity formation in early modern Spain, 1601–40* (Manchester, 2015).   14 García Hernán, *Ireland and Spain in the reign of Philip II*, pp 173–9.

at Dalkey or Howth, he arranged to sail from Drogheda on a ship from St Jean-de-Luz. He negotiated with the Portuguese captain in the hope that they would sail to Galicia, ingratiating himself with the ship's captain by saying he was going on pilgrimage, presumably to Santiago: 'I told him whither I meant to go a pilgrimage and he liked me the better for that and said he will bear me company by land or by sea.'[15] Similarly, in 1601, Richard Langton sought a passport as a pilgrim to Santiago to avoid suspicion in his diplomatic enquiries. He appears to have been working as a messenger or a spy and his work – carrying letters and information – took him to Naples, Rome, Parma and Turin. When he met Edward Bermingham at Parma, Bermingham gave him 10s. towards his pilgrimage to Santiago, while another contact who heard of his intention to go to Santiago gave him a French crown.[16]

An example of the mixed motives of those Irish who went to Santiago in the late sixteenth and early seventeenth centuries is provided by the visit of Aodh Ruadh Ó Domhnaill, who spent time in the city in 1602 (a jubilee year), with associates including Franciscan priests Flaithrí Ó Maoil Chonaire and Muiris Ó Duinnshléibhe.[17] When Aodh Ruadh Ó Domhnaill and his entourage of about twenty-five people left Ireland for Spain in January 1602, in the immediate aftermath of the Battle of Kinsale, his purpose was politics, not pilgrimage. Two different accounts of his sojourn in Spain survive from contemporary sources and some details of his journey can be recovered. Having got a suitable wind, Ó Domhnaill and his followers sailed from Castlehaven on the Cork coast on 6 January 1602. The warship had an experienced Spanish captain, but they encountered a severe storm and were blown off course. They reached the north coast of Spain on 14 January, though not at A Coruña as had been intended. Instead, they made landfall much further east, at Luarca in Asturias. From there it took them a week to reach A Coruña overland. The land route followed for this last stage of the journey to A Coruña may have been determined by January storms making any further sea voyage difficult. After a week in A Coruña, including some sightseeing at Breóghan's Tower, they set out for Santiago, spending a night at Santa Lucia, and arriving in Santiago the following day.[18] Aodh Ruadh's first two overland journeys within Spain (from Luarca to A Coruña and from A Coruña to Santiago) must have been done on horseback to be completed in the number of days indicated.

A letter written from A Coruña by an Irish priest, Patrick Sinnott, dated 4 February 1602, gave information about Aodh Ruadh Ó Domhnaill's arrival in

---

15 *Calendar of state papers Ireland, Tudor period, 1571–1575*, ed. M. O'Dowd (London, 2000), no. 233.1 (TNA, SP 63/36, no. 3(i)).   16 *Cal. S.P. Ire., 1601–3*, pp 633–4.   17 Micheline Kerney Walsh, 'Aodh Rua O'Donnell and his mission to Spain, January–September 1602', *Donegal Annual*, 41 (1989), 96–122.   18 This summary is based on Walsh (ed.), *The life of Aodh Ruadh Ó Domhnaill*, i, pp 340–3, and [Thomas Stafford], *Pacata Hibernia, or a history of the wars in Ireland during the reign of Queen Elizabeth, taken from the original chronicles* (2 vols, Dublin, 1810), i, pp 478–9, each of which contains only partial details of the journey.

Spain. Once his seasickness had passed, Aodh Ruadh enjoyed the hospitality of the earl of Caraçena in A Coruña, before departing for Santiago. Thomas Stafford's account, based on Sinnott's letter, continued:

> The next day hee went to Saint Iames of Compostella, where he was received with magnificence by the prelates, citizens, and religious persons, and his lodging was made ready for him at Saint Martins, but before hee saw it, hee visited the Archbishop, who instantly prayed him to lodge in his house; but Odonnell excused it. The nine and twentieth [January 1602] the Archbishop saying Masse with pontificall solemnity, did minister the Sacrament to Odonnell, which done hee feasted him at dinner in his house; and at his departure hee gaue him one thousand duckets. The King understanding of Odonnell's arrival, wrote unto the Earle of Caraçena concerning the reception of him, and the affaires of Ireland, which was one of the most gracious letters that ever King directed; for by it, it plainely appeared that hee would endanger his kingdome to succour the Catholikes of Ireland, to their content, and not faile therein; for the perfecting whereof, great preparations were in hand.[19]

Ó Domhnaill's journey clearly blended politics and piety in a way that had become common among the Irish in Spain. However, the long-established trade links between the two regions and the accessibility of Spain evident in the growing numbers of Irish who served in Spanish armies from the late sixteenth century are more important contexts in which to understand Irish links with Galicia than the political aspirations of Aodh Ruadh and his associates in their diplomatic negotiations with the Spanish monarch. Alongside merchants and soldiers, by the seventeenth century some of the Irish in Santiago were there because of its status as a university town where Catholics were welcome, and where they could avail of educational facilities denied them at home.

In the seventeenth century, many of the patterns already discernible in the late sixteenth century intensified. Henry O'Neill, son of the earl of Tyrone, had been welcomed 'spiritually and corporally' by the archbishop of Santiago in 1600,[20] but was essentially a political exile. Similarly, Domhnall Cam Ó Súilleabháin Béarra (1560–1618) lived in Santiago from 1604 to 1609 before moving to Madrid, where he died in exile in 1618.[21] Some Irish bishops who had been educated on the Continent maintained strong links with Spain thereafter. Thomas Walsh (1580–1654), Waterford-born archbishop of Cashel, had first gone to Santiago as a young student in 1600, where his uncle Bishop Thomas Strong was living, before joining the Irish College at Salamanca in 1602. He maintained contacts

19 [Stafford], *Pacata Hibernia*, p. 479. 20 *Cal. S.P. Spain, 1587–1603*, p. 658. 21 Emmett O'Byrne, 'O'Sullivan Beare, Domhnall' in *DIB*; Micheline Kerney Walsh, 'O'Sullivan Beare in Spain: some unpublished documents', *Archivium Hibernicum*, 45 (1990), 46–63.

with Spain throughout his life, and his appointment to Cashel was achieved with the support of the Spanish Ambassador in Rome. Having been politically active in Ireland in the 1640s and early 1650s, he was imprisoned by the Cromwellian authorities before being sent to Spain in 1653 where he resided in poor health in the Irish College at Santiago until his death the following year.[22] His contemporary biographer, William St Leger, SJ, recorded his epitaph and noted that he was buried in a place of honour in the cathedral of Santiago, 'glorious Apostle of the Spaniards'.[23]

The establishment of an Irish college at Santiago in 1605 was a significant new initiative, and was one manifestation of a more established Irish presence in the region by the beginning of the seventeenth century. Spanish support for Irish colleges in Santiago and other university towns was a form of diplomacy, following the failure of the military effort at the battle of Kinsale in December 1601. The Continental colleges played an important role in supporting the Catholic resurgence in early seventeenth-century Ireland. The small college at Santiago was founded initially to cater for the followers of Domhnall Cam Ó Súilleabháin Béarra, who had gone into exile in Spain in the aftermath of the Nine Years War (1594–1603) in Ireland. The handful of Irish students living in the college in its early years pursued studies in medicine and law at the university. However, it later functioned as a seminary, under Jesuit control, training priests for Irish dioceses, and continued in that capacity until the suppression of the Jesuit Order in Spain in 1767, after which the Irish College in Santiago was absorbed into that at Salamanca. Shortly afterwards, the Santiago college building on Rua Nova (extending to Rua Vilar at the rear) was sold in 1774 and converted to private use. Some buildings have survived, along with a statue of St Patrick in the enclosed garden for which funds had been raised by subscription in 1667.[24]

Despite the general decline in pilgrimage activity, some Irish pilgrims continued to make the journey to Santiago through the seventeenth century and beyond. In July 1608, an Irish soldier serving on the Continent was licensed to go on pilgrimage to Santiago in fulfilment of a vow.[25] Others made the journey from Ireland, generally sailing to the port of A Coruña. Dóirín Mhic Mhurchú found evidence in the register of Buen Suceso hospital at A Coruña that an occasional Irish pilgrim, ranging in age from 13 to 62, was admitted there in the late seventeenth or early eighteenth centuries. They included Juan Cobre (Carbery?) aged 25 in 1699, Patrick Macanas aged 62 from Dublin in 1735, and James Damas aged 13 and John Conway(?) aged 33, both in the period 1735 to 1753. These individuals

22 Terry Clavin, 'Walsh, Thomas' in *DIB*.   **23** Richard O'Ferrall & Robert O'Connell, *Commentarius Rinuccinianus*, ed. S. Kavanagh (6 vols, Dublin, 1932–49), v, p. 228; Patricia O Connell, *The Irish College at Santiago de Compostela, 1605–1769* (Dublin, 2007), p. 142; Anon., 'An Irish archbishop's grave in Spain', *JRSAI*, 21 (1890), p. 85.   **24** O Connell, *The Irish College at Santiago*, pp 34–5; Patricia O Connell, 'The early modern Irish college network in Iberia, 1590–1800' in T. O'Connor (ed.), *The Irish in Europe, 1580–1815* (Dublin, 2001), pp 49–64.   **25** Brendan Jennings (ed.), *Wild Geese in Spanish Flanders, 1582–1700* (Dublin, 1964), p. 109.

were explicitly described in the hospital register as Irish pilgrims. Three were discharged within two weeks; one died in the hospital.[26] Irish chaplains linked to the royal hospital in Santiago continued to cater for the needs of pilgrims through the seventeenth century and beyond.[27]

MODERN REVIVAL OF THE PILGRIMAGE

The pilgrimage to Santiago declined through the seventeenth and eighteenth centuries, to the point where in the early nineteenth century there were only a handful of pilgrims each year, with perhaps 500 in a jubilee year, almost all drawn from the local archdiocese of Santiago de Compostela.[28] Then, following new archaeological excavations in 1879 masterminded by Cardinal Miguel Payá y Rico, three sets of human bones, assumed to be those of St James and two disciples, which it was claimed had been hidden in 1589 at a time of Anglo-Spanish hostility, were rediscovered behind the high altar in the cathedral. In fact they had not been forgotten about after 1589; the sarcophagus was in its original position when the new *altar mayor* was designed in the years after 1650, and even later, Domenico Laffi, a priest from Bologna, was shown the sarcophagus when he visited in 1673.[29] It seems more likely that the relics and their container were hidden in the early eighteenth century when a further outbreak of hostilities between England and Galicia posed a threat to Santiago in 1719, after which their whereabouts no longer mattered, the pilgrimage having fallen out of favour.

The late nineteenth-century search for the relics followed decades of increased enthusiasm for local festivities on the feast of St James. The bones were declared to be authentic relics by Pope Leo XIII in 1884, and gradually became the focus of renewed interest among pilgrims.[30] In 1897 there were 965 registered pilgrims; by the 1909 jubilee year that number had grown enormously to 140,000, mostly from the archdiocese of Santiago de Compostela and mostly arriving by public transport directly to the city. Some travelled from Britain and Ireland. A shipping company used Irish newspapers to advertise a fifteen-day round trip via Liverpool to bring pilgrims to Santiago de Compostela on the RMS *Antony* in the summer of 1908.[31] The following year was a jubilee year and the archbishop of Westminster led a pilgrimage that included some Irish pilgrims.[32] Numbers declined during the First World War (1914–18), but reached 110,000 again in the next jubilee year, 1920, in what was becoming a conflation of pilgrimage and mass tourism.[33] Among the pilgrims in that year were Catholic officers and men from the British naval vessels

---

26 Mhic Mhurchú, *Bealach na bó finne*, p. 69.   27 Ofelia Rey Castelao, 'Inmigrantes Irlandeses en la Galicia del periodo moderno' in Begoña Villar García (ed.), *La emigración Irlandesa en el siglo xviii* (Málaga, 2000), pp 183–206, at p. 188.   28 Pack, 'Revival of the pilgrimage', 347.   29 Kendrick, *St James in Spain*, pp 178–9.   30 Pack, 'Revival of the pilgrimage', 335–7.   31 *Irish Independent*, 19 June, 29 June, 8 July 1908.   32 'Coming Catholic pilgrimage', *Ulster Herald*, 8 May 1909.   33 Linda Kay Davidson, 'Reformulations of the pilgrimages to Santiago de Compostela' in Pazos (ed.), *Redefining pilgrimage*, pp 159–81, at p. 168.

HMS *Valiant* and HMS *Warspite*, which anchored at Arosa Bay in March 1920 to facilitate a pilgrimage to Santiago. The 67 men, including some from Ireland, sang 'Faith of our Fathers' as they processed into the cathedral.[34]

Within Ireland, in the 1930s, there was some interest in the history of the Santiago pilgrimage. Patrick McBride used his National University of Ireland travelling scholarship to visit Madrid and was living there in 1935 when he wrote an article on medieval Irish pilgrims to Santiago for the Jesuit magazine *Irish Monthly*. McBride later became professor of Romance languages at University College, Dublin. He also described, for the same magazine early in 1935, attempts to restore Catholic education in Spain and wrote at greater length that year in another Jesuit publication, *Studies: an Irish Quarterly Review*, on the political turmoil in Spain and the challenges facing the Catholic Church there.[35] After the Second World War, Richard Hayes, a Limerick medical doctor, political activist and historian of the Irish in France, again traced the history of Irish links with Santiago (both the medieval pilgrimage and the Irish College) in an article published in *Studies* in 1948, but made no reference to contemporary Spanish politics.[36] Walter Starkie's *Spanish raggle-taggle*, a travel book first published in 1934, described his own wanderings in Spain during his summer holidays from his post as professor of Spanish at Trinity College, Dublin. He steered clear of politics, but described meeting a lone, barefoot pilgrim in the vicinity of Burgos. The barefoot man was a committed wanderer, he wore a brown cloak and had a scrip and staff, his 'hat was broad-brimmed and around it were the traditional shells that pilgrims to St James used always to wear'. Such was the man's attire that Starkie, for a moment, 'thought that I had been spirited back to the Middle Ages'.[37]

The politico-religious crusade of General Francisco Franco from the late 1930s marked a new phase in the revival of the pilgrimage, as part of the National Catholicism movement.[38] This did not go unnoticed in Ireland. The *Irish Independent* reported in July 1937 that

> Nationalists throughout Spain today celebrated the name-day of St James, the patron saint of Spain, and there were special ceremonies at Salamanca and Compostela where the shrine of the saint has escaped the ravages of the war. Prayers were offered that St James should lead Spain, now being martyred, as he was, to victory, as he has done so often in the past.[39]

---

34 'Naval pilgrimage to Santiago de Compostela', *Cork Examiner*, 6 Apr. 1920. **35** P. McBride, 'A modern Spanish crusade', *Irish Monthly*, 63:739 (Jan. 1935), 18–19; P. Mc Bride, 'The Spanish crisis', *Studies: an Irish Quarterly Review*, 24:93 (Mar. 1935), 43–59; P. McBride, 'Compostela ... and some Irish memories', *Irish Monthly*, 63:744 (June 1935), 381–5. **36** Hayes, 'Ireland's links with Compostella', 326–32. **37** Walter Starkie, *Spanish raggle-taggle: adventures with a fiddle in north Spain* (London, 1934), p. 248. **38** Lynn Talbot, 'Revival of the medieval past: Francisco Franco and the Camino de Santiago' in S. Sánchez y Sánchez & A. Hesh (eds), *The Camino de Santiago in the 21st century* (London, 2016), pp 36–56. **39** 'Report from Gibraltar', *Irish Independent*, 26 July 1937.

Most pilgrims still arrived by public transport, though Franco also encouraged more active pilgrimages by military and youth groups. The year 1938 had been designated by Pope Pius XI as a special holy year in Santiago in support of the cause of National Catholicism.[40] Franco was among those to travel from Burgos to Santiago on pilgrimage in December of that year, a widely publicized event that was reported in Irish newspapers.[41] Franco was a native of Galicia and became a strong supporter of the redevelopment of the wider region of northern Spain through investment in the pilgrimage infrastructure. This included the refurbishment of medieval hostels at Santo Domingo de la Calzada, Leon and Santiago as luxury, state-owned hotels. As motor traffic increased, the pilgrim route across northern Spain was promoted by the use of official road signs with a scallop-shell motif.[42] There was evidently a demand for leisurely rather than challenging pilgrimage journeys to the shrine of St James, as one *Irish Press* columnist mused in July 1938 regarding the possibility that the pilgrimage from Ireland might be revived:

> Aye, and we will not go on a one-sailed boat, but on a luxury liner; and when we come ashore at Vigo we will get into a motor-coach for the land part of the journey – for we will be up-to-date pilgrims, and efficient even in our prayers.[43]

With the authenticity of the relics of St James still a matter of debate, despite the controversial papal approbation in 1884, and with an eye to rural redevelopment, the 1950s saw a reorientation of marketing to emphasise the pilgrim road rather than the relics. Promoted by church and state, each jubilee year served as a target for further development of the tourist potential of the pilgrimage to attract visitors to rural northern Spain. By then, chartered flights to Santiago were possible and an Irish travel agent advertised a six-day tour for the feast of St James, 1954, on a direct *Aer Lingus* flight.[44] In Santiago, the local leader of the archconfraternity of St James, José Guerra Campos, used the preparations for the 1954 holy year deliberately to promote the idea of pilgrimage spirituality, shifting the focus away from the relics and the statue of St James the Moorslayer in the cathedral and towards the journey itself.[45] In the same year, representatives of the Spanish embassy in Dublin promoted the idea of a walking route 'for boys of all nations to follow on foot'.[46] A decade later Mary Purcell, the Catholic popular historian, reminded readers of the *Irish Independent* that the jubilee-year indulgence could be

40 Pack, 'Revival of the pilgrimage', 352; See also A.M. Pazos, 'Old and new pilgrimages in the context of the Spanish civil war' in Pazos (ed.), *Pilgrims and politics*, pp 151–60.   41 *Irish Independent*, 7 Dec. 1938.   42 Pack, 'Revival of the pilgrimage', 366.   43 Roddy the Rover, 'Seen, heard and noted', *Irish Press*, 28 July 1938. 'Roddy the Rover' was a pseudonym of Aodh de Blacam, an *Irish Press* columnist.   44 *Sunday Independent*, 4 Apr. 1954.   45 Pack, 'Revival of the pilgrimage', 360; baroque images of St James the Moorslayer had proliferated in the seventeenth century (Kendrick, *St James in Spain*, pp 147–8).   46 'Many pilgrims for Spain this year', *Irish Independent*, 11 Feb. 1954.

gained by visiting Santiago any day up to 31 December 1965. She emphasised its accessibility:

> Irish pilgrims of 1965 can get to Compostella easily. Santiago airport has connections with other Spanish cities. The cheapest way of getting there is by taking a passage from Liverpool or Southampton to Corunna or Vigo or Lisbon. Corunna is 45 and Vigo 65 miles from Santiago. Lisbon is 390 miles south, but pilgrims coming up the coast by rail or road pass by and can visit Fatima on the way.[47]

She also recommended the overland coastal route from Irun, and advised that Walter Starkie's *Road to Santiago* was a good travelling companion for those choosing the longer old pilgrim route (Camino Francés). She did not appear to consider anything other than modern transport options. On arrival in Santiago, she was impressed by the sublime sculptures in the cathedral's Portico of Glory, but was less enamoured by the swinging of the *botafumeiro*: 'the performance is not very conducive to prayer!' Other journalists also enthused that if the pilgrimage was revived, recent advances in air travel meant that 'pilgrims will be able to complete the trip in a couple of hours' compared with 'ten days under sail' in the past.[48]

The post-war movement for European cooperation, together with a growing tourist market, fed into the growth of the pilgrimage in the second half of the twentieth century. In 1950 Spain had fewer than 1 million tourists; in 2007 Galicia alone had 5.7 million tourists, 85 per cent of whom went to Santiago.[49] French interest from the 1950s helped boost the Camino Francés (Chemin St Jacques) in particular, and by the 1980s an infrastructure of pilgrim hostels to accommodate those who wished to walk the route was being re-established. The visit of Pope John Paul II to Santiago in 1982 reinforced Catholic Church sanction for the pilgrimage, though the pope's speech carefully avoided comment on the authenticity of the relics.[50]

'Authenticity' was an important promotional plank, however, and the authorities in Santiago worked to obtain Unesco World Heritage site status for the old town of Santiago in 1985, followed two years later by the adoption of the pilgrimage route as the first 'European Cultural Route' by the Council of Europe. In 1993 the Camino Francés pilgrimage route was formally recognized as 'Unesco World Heritage Patrimony for Humanity'.[51] This was extended in 2015 to encompass additional sections of the network of variant pilgrim routes in northern Spain. The Unesco designation recognized the built heritage of the route, the outstanding natural landscapes and the intangible cultural heritage associated with the Camino and was intended to support economic and social development in the region. The

---

47 'A Spanish town and an Apostle', *Irish Independent*, 1 Feb. 1965.   48 'Pilgrimage may be revived after 500 years', *Irish Independent*, 23 Feb. 1965.   49 Davidson, 'Reformulations', p. 171.   50 Pack, 'Revival of the pilgrimage', 365.   51 Davidson, 'Reformulations', p. 171.

initiative also sought to promote 'cultural dialogue between the pilgrims and the communities through which they pass'.[52]

From the early 1990s, the cathedral's pilgrim office in Santiago distinguished more clearly between those who had arrived in Santiago by mechanized means and those who had walked at least 100 km, and the issuing of the Compostela certificate was restricted to those who had made a journey of at least 100 km in a traditional way and for spiritual reasons.[53] This was a significant reduction from the 300 km stipulated in 1965, but it worked to strengthen the distinction between 'pilgrim tourists' and 'real pilgrims', gradually building up to a form of endurance tourism as some pilgrims sought to outdo others in the distances walked and the time taken.

By the early 1990s the Camino had also become a popular destination from Ireland for sponsored walks, the best-publicized being those organized as a form of fundraising for the Multiple Sclerosis Society of Ireland.[54] Some participants in those early fundraising walks were among the founding members of the Irish Society of the Friends of St James in 1992, reconstituted as Camino Society Ireland in 2015. At the close of the twentieth century the Santiago pilgrimage was becoming well integrated into the European leisure experience. Yet the continuing emphasis on jubilee years, when pilgrim numbers are greatly increased, suggests that the religious dimension of the pilgrimage phenomenon has not been forgotten. The statistics collected by the pilgrim office in Santiago cathedral indicate that the increased numbers in jubilee years are mainly accounted for by Spanish pilgrims.[55]

The recent international resurgence in the Santiago pilgrimage can be partly explained by the promotion of tourism interests, whereby an authentic heritage product is skilfully marketed for modern consumers of heritage experiences. Publicity on film and television has also helped, but its most effective supporters are probably the voluntary societies of St James that were operating in many European countries by the 1990s and whose work continues, fostering understanding of the history, art and architecture of the traditional pilgrim routes.[56] Enthusiasts for the experience of long-distance walking on historic pilgrimage routes disseminated information on the Camino Francés in particular. The 1993 jubilee year saw a huge increase in pilgrims on that route, and a guidebook in English by Alison Raju, *The Way of St James: Spain*, was first published in 1994, making it easier for English speakers to follow the route.[57] A proliferation of guidebooks in many European

---

52 Unesco, 'Routes of Santiago de Compostela: Camino Francés and the routes of northern Spain', whc.unesco.org/en/list/669, accessed 3 Mar. 2018. 53 Davidson, 'Reformulations', p. 173. 54 *Irish Independent*, 18 Jan. 1990; *Cork Examiner*, 8 Jan. 1990, 7 Jan. 1991, 28 Nov. 1991. These annual fundraising walks have continued since then. See MS Ireland, 'Camino – the Portuguese route', www.ms-society.ie/pages/get-involved/treks-and-challenges/treks/camino, accessed 14 June 2018. 55 officinadelperegrino.com/en/statistics, accessed 21 Apr. 2018. 56 Xunta de Galicia, *Directorio de asociacións de amigos do Camino de Santiago, confrarías e centros de estudos xacobeos* (Santiago de Compostela, 2015). 57 Alison Raju, *The Way of St James: Spain* (Milnthorpe, 1994). This was followed in 1999 by an extended guide, Alison Raju, *The Way of St James: Le Puy to Santiago: a walker's guide* (Milnthorpe, 1999), and later updates.

languages has ensued in recent years. As the Camino Francés commencing at St Jean Pied-de-Port or Roncesvalles has become increasingly busy in the early years of the twenty-first century, experienced walkers have looked to variant historic routes and numerous guidebooks detailing different pilgrim routes through Spain, all leading to Santiago, have been published in a variety of languages, including English.[58] A 'Celtic Camino' guidebook attempts to reconstruct a traditional Irish route from A Coruña.[59]

CONCLUSION

Whether journeying on foot, as much as feasible, all the way from their own front door or walking the last 100 km as stipulated by the authorities in Santiago as the minimum requirement for obtaining the Compostela, those who follow a medieval route to Santiago from Ireland have one thing in common. They like to believe they are adhering to a medieval tradition with a clear Irish connection. It is not that simple. The final destination is still Santiago de Compostela, as it was for medieval Irish pilgrims. But is there anything other than vague sentiment to connect the experience of the modern Irish walker to Santiago with the world of the medieval Irish pilgrim who made the hazardous journey to Galicia more than 500 years ago? Obviously, the infrastructure of travel is totally different. Few modern pilgrims, having reached Santiago on foot or by bicycle, turn around and embark on the journey home by the same means. Almost all international pilgrims simply fly home, something a medieval pilgrim could not begin to comprehend. Similarly, we struggle to comprehend some other limitations on their medieval lives – physical, cultural and religious. The stories of medieval pilgrims explored in this study of the medieval Irish connection with Santiago reflect a world that is far removed from the experience and mindset of the walkers and cyclists of today. The links back through the centuries are almost beyond recall. But yet the pull of history, as one walks a traditional route to Santiago, is incredibly strong. It is a Europe-wide experience, now evolving into a world-wide experience, and it is something in which Irish people have participated through the ages. The local Irish pilgrimage tradition is deep-rooted, and still widely celebrated, and continues to shape Irish perceptions of, and involvement with, the international Santiago phenomenon.

The fluidity that is an intrinsic part of pilgrimage allows long-established pilgrimages to evolve and retain their relevance in changing times. A rigid adherence to traditional norms and beliefs is not necessary. For most Irish people today the Santiago pilgrimage is not about devotion to St James the Great. The connection back to the medieval world persists, however, in the sense of the universal

58 Confraternity of St James, 'Books', www.csj.org.uk/product-catergory/books, accessed 23 June 2018.   59 John Rafferty, *Pilgrim guide to the Celtic Camino and the city of Santiago de Compostela* (Dublin, 2018).

attraction of pilgrimages within the Christian tradition and beyond. This finds expression in the pursuit of a physical objective, made tangible through a shrine located in a specific place, and gaining spiritual understanding along the way, in an experience that transcends the mundane and gives greater meaning to the routines and relationships of daily life.

The story of the medieval Irish pilgrims to Santiago shows that the seafaring Irish were linked into mainstream European spirituality, and that they were willing to undertake long and challenging pilgrimages in pursuit of the indulgences that they hoped would relieve them of the sufferings of Purgatory that otherwise awaited all sinners. Pilgrimages like that to Santiago had ecclesiastical support, but went beyond the norm of fixed liturgies and conformist devotions to allow the individual to take personal responsibility for the pursuit of sanctity, beyond the control of local clergy in the pre-Reformation Christian West. It may not have been their conscious objective, but, through the experiences of the journey, pilgrims would have come to a better understanding of their place in the world. Their eyes would have been opened to worlds beyond the confines of their lives to date, seeing new landscapes, new horizons, new peoples and new possibilities, while coping with the often mundane personal challenges of the arduous journey. Over time they interpreted those experiences within the context of their prior cultural, spiritual and social understanding. Through the ages, in ways that are unprescribed and difficult to define, such pilgrimages change the world, one person at a time.

Pilgrims to Santiago from medieval Ireland

Date	Details	Place	References	Notes
1222	Richard de Burgh	Clonmel	*Cal. Carew MSS*, p. 414	
1267	Fulk de Sandford, archbishop of Dublin	Dublin	*Cal. patent rolls, 1266–72*, p. 53	
1276	William de Vescy	[Dublin]	*45th deputy keeper report*, appendix ii	
1308	William le Paumer	[Co. Dublin]	*Cal. justiciary rolls, 1–7 Edward II*	Died on pilgrimage
1320	Edmund Butler, justiciar of Ireland, his wife and son	[Ormond]	*Cal. papal letters;* Grace's annals, pp 98–9	Petitioned to be released from vow
1428	Aodh Mág Uidhir	Fermanagh	*AFM*, 1428	Died on return
1428	Tomás Óg Mág Uidhir, first pilgrimage	Fermanagh	*AFM*, 1428	
1430	Tomás Óg Mág Uidhir, second pilgrimage	Fermanagh	*AU*, 1480	
1445	Mairgréag an Einigh Ní Chearbhaill	Offaly	*A.Lecan*, p. 211	
1445	Tomaltach mac Diarmada	Moylurg	*A.Lecan*, p. 211	
1445	Mac Eochagain	Leinster	*A.Lecan*, p. 211	
1445	Evilin Ó Fearghail/wife of Piers Dalton	Leinster	*A.Lecan*, p. 211	Died in Spain
1445	Gerott Fitzgerald		*A.Lecan*, p. 211	Died in Spain
1445	Ó Drisceoil Óg	Collybeg, west Cork	*A.Lecan*, p. 211	Died at sea
1445	Many more noble and ignoble persons		*A.Lecan*, p. 211	
1451	An Calbhach Ó Conchobhair Fáilghe	Offaly	*A.Lecan*, p. 230	
1456	Many people went for jubilee year		*A.Lecan*, p. 249	
1462	Many people went for jubilee year		*A.Conn*, p. 513	

Date	Details	Place	References	Notes
1472	Finghin Ó Drisceoil Mór	West Cork	*A.LCé*, pp 172–3; AFM	Died after return
1472	Tadhg son of Finghin Ó Drisceoil	West Cork	*A.LCé*, pp 172–3: AFM	Died after return
1473	Mayor James Rice, first pilgrimage	Waterford	Morrissey, *Statute rolls*, p. 55	
1473	Mayor John Fowling	Drogheda	Morrissey, *Statute rolls*	
1473	400 pilgrims on *Mary* of London	New Ross/ Waterford	Mac Niocaill, *Na Buirgéisi*	
1479	David Lombard	Blarney, Co. Cork	NLI Report on Lombard MSS	
1483-4	Mayor James Rice, second pilgrimage	Waterford	Connolly, *Statute Rolls*, p. 39	
1483-4	Patrick Mulgane, bailiff	Waterford	Connolly, *Statute Rolls*, p. 39	
1483-4	Philip Bryan, bailiff	Waterford	Connolly, *Statute Rolls*, p. 39	
1501	Domhnall son of Brian Ó hUiginn	Connacht	*AFM*, 1501	
1501	Ó Ceallaigh, buried in Franciscan friary	Kilconnell, Co. Galway	Ó Clabaigh, *JGAHS* (2007)	
1501	Edmund, son of Richard Burke		*AFM*, 1501	Taken hostage on return
1507	Domhnall son of Tadhg Ó Fiaich		*AFM*, 1507	Drowned at sea
1507	James Barry 'Roe', Lord Barrymore	Cork	*AFM*, 1507	Drowned at sea
1507	'many of the chiefs of his people' attended Lord Barrymore on pilgrimage.	Cork	*AFM*, 1507	Drowned at sea
1512?	Margaret Athy	Galway	Walsh, *JGAHS* (1992)	
1518?	Feidhlimidh son of Brian Mág Uidhir	Fermanagh	*AU*; *AFM*	Died after return
1520	David, Dominican	Athenry, Co. Galway	Fenning, 'Irish material', *Archivum Fratrum Praedicatorum* (1969)	
1572	Henry Dillon	Leinster	TNA, SP 63/36, no. 3(i)	Via Italy
1574?	Thomas Field, SJ	Limerick	*Cork Examiner*, 6 Oct. 1969	Rome also

Date	Details	Place	References	Notes
1580	Margery Barnwall and her servant girl	Leinster	Hogan, *Distinguished Irishmen*, pp 34–7	Rome also
1600	Henry O'Neill, aged 13	Tyrone	*Cal. S.P. Spain*, 1587–1603, p. 658	Exile/military
1602	Aodh Ruadh Ó Domhnaill	Donegal	Stafford, *Pacata Hib.*	Diplomacy
1602	Flaithrí Ó Maoil Chonaire	Roscommon	Stafford, *Pacata Hib.*	Diplomacy
1602	Muiris Ó Duinnshléibhe	Donegal	Stafford, *Pacata Hib.*	Diplomacy
1602	John Burke	Limerick	Stafford, *Pacata Hib.*, pp 329, 379	
1602	25 accompanied Aodh Ruadh Ó Domhnaill	[Donegal]		Exile/military
1605	Domhnall Cam Ó Suilleabháin Béarra	Cork	*Archivium Hibernicum*, 45 (1990), 46–63	Exile
1608	Domhnall Ó Fearghail, soldier in Henry O'Neill's regiment	Leinster	Jennings, *Wild geese*, p. 109	Military
1699	Juan Cobre (Carbery?), aged 25		Mhic Mhurchú, *Bealach na bó finne*	A Coruña hospital register
1735	Patrick Macanas, aged 62	Dublin	Mhic Mhurchú, *Bealach na bó finne*	A Coruña hospital register
1735–53	James Damas (Thomas), aged 13		Mhic Mhurchú, *Bealach na bó finne*	A Coruña hospital register
1735–53	John Conway?, aged 33		Mhic Mhurchú, *Bealach na bó finne*	A Coruña hospital register

Vowed to go but could not

Date	Details	Place	References	Notes
1343	Elizabeth de Burgh		*Cal. papal petitions*, i, *1342–1419*, pp 22–3	
1343	Matilda de Burgh and servants	[England]	*Cal. papal petitions*, i, *1342–1419*, p. 74	

Churches dedicated to St James the Great

Place	Date of source	Category	County	Diocese	Source
Ulster					
Rathmullan (Rathmaylyn)	1496	Vicarage	Down	Down	*Cal. papal letters*, xvi, p. 437
Laragh	1837	Church	Cavan	Kilmore	OS letters, p. 122
Drumnakill	1300	Chapel	Antrim	Connor	Reeves, *Down & Connor*, pp 282–3
Leinster					
Gaulskill			Kilkenny	Ossory	Carrigan, *Ossory*, iv, pp 139–40
Kilmokevogue (Glenmore)	c.1500; 1837		Kilkenny	Ossory	Carrigan, *Ossory*, iv, pp 92–4; OS letters, p. 143
Killokighan	c.1500		Kilkenny	Ossory	Moran, *Spic. Oss*, i, p. 8
Mallardstown	c.1500		Kilkenny	Ossory	Moran, *Spic. Oss*, i, p. 9
Athboy	1406; 1434	Rectory	Meath	Meath	*Cal. papal letters*, vi, p. 111; viii, 503, 512
Athlumney	1837		Meath	Meath	OS letters, p. 141
Horetown		Parish church, on site of older Carmelite priory	Wexford	Ferns	Moore, *Archaeological inventory*, no. 1244
Dunbrody	1615		Wexford	Ferns	Hore, *Wexford*, ii, pp 247–60; vi, p. 269
Ballyhack	1591		Wexford	Ferns	*Hist. Ire.*, 24:3 (2016), 17, 18

Place	Date of source	Category	County	Diocese	Source
Horeswood		Modern	Wexford	Ferns	*Hist. Ire.*, 24:3 (2016), 18, 19
Newtown (Tyrrellspass)	1515	Rectory	Westmeath	Meath	*Cal. papal letters*, xx, p. 216; OS letters, pt 2, p. 12
Kilbeggan	1837	Modern	Westmeath	Meath	OS letters, pt 1, p. 318
Dublin	1190s	Parish church	Dublin city	Dublin	Gilbert, *Reg. St Thomas*, p. 284
Usk	1565	Parish church	Kildare	Kildare	*Ir. Fiants, Eliz.* 740
Ballyisonan	1502	Parish church	Kildare	Kildare	*Cal. papal letters*, xvii, pt 1, p. 565; *Cal. patent rolls, Henry 8*, p. 31
Rosenallis		Modern	Kildare	Kildare	Brandon, *To whom we dedicate*
Castledermot	1837	Parish church	Kildare	Glendalough	OS letters, pt 2, p. 96
Palmerstown	1540	Chapel (fair & well)	Dublin	Dublin	White, *Extents*, p. 57; *Ir. Fiants, Eliz.* 2449 (1574); *Ir. Fiants, Eliz.* 4012 (1582)
Drogheda	1542	Chapel in church	Louth	Dublin	*JLAS* 6 (1926), 92
Kilkenny town	Demolished 1360	Chapel	Kilkenny	Ossory	www.excava-tions.ie/ report/2001/ kilkenny/ 0006640
Kiljames	1837	Chapel in Kiljames townland, Thomastown	Kilkenny	Ossory	OS letters, pt 2, p. 340–1; Carrigan, *Ossory*, iv, p. 237
St Mullins		Small chapel	Carlow	Leighlin	*JRSAI*, 22 (1892), 384

Place	Date of source	Category	County	Diocese	Source
Munster					
Dangandonovan	1190s	Rectory	Cork	Cloyne	MacCotter, *Medieval Cloyne*, p. 169
Adare	1497	Trinitarian house	Limerick	Limerick	*Cal. papal letters*, xvii, pt 2, p. 65
Borrisoleigh (Two Mile Borris)	1514	Vicarage	Tipperary	Cashel	*Cal. papal letters*, xx, p. 174; xix, p. 205
Peppardstown	1516	Vicarage	Tipperary	Cashel	*Cal. papal letters*, xx, p. 466
Nantinan	Early 17th c.	Parish church	Limerick	Limerick	Lenihan, *Limerick*, p. 563
Stradbally, Co. Waterford	13th c.	Church	Waterford	Waterford	www.excavations.ie/report/2001/Waterford/0007182
Waterford	1482	Chantry chapel in cathedral	Waterford	Waterford	Byrne, *Waterford 1470*
Mallow	Modern	Parish church	Cork	Cloyne	Brandon, *To whom we dedicate*
Durrus	Modern	Parish church	Cork	Cork	Brandon, *To whom we dedicate*
Ringrone	Modern	Parish church	Cork	Cork	Brandon, *To whom we dedicate*
Cork city	16th c.	Chantry chapel in Christ Church	Cork	Cork	Caulfield, 'Original documents'
Ballyheigue	Modern	Parish church	Kerry	Ardfert & Aghadoe	Brandon, *To whom we dedicate*
Dingle	1837	Parish church	Kerry	Kerry	OS letters, p. 110
Killorglin	Modern	Parish church	Kerry	Kerry	www.excavations.ie/report/2004/Kerry/0011887
Limerick	Pre-Reformation	Side chapel in St Mary's cathedral	Limerick	Limerick	*JRSAI*, 28 (1898), 38

Place	Date of source	Category	County	Diocese	Source
Connacht					
Claregalway	1480	Vicarage	Galway	Galway	*Cal. papal letters*, xiii, p. 88, 700
Rahoon	1685	Chapel	Galway	Annaghdown	O'Flaherty, *Chorographical desc.* 1684
Newcastle	*c.*1510	Chapel	Galway	Galway	*JGAHS*, 42 (1989–90), 150–5
Ballybane	1200	Ruins of St James's chapel	Galway	Galway	Higgins, *St James's church & cemetery*, 1996
Galway	*c.*1510	Altar in St Nicholas's	Galway	Galway	Higgins & Herringklee, *Monuments*, 1992
Kilgefin	1837	Parish church	Roscommon	Elphin	OS letters, pt 1, p. 116

Note: Pagination of OS letters refers to original manuscript pagination in the volumes for the relevant county; these page numbers are cited in the margins of both the Flanagan and Herity editions of the letters.

Wells dedicated to St James the Great

	County	Locality	Source	Date of reference	Notes
Ulster					
None identified					
Leinster					
	Carlow	St Mullins	MacNeill, *Festival*, pp 263–4		
	Dublin	Kilgobbin	*Rep. Nov.* 2:1 (1957–8), 84		Uncertain
	Dublin	Palmerstown	*Rep. Nov.* 2:1 (1957–8), 75		Chapel and fair of St James
	Dublin	Cothlanstown			Well with pattern day 25 July
	Dublin	Dublin city	*Rep. Nov.* 2:1 (1957–8), 79–80	1757	
	Dublin	James's Street	*Holinshed's Irish chronicle*	1577	
	Dublin	Jamestown	*JRSAI*, 31 (1901), 252		
	Kildare	Coughlanstown west, Ballybought parish	*JKAS* 16 (1977–86), 154–5		
	Kildare	Corballis, Kineagh parish	*JKAS* 16 (1977–86), 152		
	Kildare	Abbeylands, Castledermot parish	*JKAS* 16 (1977–86), 150–1	1837	Parish dedicated to St James
	Kilkenny	Kilmokevogue	OS letters, pt 2, p. 177	1837	
	Kilkenny	Kilbeacon	OS letters, pt 2, p. 146	1837	Well dedicated to St Luke but pattern on St James's day
	Louth	Muchgrange, Cooley	*JLAHS* 24 (1997–2000), 342	1835	

County	Locality	Source	Date of reference	Notes
Meath	Athboy	French, *Meath holy wells*, p. 88		Parish dedicated to St James
Waterford		Logan, *Holy wells*, p. 42		Pattern 25 July
Wexford	Tomhaggard	OS letters, pt 2, p. 200		
Wexford	Kerloge, Wexford town	OS letters, pt 1, p. 375; *Jn. Wexford Hist. Soc.* 9 (1983–4)	1837	Pattern abolished, *c.*1820; also St Tulloge
Wicklow	Kerrikee, Glenmalure	O'Hanlon, *Lives of Irish saints*, 25 July		
Wicklow	Leitrim	*Archaeological inventory, Wicklow*		
Munster				
Cork	Balleenbrack	*Archaeological inventory, Cork*, pt i, p. 281		
Kerry	Corkaguiny	*JRSAI*, 90 (1960), 67		
Limerick	Ballinlough	*JRSAI* 85 (1955), 198		
Limerick	Tervoe	*JRSAI* 85 (1955), 198		
Limerick	Ardgoul north, par Nantinan	*JRSAI* 85 (1955), 198	1837	Fair on St James's day
Limerick	Ballymacave	*JRSAI* 85 (1955), 198		
Tipperary	Kilkip West	Historic Monuments Viewer, TN023-050		
Tipperary	Churchfield	Historic Monuments Viewer, TS059-015		
Tipperary	Peppardstown	Historic Monuments Viewer, TS062-089		Church dedication also
Connacht				
Galway	Newcastle	*JGHAS* 60 (2008), p. 149	1835	
Galway	Rahoon	*JGHAS* 60 (2008), p. 148	1685	
Sligo	Ummeraroe	OS letters, p. 245; Logan, *Holy wells*, p. 43	1837	
Roscommon	Kilgefin	OS letters, pt 1, p. 116; Logan, *Holy wells*, p. 43		

Note: Pagination of OS letters refers to original manuscript pagination in the volumes for the relevant county; these page numbers are cited in the margins of both the Flanagan and Herity editions of the letters.

APPENDIX 4

Fairs on St James's Day

Place	County	Date	Holder	Province	Source	Notes
Adare	Limerick	1226	Geofrey de Maricso	Munster	Gwynn & Hadcock, p. 217	
Ballynynthea	Limerick	1607	Fitzharris	Munster	*Fairs & Markets rep.*	
Castlecoole	Fermanagh	1620	Basset	Ulster	*Fairs & Markets rep.*	
Cloghmagheradunnagh	Antrim	1610	Antrim	Ulster	*Fairs & Markets rep.*	In Route
Connahie als Kinastallon	Cork	1613	Boyle	Munster	*Fairs & Markets rep.*	
Dublin	Dublin	pre–16th c.	City	Leinster	*Holinshed's Irish chronicle*	
Freshford	Kilkenny	1675	Mand	Leinster	*Fairs & Markets rep.*	
Graunamenagh	Tipperary	1632	Waller	Munster	*Fairs & Markets rep.*	
Galbally	Limerick	1620	Thomond	Munster	*Fairs & Markets rep.*	
Kilconnell	Galway	1616	Clanricard	Munster	*Fairs & Markets rep.*	St James on wall tomb in friary
Kisnebrosny	King's Co.	1619	Medhop	Leinster	*Fairs & Markets rep.*	
Legan	Fermanagh	1629	Balfour	Ulster	*Fairs & Markets rep.*	
Limerick	Limerick	1291	city	Munster	*Fairs & Markets rep.*	Confirmed 1551
Loughanstown	Dublin	1678	Domville	Leinster	*Fairs & Markets rep.*	
Middenaghmore	Cork	1611	Hurley	Munster	*Fairs & Markets rep.*	
Nantinan	Limerick	1707	Boyle	Munster	*Fairs & Markets rep.*	Holy well

Place	County	Date	Holder	Province	Source	Notes
Neal	Mayo	1612	Browne	Connacht	*Fairs & Markets rep.*	
Newtowngore	Mayo	1612	Gore	Connacht	*Fairs & Markets rep.*	
Palmerstown	Dublin	1603	Lombard	Leinster	*Fairs & Markets rep.*	St James chapel dedication
St Mullins	Carlow			Leinster	*Hist. Ire.*, 24:3 (2016)	Pattern day 25 July
Tracton	Cork	1609	Boyle	Munster	*Fairs & Markets rep.*	
Whitechurch	Waterford	1607	Fitzgerald	Munster	*Fairs & Markets rep.*	

Bibliography

MANUSCRIPTS

British Library, Additional 4813 (NLI microfilm P 17). Robert Ware's notes on Dublin churches [c.1680].

British Library, Sloane MS 1449. The church history of Ireland.

The National Archives (Kew). SC 8/148/7385. Petition of Thomas Woodstock and others [1388].

The National Archives (Kew). SP 63. State papers, Ireland.

National Library of Ireland. John Ainsworth, Reports on private collections, no. 46.

Royal Irish Academy, MS 23 E 25, *Leabhar na hUidhre*.

Royal Irish Academy, MS 23 P 16, *Leabhar Breac*.

Royal Irish Academy, MS 24 P 1, Devotional miscellany.

Royal Irish Academy, MS 24 P 25, *Leabhar Chlainne Suibhne*.

Royal Irish Academy, MS 3 B 22, Devotional miscellany.

Royal Irish Academy, MS 3 B 23, Devotional miscellany.

Royal Irish Academy, MS D ii 1, Book of Uí Mhaine.

Trinity College, Dublin, MS 667. Latin miscellany, late fifteenth century.

PRINTED PRIMARY SOURCES

Atkinson, Robert (ed.), *The passions and the homilies from Leabhar Breac: text, translation and glossary*, Todd Lecture Series, 2 (Dublin, 1887).

Bergin, Osborn, *Irish bardic poetry* (Dublin, 1970).

Bieler, Ludwig (ed.), *The Irish penitentials*, Scriptores Latini Hiberniae, v (Dublin, 1963).

Borde, Andrew, *The fyrst boke of the introduction of knowledge*, ed. F.J. Furnivall, EETS extra ser. (London, 1870).

Breatnach, P.A., 'Ar bhás Aodha an Éinigh Mhéig Uidhir, AD 1428', *Éigse*, 21 (1986), 37–52.

B[urton], R., *The history of the kingdom of Ireland* (London, 1693).

Butler, Richard (ed.), *Registrum Prioratus Omnium Sanctorum juxta Dublin*, Irish Archaeological Society (Dublin, 1845).

Byrne, N.J. (ed.), *The great parchment book of Waterford: Liber antiquissimus civitatis Waterfordiae* (Dublin, 2007).

Byrne, Niall (ed. & trans.), with Michael Byrne, *The register of St Saviour's chantry of Waterford: Registrum cantariae S. Salvatoris Waterfordensis. BL, Harleian MS 3765* (Dublin, 2013).

Calendar of the Carew manuscripts preserved in the archiepiscopal library at Lambeth (6 vols, London, 1867–73).

Calendar of documents relating to Ireland [1171–1307] (5 vols, London, 1875–86).

Calendar of entries in the papal registers relating to Great Britain and Ireland: papal letters (London, 1893–).

Calendar of the justiciary rolls, or proceedings in the court of the justiciar of Ireland, I–VII years of Edward II, ed. H. Wood, A.E. Langman & M. Griffith (Dublin, 1956).

Calendar of the patent rolls preserved in the Public Record Office (London, 1906–).

Calendar of state papers Ireland: Tudor period, 1571–1575, ed. Mary O'Dowd (London, 2000).

Calendar of the state papers relating to Ireland (24 vols, London, 1860–1911).

Caulfield, Richard (ed.), 'Original documents relating to the county and city of Cork', *Gentlemen's Magazine*, ser. 3, vol. 12 (June 1862).

Connolly, Philomena (ed.), *Statute rolls of the Irish parliament, Richard III–Henry VIII* (Dublin, 2002).

Cunningham, Bernadette (ed.), 'Clanricard letters: letters and papers, 1605–1673, preserved in the National Library of Ireland, manuscript 3111', *JGAHS*, 48 (1996), 162–208.

Dineley, Thomas, *Observations in a voyage through the kingdom of Ireland*, ed. J. Graves & E.P. Shirley (Dublin, 1870).

Erasmus, *Ten colloquies*, ed. & trans. C.R. Thompson (New York, 1986).

Esposito, Mario (ed.), *Itinerarium Symonis Semeonis ab Hybernia ad Terram Sanctam*, Scriptores Latini Hiberniae, iv (Dublin, 1960).

Fenning, Hugh, 'Irish material in the registers of the Dominican Masters General (1360–1649)', *Archivum Fratrum Praedicatorum*, 39 (1969), 249–366.

Forty-fifth annual report of the deputy keeper of the public records (London, 1885).

Freeman, A.M. (ed.), *Annála Connacht: the annals of Connacht, AD 1224–1544* (Dublin, 1944).

Gerson, Paula, Annie Shaver-Crandell & Alison Stones, with Jeanne Krochalis (eds), *The pilgrim's guide: a critical edition, ii: the text* (London, 1998).

Gilbert, J.T. (ed.), *Account of facsimiles of national manuscripts of Ireland* (London, 1884).

Gilbert, J.T. *Calendar of ancient records of Dublin*, i (Dublin, 1889).

Gilbert, J.T. (ed.), *Chartularies of St Mary's abbey, Dublin ... and annals of Ireland, 1162–1370* (2 vols, London, 1884–6).

Gilbert, J.T. (ed.), *Register of the abbey of St Thomas the Martyr* (London, 1889).

Grace, James, *Annales Hiberniae*, ed. Richard Butler (Dublin, 1842).

Greene, David (ed.), *Duanaire Mheig Uidhir* (Dublin, 1972).

Hammerich, L.L. (ed.), *Visiones Georgii: visions quas in purgatorio Sancti Patricii vidit Georgius Miles de Ungaria, AD mcccliii* (Copenhagen, 1930).

Hardiman, James, 'The pedigree of Doctor Dominick Lynch, regent of the Colledge of St Thomas of Aquin, in the City of Seville, AD 1674, from a coeval MS', *Miscellany of the Irish Archaeological Society*, i (1846), 44–90.

Heist, W.W. (ed.), *Vitae sanctorum Hiberniae ex codice olim Salmanticensi nunc Bruxellensi* (Brussels, 1965).

Hennessy, W.M. (ed.), *The Annals of Loch Cé: a chronicle of Irish affairs from AD 1014 to AD 1590* (2 vols, London, 1871).

Hennessy, W.M., & Bartholomew MacCarthy (eds), *Annála Uladh: Annals of Ulster from the earliest times to the year, 1541* (4 vols, Dublin, 1887–1901; reprint Dublin, 1998).

Herity, Michael (ed.), *Ordnance Survey letters: Meath* (Dublin, 2001).

Herity, Michael (ed.), *Ordnance Survey letters: Galway* (Dublin, 2009).

Herity, Michael (ed.), *Ordnance Survey letters: Roscommon* (Dublin, 2010).

Herity, Michael (ed.), *Ordnance Survey letters: Londonderry, Fermanagh, Armagh-Monaghan, Louth, Cavan-Leitrim* (Dublin, 2012).

Holinshed, Raphaell, *Holinshed's Irish chronicle: the historie of Irelande from the first inhabitation thereof, unto the yeare 1509, and continued till the yeare 1547 by Richard Stanyhurst*, ed. L. Miller & E. Power (Dublin, 1979).

Hyde, Douglas (ed.), *Gabhaltais Shearluis Mhóir: the conquests of Charlemagne, edited from the Book of Lismore and three other vellum MSS* (London, 1917).

Irish fiants of the Tudor sovereigns ... with a new introduction by Kenneth Nicholls (4 vols, Dublin, 1994; reprinted from *Reports of the deputy keeper of the public records in Ireland*, 1875–90).

Jacobus de Voragine, *The Golden Legend: readings on the saints*, trans. W.G. Ryan (2 vols, Princeton, NJ, 1993).

Jennings, Brendan (ed.), 'Brevis synopsis Provinciae Hiberniae FF. Minorum', *Analecta Hibernica*, 6 (1934), 139–91.

Jennings, Brendan (ed.), 'Brussels MS 3947: Donatus Moneyus, de Provincia Hiberniae S. Francisci', *Analecta Hibernica*, 6 (1934), 12–138.

Jennings, Brendan (ed.), 'Miscellaneous documents I, 1588–1634', *Archivium Hibernicum*, 12 (1946), 70–200.

Jennings, Brendan (ed.), *Wild Geese in Spanish Flanders: documents relating chiefly to Irish regiments* (Dublin, 1964).

Jones, David (ed.), *Friars' tales: thirteenth-century exempla from the British Isles* (Manchester, 2011).

Keating, Geoffrey, *Foras feasa ar Éirinn*, ed. D. Comyn & P.S. Dinneen (4 vols, London, 1902–14).

Kemp, B.R. (ed.), *Reading Abbey cartularies: British Library manuscripts: Egerton 3031, Harley 1708 and Cotton Vespasian E XXV, 1*, Camden 4th ser., 31 (London, 1986).

Lewis, B.K. (ed.), *Medieval Welsh poems to saints and shrines* (Dublin, 2015).

Lombard, Peter, *De regno Hiberniae*, ed. P.F. Moran (Dublin, 1868).

Lynch, John, *The portrait of a pious bishop, or the life and death of the most Rev. Francis Kirwan, bishop of Killala*, ed. C.P. Meehan (Dublin, 1884).

Lynch, John, *De praesulibus Hiberniae*, ed. J.F. O'Doherty (2 vols, Dublin, 1944).

Macalister, R.A.S. (ed.), *Lebor Gabála Érenn: the book of the taking of Ireland* (5 vols, Dublin, 1938–56).

Macalister, R.A.S. (ed.), *The Book of Mac Carthaigh Riabhach, otherwise the Book of Lismore*. Facsimile (Dublin, 1950).

McKenna, Lambert (ed. & trans.), *Aithdioghluim dána* (2 vols, London, 1935–40).

McKenna, Lambert (ed.), *Dioghluim dána* (Dublin, 1938).

Mc Manus, Damian, & Eoghan Ó Raghallaigh (eds), *A bardic miscellany: five hundred bardic poems from manuscripts in Irish and British libraries* (Dublin, 2010).

Mac Mathúna, Séamus, *Immram Brain: Bran's journey to the land of the women* (Tubingen, 1985).

McNeill, Charles (ed.), *Calendar of Archbishop Alen's register, c.1172–1534* (Dublin, 1950).

Meech, S.B., & H.E. Allen (eds), *The Book of Margery Kempe*, EETS original ser., 212 (London, 1940).

Moran, P.F. (ed.), *Spicilegium Ossoriense, being a collection of original letters and papers illustrative of the history of the Irish church*, 1st series (Dublin, 1874).

Morrissey, J.F. (ed.), *Statute rolls of the parliament of Ireland: twelfth and thirteenth to the twenty-first and twenty-second years of the reign of King Henry the Fourth* (Dublin, 1939).

Moseley, C.W.R.D. (trans.), *The travels of Sir John Mandeville* (London, 2005).

Mulchrone, Kathleen (ed.), *Bethu Phátraic: the tripartite Life of Patrick* (Dublin, 1939).

Murphy, Denis (ed.), *Annals of Clonmacnoise from the earliest period to AD 1408, translated into English by Conell Mageoghagan, AD 1627* (Dublin, 1896).

Murphy, Gerard, 'Two Irish poems written from the Mediterranean in the thirteenth century', *Éigse*, 7:2 (1953), 74–9.

Ní Urdail, Meidhbhín (ed.), 'A poem on the adventures abroad and death of Donnchadh son of Brian Bóraimhe', *ZCP*, 59 (2912), 169–99.

Ó Cuív, Brian, 'A pilgrim poem', *Éigse*, 13:2 (1970), 105–9.

Ó Cuív, Brian, 'A poem on the infancy of Christ', *Éigse*, 15:2 (1973), 93–102.

O'Donovan, John (ed.), 'The annals of Ireland from the year 1443 to 1468 translated from the Irish by Dudley Firbisse, or as he is more usually called, Duald Mac Firbis, for Sir James Ware in the year, 1666' in *Miscellany of the Irish Archaeological Society*, 1 (Dublin, 1846), pp 198–302.

O'Donovan, John (ed.), *Annála ríoghachta Éireann: Annals of the kingdom of Ireland, by the Four Masters, from the earliest period to the year, 1616* (2nd ed., 7 vols, Dublin, 1856).

O'Donovan, John (ed.), 'Letter of Florence Mac Carthy to the earl of Thomond, on the ancient history of Ireland', *Journal of the Kilkenny and South-East Ireland Archaeological Society*, new ser., 1:1 (1856), 203–29.

O'Ferrall, Richard, & Robert O'Connell, *Commentarius Rinuccinianus*, ed. S. Kavanagh (6 vols, Dublin, 1932–49).

O'Flaherty, Roderic, *A chorographical description of West or h-Iar Connaught*, ed. J. Hardiman (Dublin, 1846).

O'Flanagan, M. (ed.), *Letters containing information relative to the antiquities of the county of Kerry ... Ordnance Survey, 1841* [typescript] (Bray, 1935).

O'Grady, S.H., *Silva Gadelica (I–XXXI): a collection of tales in Irish*, [I] Irish text; [II] translation and notes (London, 1892).

Ó Maonaigh, Cainneach (ed.), *Smaointe beatha Chríost .i. innsint Ghaelge a chuir Tomás Gruamdha Ó Bruacháin (fl. c.1450) ar an* Meditationes vitae Christi (Dublin, 1944).

Ó Muraíle, Nollaig (ed.), *Leabhar mór na ngenealach: the great book of Irish genealogies, compiled (1645–66) by Dubhaltach Mac Fhirbhisigh* (5 vols, Dublin, 2003).

Ó Muraíle, Nollaig (ed.), *Turas na dtaoiseach nUltach as Éirinn: from Ráth Maoláin to Rome* (Rome, 2007).

Ó Riain, Pádraig (ed.), *Corpus genealogiarum sanctorum Hiberniae* (Dublin, 1985).

Ó Riain, Pádraig (ed.), *Four Irish martyrologies: Drummond, Turin, Cashel, York* (London, 2002).

Orrery, Roger Boyle, earl of, *Poems on most of the festivals of the church* (London, 1681).

Oskamp, H.P.A. (ed. & trans.), *The voyage of Máel Dúin: a study in early Irish voyage literature, followed by an edition of Immram Curaig Maele Dúin from the Yellow Book of Lecan* (Groningen, 1970).

O'Sullivan Beare, Philip, *Patricana decas* (1629).

Plummer, Charles (ed.), *Vitae sanctorum Hiberniae* (2 vols, Oxford, 1910).

Plummer, Charles (ed.), *Bethada náem nÉrenn: Lives of the Irish saints* (2 vols, Oxford, 1922).

Plummer, Charles (ed.), *Miscellanea hagiographica Hibernica* (Brussels, 1925).

Powell, Susan (ed.), *John Mirk's* Festial*: edited from British Library MS Cotton Claudius A.II.*, EETS original ser., 335 (2 vols, Oxford, 2011).

Refaussé, Raymond, with Colm Lennon (eds), *The registers of Christ Church cathedral, Dublin* (Dublin, 1998).

Report of the commissioners appointed to inquire into the state of the fairs and markets in Ireland, House of Commons, 1852–3 [1674], xli.

Rochford, Robert, *The Life of the glorious bishop St Patricke ... together with the Lives of the holy virgin S. Bridgit and of the glorious abbot Saint Columbe*, English Recusant Literature, 210 (St Omer, 1625; reprint London, 1974).

Shepherd, S.H.A. (ed.), *Turpines story: a Middle English translation of the Pseudo-Turpin Chronicle*, EETS original ser., 322 (Oxford, 2004).

Smith, Brendan (ed.), *The register of Nicholas Fleming, archbishop of Armagh, 1404–1416* (Dublin, 2003).

Smith, Peter J., *Three historical poems ascribed to Gilla Cóemáin: a critical edition of the work of an eleventh-century Irish scholar* (Münster, 2007).

Stafford, Thomas, *Pacata Hibernia, or a history of the wars in Ireland during the reign of Queen Elizabeth, taken from the original chronicles* (2 vols, Dublin, 1820).

Stanihurst, Richard, *De vita Sancti Patricii* (Antwerp, 1587).

Stokes, Whitley, 'The Gaelic abridgement of the Book of Ser Marco Polo', *ZCP*, 1 (1896–7), 245–73, 362–408, 603; 2 (1898), 222–3.

Stokes, Whitley, 'The Gaelic Maundeville', *ZCP*, 2 (1898), 1–63, 226–312, 603–4.

Stokes, Whitley (ed.), *Félire Óengusso, the martyrology of Oengus the Culdee* (London, 1905; reprint Dublin, 1984).

Stones, Alison, & Jeanne Krochalis, with Paula Gerson & Annie Shaver-Crandel (eds), *The pilgrim's guide to Santiago de Compostela: critical edition, i: the manuscripts* (London, 1998).

Sughi, Mario Alberto (ed.), *Registrum Octaviani alias Liber Niger: the register of Octavian de Palatio, archbishop of Armagh, 1478–1513* (2 vols, Dublin, 1999).

Tresham, E. (ed.), *Rotulorum patentium et clausorum cancellariae Hiberniae calendarium* (Dublin, 1828).

Walsh, Paul (ed.), *Beatha Aodha Ruaidh Uí Dhomhnaill: the life of Aodh Ruadh Ó Domhnaill transcribed from the book of Lughaidh Ó Cléirigh* (2 vols, London, 1948–57).

Ward, Hugh, *Sancti Rumoldi* (Louvain, 1662).

Warren, F.E. (ed.), *The Sarum missal in English* (2 vols, London, 1913).

White, N.B. (ed.), *Irish monastic and episcopal deeds, AD 1200–1600* (Dublin, 1936)

White, N.B. (ed.), *Extents of Irish monastic possessions, 1540–1541* (Dublin, 1943).

Wickham Legg, J. (ed.), *The Sarum missal, edited from three early manuscripts* (Oxford, 1916).

Williams, Bernadette (ed.), *Annals of Ireland by Friar John Clyn* (Dublin, 2007).

SECONDARY SOURCES

Almazán, Vicente (ed.), *Actas del II Congreso Internacional de Estudios Jacobeos* [Ferrol 1996]: *rutas Atlánticas de peregrinación a Santiago de Compostela* (2 parts, [Santiago de Compostela, 1999]).

Anon., 'An Irish archbishop's grave in Spain', *JRSAI*, 21 (1890), 85.

Barnes, R.E., & C. Branfoot (eds), *Pilgrimage: the sacred journey* (Oxford, 2006).

Barral Iglesias, Alejandro, & Ramón Yzquierdo Perrín, *Santiago cathedral: a guide to its art treasures* (3rd ed., Leon, 2009).

Bartlett, Robert, *Why can the dead do such great things? Saints and worshippers from the martyrs to the Reformation* (London, 2013).

Bell, A.R., & R.S. Dale, 'The medieval pilgrimage business', *Enterprise and Society*, 12:3 (2011), 601–27.

Bennett, Isabel, 'Some aspects of the connections between Dingle and Spain', *CSJ Bulletin*, 59 (May 1997), 34–40.

Bennett, Michael, 'Late medieval Ireland in a wider world' in B. Smith (ed.), *The Cambridge history of Ireland, i, 600–1550* (Cambridge, 2018), pp 329–52.

Bernard, Jacques, 'The maritime intercourse between Bordeaux and Ireland, *c.*1450–*c.*1520', *Irish Economic and Social History*, 7 (1980), 7–21.

Berry, H.F., 'Notes of a statement dated 1634, regarding St Thomas's Court and St Katherine's churchyard, Dublin', *JRSAI*, 37:4 (1907), 393–6.

Birch, D.J., *Pilgrimage to Rome in the Middle Ages: continuity and change* (Woodbridge, 1998).

Bissell, Tom, *Apostle: travels among the tombs of the twelve* (London, 2016).

Bourke, Cormac, 'The *Domnach Airgid* in 2006', *Clogher Record*, 19:1 (2006), 31–42.

Bradley, John, 'The topography and layout of medieval Drogheda', *JLAHS*, 19:2 (1978), 98–127, and folded maps.

Bradley, John (ed.), *Settlement and society in medieval Ireland: studies presented to F.X. Martin* (Kilkenny, 1988).

Brady, Karl, & Chris Corlett, 'Holy ships: ships on plaster at medieval ecclesiastical sites in Ireland', *Archaeology Ireland*, 18:2 (2004), 28–31.

Brandon, E.A., *To whom we dedicate* (Dundalk, 1954).

Branfoot, Crispin, 'Pilgrimage in South Asia: crossing boundaries of space and faith' in Barnes & Branfoot (eds), *Pilgrimage: the sacred journey*, pp 45–79.

Breatnach, P.A., 'The chief's poet', *Proc. RIA*, 83C (1983), 37–79.

Bredero, A.H., *Christendom and Christianity in the Middle Ages* (Grand Rapids, 1994).

Brierley, John, *A pilgrim's guide to the Camino de Santiago. St Jean – Roncesvalles – Santiago: a practical and mystical manual for the modern day pilgrim* (Forres, 2003; reprint 2017).

Brindley, Anna, & Annaba Kilfeather, *Archaeological inventory of County Carlow* (Dublin, 1993).

Burke, W.P., *History of Clonmel* (Clonmel, 1907, 3rd ed., 2010).

Butler, T.C., *Journey of an abbey, 1292–1972* (Dublin, [1973]).

Byrne, Michael, *Waterford 1470: Dean John Collyn and the chantry chapel of St Saviour* (Drogheda, 2013).

Campbell, Ian, 'Planning for pilgrims: St Andrews as the second Rome', *Innes Review*, 64:1 (2013), 1–22.

Campbell, Kieran, 'The archaeology of medieval Drogheda', *Archaeology Ireland*, 1:2 (1987), 52–6.

Carballeira Debasa, Ana Maria, 'The pilgrims' Way of St James and Islam: pilgrimage, politics and militias' in Pazos (ed.), *Pilgrims and politics*, pp 9–27.

Carey, John, '*Lebor Gabála* and the legendary history of Ireland' in Helen Fulton (ed.), *Medieval Celtic literature and society* (Dublin, 2005), pp 32–48.

Carney, James, 'Literature in Irish, 1169–1534' in Cosgrove (ed.), *NHI*, ii, pp 688–707.

Cartwright, Jane (ed.), *Celtic hagiography and saints' cults* (Cardiff, 2003).

Cartwright, Jane, 'The harlot and the hostess: a preliminary study of the Middle Welsh lives of Mary Magdalene and her sister Martha' in Cartwright (ed.), *Celtic hagiography*, pp 77–101.

Carus Wilson, E.M., 'The overseas trade of Bristol' in E. Power and M.M. Postan (eds), *Studies in English trade in the fifteenth century* (London, 1933), pp 183–246.

Carville, Geraldine, *The heritage of Holy Cross* (Belfast, 1973).

Castiñeiras, Manuel, 'Didacus Gelmirius, patron of the arts: Compostela's long journey: from the periphery to the center of Romanesque art' in Xunta de Galicia (ed.), *Compostela and Europe*.

Castiñeiras, Manuel, 'The reason for a traveling exhibition: Diego Gelmírez, genius and traveling spirit of Romanesque' in Xunta de Galicia (ed.), *Compostela and Europe*.

Charles-Edwards, T.M., 'The social background to Irish *peregrinatio*', *Celtica*, 11 (1976), 43–59.

Cherry, John, 'The depiction of St James Compostela on seals' in Sarah Blick (ed.), *Beyond pilgrim souvenirs and secular badges: essays in honour of Brian Spencer* (Oxford, 2007), pp 37–47.

Childs, Wendy, 'English ships and the pilgrim route to Santiago' in Almazán (ed.), *Actas del II Congreso Internacional de Estudios Jacobeos,* i, pp 79–91.

Childs, Wendy, 'The perils, or otherwise, of maritime pilgrimage to Santiago de Compostela in the fifteenth century' in Stopford (ed.), *Pilgrimage explored*, pp 123–43.

Childs, Wendy, & Timothy O'Neill, 'Overseas trade' in Cosgrove (ed.), *NHI*, ii, pp 492–524.

Clark, Mary, & Raymond Refaussé (eds), *Directory of historic Dublin guilds* (Dublin, 1993).

Clarke, Howard (ed.), *Dublin, part 1, to 1610*, Irish Historic Towns Atlas, 11 (Dublin, 2002).

Cleary, Gregory, 'Saint Francis and Ireland', *Studies: an Irish Quarterly Review*, 15:60 (1926), 542–56.

Clyne, Miriam, 'Excavation at St Mary's cathedral, Tuam, Co. Galway', *JGAHS*, 41 (1987–8), 90–103.

Clyne, Miriam, 'A medieval pilgrim: from Tuam to Santiago de Compostela', *Archaeology Ireland*, 4:3 (1990), 21–2.

Cogan, Anthony, *The diocese of Meath, ancient and modern* (3 vols, Dublin, 1862–70).

Connolly, Michael, 'Medieval Tralee uncovered', *Kerry Magazine*, 15 (2005), 18–22.

Cooke, Jim, 'The obelisks of greater Dublin', *Dublin Historical Record*, 56:2 (2003), 146–60.

Cosgrove, Art (ed.), *A new history of Ireland*, ii: *medieval Ireland, 1169–1534* (Oxford, 1987).

Cosgrove, Art, 'Anglo-Ireland and the Yorkist cause, 1447–60' in Cosgrove (ed.), *NHI*, ii, pp 557–68.

Cotter, F.J., *The Friars Minor in Ireland, from their arrival to 1400*, ed. R.A. McKelvie (New York, 1994).

Cox, Ian (ed.), *The scallop: studies of a shell and its influences on mankind* (London, 1957).

Craig, Leigh Ann, '"Stronger than men and braver than knights": women and the pilgrimages to Jerusalem and Rome in the later Middle Ages', *Journal of Medieval History*, 29:3 (2003), 153–75.

Cross, F.L., & E.A. Livingstone (eds), *The Oxford dictionary of the Christian church* (3rd ed., Oxford, 1997).

CSJ, *Pilgrims from the British Isles to Santiago de Compostela in the Middle Ages*, CSJ Conference proceedings (London, 1991; reprint, 2014).

Cullen, L.M., 'The port and the local economy' in Tom Dunne (ed.), *New Ross: Rosponte: Ros Mhic Treoin: an anthology celebrating 800 years* (Wexford, 2007), pp 243–51.

Cunningham, Bernadette, *The Annals of the Four Masters: Irish history, kingship and society in the early seventeenth century* (Dublin, 2010).

Cunningham, Bernadette, 'The view from Breoghán's tower' in S. Ryan (ed.), *Treasures of Irish Christianity, volume III, to the ends of the earth* (Dublin, 2015), pp 46–9.

Cunningham, Bernadette, & Raymond Gillespie, 'Holy Cross abbey and the Counter Reformation in Tipperary', *Tipperary Historical Journal*, [4] (1991), 171–80.

Cunningham, Bernadette, & Raymond Gillespie, 'The cult of St David in Ireland before 1700' in J.R. Guy & W.G. Neely (eds), *Contrasts and comparisons: studies in Irish and Welsh church history* (Llandysul, 1999), pp 27–42.

D'Alton, John, *The history of Drogheda, with its environs* (2 vols, Dublin, 1844).

Daly, Leo, & Ronan Casey, 'Extracts from the excavation reports [Mullingar]', *Westmeath Examiner*, 21 Oct. 2000, p. 9.

Davey, Francis, *William Wey: an English pilgrim to Compostella in 1456*, CSJ (London, 2000).

Davidson, L.K., 'Reformulations of the pilgrimages to Santiago de Compostela' in A.M. Pazos (ed.), *Redefining pilgrimage: new perspectives on historical and contemporary pilgrimage* (London, 2014), pp 159–81.

Davies, Horton & Marie-Hélène, *Holydays and holidays: the medieval pilgrimage to Compostela* (Lewisburg, 1982).

Dawn, Maggi, *The accidental pilgrim: new journeys on ancient pathways* (London, 2012).

de Barra, Mícheál, *An bóthar go Santiago* (Dublin, 2007).

de Cléir, Síle, *Popular Catholicism in 20th-century Ireland: locality, identity and culture* (London, 2017).

de Courcy Ireland, John, 'A survey of early maritime trade and ships' in M. McCaughan & J.C. Appleby (eds), *The Irish Sea: aspects of maritime history* (Belfast, 1989), pp 21–5.

Dennett, Laurie, *The origins of holy years and the Compostela*, CSJ Occasional Paper 7 (London, 2004).

Dickinson, J.C., *The shrine of Our Lady of Walsingham* (Cambridge, 1956).

Ditchburn, David, '"Saints at the door don't make miracles"? The contrasting fortunes of Scottish pilgrimage, c.1450–1550' in J. Goodare, & A.A. MacDonald (eds), *Sixteenth-century Scotland: essays in honour of Michael Lynch* (Leiden, 2008), pp 69–98.

Dominquez Garcia, Javier, 'St James and Santiago de Compostela' in L.J. Taylor et al. (eds), *Encyclopedia of medieval pilgrimage* (Leiden, 2010), pp 707–11.

Doran, Linda, 'Lords of the river valleys: economic and military lordship in the Carlow corridor, c.1200–1350: European model in an Irish context' in L. Doran & J. Lyttleton (eds), *Lordship in medieval Ireland* (Dublin, 2007), pp 99–129.

Dufficy, Maurice, 'The story of St James' church, James' Street, Dublin', *Dublin Historical Record*, 29:2 (1976), 66–9.

Duffy, Eamon, *The stripping of the altars: traditional religion in England, 1400–1580* (New Haven, 1992).

Duffy, Eamon, 'The dynamics of pilgrimage in late medieval England' in Morris & Roberts (eds), *Pilgrimage: the English experience*, pp 164–77.

Duffy, Paul, & Tadhg O'Keeffe, 'A stone shrine for a relic of St Thomas Becket in Dublin?' *Archaeology Ireland*, 31:4 (2017), 18–22.

Dunn, Maryjane, & L.K. Davidson, *Pilgrimage to Compostela in the Middle Ages: a book of essays* (New York, 1996).

Dunning, P.J., 'Irish representatives and Irish ecclesiastical affairs at the Fourth Lateran Council' in Watt, Morrall & Martin (eds), *Medieval studies presented to Aubrey Gwynn*, pp 114–32.

Edwards, G.R., 'Purgatory: birth or evolution', *Journal of Ecclesiastical History*, 36 (1985), 634–46.

Eliade, Mircea (ed.), *The encyclopedia of religion* (16 vols, New York, 1987).

Evans, J. Wyn, 'St David and St Davids: some observations on the cult, site and buildings' in Cartwright (ed.), *Celtic hagiography*, pp 10–25.

Feehan, John, *Cruachán Éile in Uíbh Fhaíli; Croghan, County Offaly, Ireland* ([Tullamore], 2011).

Ffrench, J.F.M., 'St Mullins, Co. Carlow', *JRSAI*, 22 (1892), 377–88.

FitzPatrick, Liz, 'Mairgréag an-Einigh Ó Cearbhaill: "the best of the women of the Gaedhil"', *JKAS*, 18 (1992–3), 20–38.

Fitzpatrick, Martin, 'Pilgrimage to Santiago de Compostela', *Archaeology Ireland*, 24:4 (2010), 14–17.

Flanagan, Marie Therese, *The transformation of the Irish church in the twelfth century* (Woodbridge, 2010).

Fletcher, A.J., 'Preaching in late-medieval Ireland: the English and the Latin tradition' in A.J. Fletcher & R. Gillespie (eds), *Irish preaching, 700–1700* (Dublin, 2001), pp 56–80.

Fletcher, R.A., *St James's catapult: the life and times of Diego Gelmírez* (Oxford, 1984).

Flower, Robin, *Catalogue of Irish manuscripts in the British Library*, II (London, 1926; reprint, Dublin, 1992).

Foley, Áine, *The abbey of St Thomas the Martyr, Dublin* (Dublin, 2017).

Follett, Westley, *Céli Dé in Ireland: monastic writing and identity in the early Middle Ages* (Woodbridge, 2006).

Follett, Westley, 'Religious texts in the Mac Aodhagáin library in Lower Ormond', *Peritia*, 25 (2014), 213–29.

Freeman, Charles, *Holy bones, holy dust: how relics shaped the history of medieval Europe* (New Haven, 2011).

French, Noel, *Meath holy wells* (Trim, 2012).

Freund, René, *The road to Santiago: walking the Way of St James* (London, 2016) [originally published as *On foot to the end of the world* (2006)].

Furlong, Nicholas, 'Life in Wexford port, 1600–1800' in K.Whelan (ed.), *Wexford history and society* (Dublin, 1987), 150–72.

Gabriele, Matthew, *An empire of memory: the legend of Charlemagne, the Franks and Jerusalem before the First Crusade* (Oxford, 2011).

Gaffney, W.J., *The early history of St Peter's church, Marlow, 1846–1912* ([Marlow], 1974).

García Hernan, Enrique, *Ireland and Spain in the reign of Philip II* (Dublin, 2009).

Garton, Tessa, 'The influence of pilgrimage on artistic traditions in medieval Ireland' in M. Cormack (ed.), *Saints and their cults in the Atlantic world* (Columbia, SC, 2007), pp 174–201.

Geissel, Hermann, *A road on the long ridge: in search of the ancient highway on the Esker Riada* (Newbridge, 2006).

Gibbons, Michael, & Myles Gibbons, 'Inishglora: "the western threshold between land and wave"' in J. Higgins (ed.), *Recent explorations and discoveries in Irish heritage* (Galway, 2017), pp 24–40.

Gibson, David, *Walking in my shadow: a pilgrim walk to Santiago* (Dublin, 2002).

Goitein, S.D., 'The unity of the Mediterranean world in the "middle" Middle Ages', *Studia Islamica*, 12 (1960), 29–42.

Goodman, Anthony, *Margery Kempe and her world* (London, 2002).

Gosling, Paul, *Archaeological inventory of County Galway, i, West Galway* (Dublin, 1993).

Gougaud, Louis, *Les chrétientés celtiques* (Paris, 1911).

Gougaud, Louis, *Gaelic pioneers of Christianity* (London, 1933).

Greve, Anja, 'Pilgrims and fashion: the functions of pilgrims's garments' in S. Blick & R. Tekippe (eds), *Art and architecture of late medieval pilgrimage in northern Europe and the British Isles: texts* (Leiden, 2005), pp 3–27.

Gwynn, Aubrey, 'Archbishop FitzRalph and George of Hungary', *Studies: an Irish Quarterly Review*, 24:96 (1935), 558–72.

Gwynn, Aubrey, *The medieval province of Armagh* (Dundalk, 1946).

Gwynn, Aubrey, 'Ireland and the Continent in the eleventh century', *IHS*, 8:31 (1953), 193–216.

Gwynn, Aubrey, *Cathal Óg Mac Maghnusa and the Annals of Ulster*, ed. N. Ó Muraíle (Enniskillen, 1998).

Gwynn, Aubrey, & D.F. Gleeson, *A history of the diocese of Killaloe* (Dublin, 1962).

Gwynn, Aubrey, & R.N. Hadcock, *Medieval religious houses: Ireland* (Dublin, 1970).

Harbison, Peter, *Pilgrimage in Ireland: the monuments and the people* (London, 1991).

Harbison, Peter, 'An ancient pilgrimage "relic-road" in north Clare', *The Other Clare*, 24 (2000), 55–9.

Hardiman, James, *The history of the town and county of the town of Galway from the earliest period to the present time* (Dublin, 1820).

Haren, M.J., 'The religious outlook of a Gaelic lord: a new light on Thomas Óg Maguire', *IHS*, 25:98 (1986), 195–7.

Haren, M.J., & Yolande de Pontfarcy (eds), *The medieval pilgrimage to St Patrick's Purgatory, Lough Derg and the European tradition* (Clogher, 1988).

Hartwell Jones, G., 'Celtic Britain and the pilgrim movement', *Y Cymmrodor*, 23 (1912).

Hayden, A.R., *Trim Castle, Co. Meath: excavations 1995–8* (Dublin, 2011).

Hayes, Richard, 'Ireland's links with Compostella', *Studies: an Irish Quarterly Review*, 37:147 (Sep. 1948), 326–32.

Henderson, Phinella, *Pre-Reformation pilgrims from Scotland to Santiago de Compostela*, CSJ Occasional Paper 4 (London, 1997).

Hennig, John, 'Studies in the Latin texts of the *Martyrology of Tallaght*, of *Félire Oengusso* and of *Félire húi Gormáin*', *Proc. RIA*, 69C4 (1970), 45–112.

Herbert, Máire, *Iona, Kells and Derry: the history and hagiography of the monastic familia of Columba* (Oxford, 1988).

Higgins, Jim, *The stone carving collection, Convent of Mercy, Francis St., Galway* (Galway, 1989).

Higgins, Jim, *St James' church and cemetery, Gleninagh Heights, Galway* (Galway, c.1996).

Higgins, Jim, *The stone carving collection at National University of Ireland Galway: a corpus of late-medieval and post-medieval sculpture from Galway city*. Galway's Heritage in Stone, Catalogue 3 (Galway, 2011).

Higgins, Jim, & Aisling Parsons, *St Mary's cathedral (Church of Ireland) Tuam: an architectural, archaeological and historical guide* (Tuam, 1995).

Higgins, Jim, & Susan Heringklee (eds), *Monuments of St Nicholas's collegiate church, Galway: a historical, genealogical and archaeological record* (Galway, 1992).

Hill, Peter, *Whithorn & St Ninian: the excavation of a monastic town, 1984–91* (Stroud, 1997).

Hogan, Edmund, *Distinguished Irishmen of the sixteenth century* (London, 1894).

Hogg, A.V., 'The collegiate church of St Mary, Gowran, County Kilkenny, and its monuments', *JRSAI*, 40:4 (1910), 340–5.

Hore, P.H. (ed.), *History of the town and county of Wexford* (6 vols, London, 1900–11).

Howard, D.R., *Writers and pilgrims: medieval pilgrimage narratives and their posterity* (Berkeley, 1980).

Hughes, Kathleen, 'The changing theory and practice of Irish pilgrimage', *Journal of Ecclesiastical History*, 11 (1960), 143–51.

Hunt, John, *Irish medieval figure sculpture, 1200–1600: a study of Irish tombs* (2 vols, Dublin & London, 1974).

Hunt Museum, *The Hunt Museum essential guide* (London, 2002).

Hurlock, Kathryn, *Wales and the Crusades, c.1095–1291* (Cardiff, 2011).

Hurlock, Kathryn, *Britain, Ireland and the Crusades, c.1000–1300* (London, 2013).

Hurtley, Jacqueline, *Walter Starkie, 1894–1976: an odyssey* (Dublin, 2013).

Huws, Daniel, *Medieval Welsh manuscripts* (Aberystwyth, 2000).

Jackson, Patricia, 'The holy wells of Co. Kildare', *JKAS*, 16 (1977–86), 133–61.

James, M.K., *Studies in the medieval wine trade* (Oxford, 1971).

Kelly, Fergus, *A guide to early Irish law* (Dublin, 1988).

Kelly, Maria, *A history of the Black Death in Ireland* (London, 2001).

Kemp, Brian, 'The miracles of the hand of St James', *Berkshire Archaeological Journal*, 65 (1970), 1–19.

Kemp, Brian, 'The hand of St James at Reading Abbey', *Reading Medieval Studies*, 16 (1990), 3–22.

Kendrick, T.D., *St James in Spain* (London, 1960).

Kenny, Gillian, *Anglo-Irish and Gaelic women in Ireland, c.1170–1540* (Dublin, 2007).

Kerney Walsh, Micheline, 'Aodh Rua O'Donnell and his mission to Spain, January–September 1602', *Donegal Annual*, 41 (1989), 96–122.

Kerney Walsh, Micheline, 'O'Sullivan Beare in Spain: some unpublished documents', *Archivium Hibernicum*, 45 (1990), 46–63.

Kerns, Vincent, 'The traditional doctrine of Purgatory', *Irish Ecclesiastical Record*, 80 (1953), 326–42.

Kevin, Tony, *Walking the Camino: a modern pilgrimage to Santiago* (Victoria, 2007).

King, Heather, 'Late medieval crosses in County Meath, c.1470–1635', *Proc. RIA*, 84C2 (1984), 79–115.

Koldeweij, A.M., 'Lifting the veil on pilgrim badges' in Stopford (ed.), *Pilgrimage explored*, pp 11–88.

Krasnodebska-D'Aughton, Malgorzata, 'Relics and riches: familiarizing the unknown in a fourteenth-century pilgrimage account from Ireland' in M. Boulton & J. Hawkes, with M. Herman (eds), *The art, literature and material culture of the medieval world* (Dublin, 2015), pp 111–24.

Kurth, Willi (ed.), *The complete woodcuts of Albrecht Dürer* (New York, 1927; reprint 1963).

Lanigan Wood, Helen, 'Ecclesiastical sites in County Fermanagh from the early Christian period until the end of the medieval period' in C. Foley & R. McHugh, *An archaeological survey of County Fermanagh, vol. 1, pt 2: the early Christian and medieval periods* (Newtownards, 2014), pp 637–65.

Leask, H.J., 'The collegiate church of St Nicholas, Galway: a study of the structure', *JGAHS*, 17 (1936–7), 1–23.

Lenihan, Maurice, *Limerick, its history and antiquities* (Dublin, 1866).

Leslie, Shane, *Saint Patrick's Purgatory: a record from history and literature* (London, 1932).

Logan, Patrick, *The holy wells of Ireland* (Gerrards Cross, 1980).

Lomax, D.W., 'The first English pilgrims to Santiago de Compostela' in H. Mayr-Harting & R.I. Moore (eds), *Studies in medieval history presented to R.H.C. Davis* (London, 1985), 165–75.

Lubin, Helen, *The Worcester pilgrim* (Worcester, 1990).

Mac Brádaigh, Frainc, *Cá bhfuil Walsingham? 'The fumbles of our funny God'* (Dublin, 2010).

Mac Brádaigh, Frainc, *Conair na Fraince go Santiago: Le Puy-en-Velay go Pamplona na Spáinne* (Dublin, 2014).

McBride, P., 'A modern Spanish crusade', *Irish Monthly*, 63:739 (Jan. 1935), 18–19.

McBride, P., 'The Spanish crisis', *Studies: an Irish Quarterly Review*, 24:93 (Mar. 1935), 43–59.

McBride, P., 'Compostela ... and some Irish memories', *Irish Monthly*, 63:744 (June 1935), 381–5.

MacCotter, Paul, *A history of the medieval diocese of Cloyne* (Dublin, 2013).

Mac Craith, Mícheál, 'Tadhg Ó Cianáin agus Loreto', *Bliainiris*, 11 (2016), 78–128.

MacCulloch, Diarmaid, *Reformation: Europe's house divided, 1490–1700* (London, 2003).

MacCulloch, Diarmaid, *A history of Christianity* (London, 2009).

McEneaney, Eamonn, *A history of Waterford and its mayors: from the 12th century to the 20th century* (Waterford, 1995).

McEneaney, Eamonn, 'Politics and the art of devotion in late fifteenth-century Waterford' in Moss, Ó Clabaigh & Ryan (eds), *Art and devotion*, pp 33–50.

McEneaney, Eamonn, with Rosemary Ryan (eds), *Waterford treasures: a guide to the historical and archaeological treasures of Waterford city* (Waterford, 2004).

McGuire, James, & James Quinn (eds), *Dictionary of Irish biography* (9 vols, Cambridge, 2009).

McKenzie, C.J., E.M. Murphy & C.J. Donnelly (eds), *The science of a lost medieval Gaelic grave-yard: the Ballyhanna research project*, TII Heritage, 2 (Dublin, 2015).

McLellan, Damien, 'Reclaiming an Irish "Way of St James"', *History Ireland*, 24:3 (2016), 16–19.

McMahon, Mary, *St Audoen's church, Cornmarket, Dublin: archaeology and architecture* (Dublin, 2006).

McManus, Brendan, *Redemption road: grieving on the Camino* (Blackrock, Co. Dublin, 2014).

McNamara, Martin, *The Apocrypha in the Irish church* (Dublin, 1975).

MacNeill, Máire, *The festival of Lughnasa* (Oxford, 1962).

Mac Niocaill, Gearóid, *Na Buirgéisí, xii–xv aois* (2 vols, Baile Átha Cliath, 1964).

Mac Niocaill, Gearóid, 'Dhá leagan de scéal Phíoláit', *Celtica*, 7 (1966), 207–13.

Maher, Michael, '*Peregrinatio pro Christo*: pilgrimage in the Irish tradition', *Milltown Studies*, 43 (1999), 5–39.

Martin, F.X., 'The Irish Augustinian reform movement in the fifteenth century' in Watt, Morrall & Martin (eds), *Medieval studies presented to Aubrey Gwynn*, pp 230–64.

Martyn, Adrian, *The tribes of Galway, 1124–1642* ([Galway], 2016).

Matthews, John & Caitlín, *The encyclopaedia of Celtic myth and legend* (London, 2002).

Meenan, Rosanne, 'A survey of late medieval and early post-medieval Iberian pottery from Ireland' in D. Gaimster & M. Redknap (eds), *Everyday and exotic pottery from Europe, c.650–1900* (Oxford, 1992), pp 186–93.

Menard, R.R., 'Transport costs and long-range trade, 1300–1800: was there a European "transport revolution" in the early modern era?' in J.D. Tracy (ed.), *The political economy of merchant empires* (Cambridge, 1997), pp 228–75.

Meri, J.W., 'The etiquette of devotion in the Islamic cult of saints' in J. Howard-Johnston & P.A. Hayward (eds), *The cult of saints in late antiquity and the early Middle Ages* (Oxford, 1999), pp 263–86.

Mhic Mhurchú, Dóirín, *Bealach na bó finne* (Dublin, 1994).

Moloney, Colm, Louise Baker, Jonathan Millar & Damian Shiels, *Guide to the excavations at Ardreigh, County Kildare* (Dublin, 2016).

Moody, T.W., F.X. Martin & F.J. Byrne (eds), *A new history of Ireland*, ix: *maps, genealogies, lists* (Oxford, 1984).

Moore, A.W., *A history of the Isle of Man* (2 vols, London, 1900).

Moore, Fionnbarr, *Ardfert cathedral: summary of excavation results* (Dublin, 2007).

Moore, Michael J., *Archaeological inventory of County Wexford* (Dublin, 1996).

Morgan, Hiram, *Ireland 1518: Archduke Ferdinand's visit to Kinsale and the Dürer connection* (Cork, 2015).

Morgan, Nigel, 'The calendar and litany of Reading Abbey', *Reading Medieval Studies*, 42 (2016), 89–102.

Morris, Colin, 'Pilgrimage to Jerusalem in the late Middle Ages' in Morris & Roberts (eds), *Pilgrimage: the English experience*, pp 141–63.

Morris, Colin, & Peter Roberts (eds), *Pilgrimage: the English experience from Beckett to Bunyan* (Cambridge, 2002).

Morrison, S.S., *Women pilgrims in late medieval England: private piety as public performance* (London, 2000).

Moss, Rachel, 'Permanent expressions of piety: the secular and the sacred in late medieval stone sculpture' in Moss, Ó Clabaigh & Ryan (eds), *Art and devotion*, pp 72–97.

Moss, Rachel, Colmán Ó Clabaigh & Salvador Ryan (eds), *Art and devotion in late medieval Ireland* (Dublin, 2006).

Mueller-Lisowski, Käte, 'La légende de St Jean dans la tradition irlandaise et le druide Mog Ruith', *Études Celtiques*, 3 (1938), 46–70.

Murphy, Donald, 'Archaeological excavations at the Magdalene Tower, Drogheda, County Louth', *JLAHS*, 24:1 (1997), 75–128.

Murray, Griffin, *The Cross of Cong: a masterpiece of medieval Irish art* (Sallins, 2014).

Murtagh, Natasha & Peter, *Buen Camino! A father-daughter journey from Croagh Patrick to Santiago de Compostela* (Dublin, 2011).

Ní Mharcaigh, Máirín, 'The medieval parish churches of south-west County Dublin', *Proc. RIA*, 97C (1997), 245–96.

Niles, J.D., 'The ideal depiction of Charlemagne in "Le Chanson de Roland"', *Viator*, 7 (1976), 123–39.

Nilson, Ben, 'The medieval experience at the shrine' in Stopford (ed.), *Pilgrimage explored*, pp 95–122.

Nolan, J.P., 'Galway castles and their owners in 1574', *JGAHS*, 1 (1901), 109–23.

Nugent, Louise, 'Pilgrimage in medieval Ireland, AD 600–1600', 3 vols (PhD, University College, Dublin, 2009).

Nugent, Louise, 'Medieval pilgrim's tokens and other souvenirs in Ireland: a review of the archaeological and historical evidence' in J. Higgins, A. Conneely & M. Gibbons (eds), *Irish maritime heritage: proceedings of the 3rd Galway International Heritage Conference, 2013* (Galway, 2013).

O'Brien, A.F., 'The development and evolution of the medieval borough and port of Dungarvan, Co. Waterford, c.1200 to c.1530', *JCHAS*, 92 (1987), 85–94.

O'Brien, A.F., 'Commercial relations between Aquitaine and Ireland, c.1000 to c.1500' in Jean-Michel Picard (ed.), *Aquitaine and Ireland in the Middle Ages* (Dublin, 1995), pp 31–80.

O'Brien, Caimin, *Stories from a sacred landscape: Croghan Hill to Clonmacnoise* (Tullamore, 2006).

O'Brien, Niall, 'Wexford apprentices in sixteenth-century Bristol', *Journal of the Wexford Historical Society*, 23 (2011–12), 169–76.

Ó Clabaigh, Colmán, *The Franciscans in Ireland, 1400–1534* (Dublin, 2002).

Ó Clabaigh, Colmán, 'The mendicant friars in the medieval Diocese of Clonfert', *JGAHS*, 59 (2007), 25–36.

Ó Clabaigh, Colmán, 'Anchorites in late medieval Ireland' in Liz Herbert McAvoy, *Anchoritic traditions of medieval Europe* (Woodbridge, 2010), pp 153–77.

Ó Clabaigh, Colmán, *The friars in Ireland, 1224–1540* (Dublin, 2012).

Ó Clabaigh, Colmán, & Michael Staunton, 'Thomas Becket and Ireland' in E. Mullins & D. Scully (eds), *Listen, O Isles, unto me: studies in medieval word and image in honour of Jennifer O'Reilly* (Cork, 2011), pp 87–101.

Ó Cléirigh, Cormac, 'The O'Conor Faly lordship of Offaly, 1395–1513', *Proc. RIA*, 96C (1996), 87–102.

O Connell, Patricia, 'The early modern Irish college network in Iberia, 1590–1800' in O'Connor (ed.), *The Irish in Europe, 1580–1815*, pp 49–64.

O Connell, Patricia, *The Irish College at Santiago de Compostela, 1605–1769* (Dublin, 2007).

O'Connor, John, *The Galway Augustinians* (Dublin, 1979).

O'Connor, Thomas (ed.), *The Irish in Europe, 1580–1815* (Dublin, 2001).

O'Connor, Thomas, *Irish voices from the Spanish Inquisition: migrants, converts and brokers in early modern Iberia* (Basingstoke, 2016).

Ó Corráin, Donnchadh (ed.), *Clavis litterarum Hibernensium: medieval Irish books and texts (c.400–c.1600)* (3 vols, Turnhout, 2017).

Ó Cuív, Brian, *Catalogue of Irish manuscripts in the Bodleian Library at Oxford* (2 vols, Dublin, 2001).

Ó Danachair, Caoimhín, 'The holy wells of Co. Limerick', *JRSAI*, 85 (1955), 193–217.

O'Dowd, Peadar, 'Holy wells of Galway city', *JGAHS*, 60 (2008), 136–53.

Ó Dufaigh, Seosamh, 'The Mac Cathmhaoils of Clogher', *Clogher Record*, 2:1 (1957), 25–49.

Ó Fiaich, Tomás, *Gaelscrínte san Eoraip* (Baile Átha Cliath, 1986).

Ó Fiannachta, Pádraig, 'Oilithireacht ón Daingean go Santiago de Compostella', *Irisleabhar Mha Nuad*, 2007, 167–90.

Ó Floinn, Raghnall, *Irish shrines and reliquaries of the Middle Ages* (Dublin, 1994).

Ó Floinn, Raghnall, 'The late-medieval relics of Holy Trinity church, Dublin' in J. Bradley, A.J. Fletcher & A. Simms (eds), *Dublin in the medieval world: studies in honour of Howard B. Clarke* (Dublin, 2009), pp 369–89.

O'Hanlon, John, *Lives of the Irish saints*, vii (Dublin, 1873).

O'Keeffe, John, 'Early pilgrims to Santiago from Ireland', *CSJ Bulletin*, 57 (1996), 28–9.

O'Laverty, James, *An historical account of the diocese of Down and Connor* (5 vols, Dublin, 1878–95).

O'Loughlin, Thomas, *Journeys on the edges: the Celtic tradition* (London, 2000).

Ó Mainnín, M.B., 'Dán molta ar Eoin Mac Domhnaill, "Tiarna na nOileán" (+1503)' in M. Mac Craith & P. Ó Héalaí (eds), *Diasa díograise: aistí i gcuimhne ar Mháirtín Ó Briain* (Indreabhán, 2009), 413–35.

O'Meara, J.J., 'In the wake of the saint: the Brendan Voyage, an epic crossing of the Atlantic by leather boat' in Wooding (ed.), *The Otherworld voyage*, pp 109–12.

Ó Muirthile, Liam, *Oilithreach pinn* (Dublin, 2017).

O'Neill, Timothy, *Merchants and mariners in medieval Ireland* (Dublin, 1987).

O'Neill, Timothy, 'A fifteenth-century entrepreneur: Germyn Lynch, fl. 1441–1483' in J. Bradley (ed.), *Settlement and society*, pp 412–18.

O'Neill, Timothy, 'Trade and shipping on the Irish Sea in the later Middle Ages' in M. McCaughan & J.C. Appleby (eds), *The Irish Sea: aspects of maritime history* (Belfast, 1989), pp 27–32.

O'Reilly, P.J., 'The Christian sepulchral *leacs* and freestanding crosses of the Dublin half barony of Rathdown', *JRSAI*, 31:2 (1901), 134–61.

Ó Riain, Pádraig, *A dictionary of Irish saints* (Dublin, 2011).

Ó Riain-Raedel, Dagmar, 'The Irish medieval pilgrimage to Santiago de Compostela', *History Ireland*, 6:3 (1998), 17–21.

O'Scea, Ciaran, 'The devotional world of the Irish Catholic exile in early modern Galicia, 1598–1666' in O'Connor (ed.), *The Irish in Europe, 1580–1815*, pp 27–48.

O'Scea, Ciaran, 'Irish emigration to Castille in the opening years of the seventeenth century' in Patrick J. Duffy (ed.), *To and from Ireland: planned migration schemes, c.1600–2000* (Dublin, 2004), pp 17–37.

O'Scea, Ciaran, *Surviving Kinsale: Irish emigration and identity formation in early modern Spain, 1601–40* (Manchester, 2015).

O'Sullivan, Aidan, & Colin Breen, *Maritime Ireland* (Stroud, 2007).

O'Sullivan, M.D., *Old Galway: the history of a Norman colony in Ireland* (Cambridge, 1942).

Ohler, Norbert, *The medieval traveller* (Woodbridge, 2010).

Olson, Katharine K., '"Ar ffordd Pedr a Phawl": Welsh pilgrimage and travel to Rome, c.1200–c.1530', *Welsh History Review*, 24:2 (2008), 1–39.

Pack, Sasha, 'Revival of the pilgrimage to Santiago de Compostela: the politics of religious, national and European patrimony, 1879–1988', *Journal of Modern History*, 82:2 (2010), 335–67.

Pazos, Antón M. (ed.), *Pilgrims and politics: rediscovering the power of the pilgrimage* (Farnham, 2012).

Pazos, Antón M., 'Old and new pilgrimages in the context of the Spanish civil war' in Pazos (ed.), *Pilgrims and politics*, pp 151–60.

Prescott, H.F.M., *Jerusalem journey: pilgrimage to the Holy Land in the fifteenth century* (London, 1954).

Prunty, Jacinta, & Paul Walsh, *Galway/Gaillimh*, Irish Historic Towns Atlas, 28 (Dublin, 2017).

Quinn, Billy, L.G. Lynch & Declan Moore, 'Excavations at Terryland, Galway', *JGAHS*, 66 (2014), 46–5.

Rabe, Cordula, *Camino de Santiago: Way of St James from the Pyrenees to Santiago* (Munich, 2007).

Rae, E.C., 'The Rice monument in Waterford cathedral', *Proc. RIA*, 69C (1970), 1–14.

Rafferty, John, *Pilgrim guide to the Celtic Camino and the city of Santiago de Compostela* (Dublin, 2018).

Recio Morales, Óscar, *Ireland and the Spanish empire, 1600–1825* (Dublin, 2010).

Rees, Mona, & Terry John, *Pilgrimage: a Welsh perspective* (Llandysul, 2002).

Reeves, William, *Ecclesiastical antiquities of Down, Connor, and Dromore* (Dublin, 1847).

Rekdal, Jan Erik, 'The Irish ideal of pilgrimage as reflected in the tradition of Colum Cille (Columba)' in Ailbhe Ó Corráin (ed.), *Proceedings of the third symposium of Societas Celtologica Nordica held in Oslo, 1–2 November 1991* (Uppsala, 1994), pp 67–83.

Rey Castelao, Ofelia, 'Inmigrantes Irlandeses en la Galicia del periodo moderno' in Begoña Villar García (ed.), *La emigración Irlandesa en el siglo xviii* (Málaga, 2000), pp 183–206.

Ritari, Katya, *Pilgrimage to Heaven: eschatology and monastic spirituality in early medieval Ireland* (Turnhout, 2016).

Ritari, Katja, '"Whence is the origin of the Gaels?" Remembering the past in Irish pseudohistorical poems', *Peritia*, 28 (2017), 155–76.

Rock, Daniel, *The church of our fathers as seen in St Osmund's rite for the cathedral at Salisbury* (London, 1903).

Roe, H.M., *Medieval fonts of Meath* ([Meath], 1968).

Ronan, Myles, 'Union of the dioceses of Glendaloch and Dublin in 1216', *JRSAI*, 60:1 (1930), 56–72.

Roudier, Jean, *Saint Jacques en Bretagne: culte et patrimoine* (Ploudalmézeau, 2005).

Rowlands, Eurys, 'The continuing tradition' in A.O.H. Jarman & G. Rees Hughes (eds), *A guide to Welsh literature, 1282–c.1550* (Cardiff, 1997).

Ryan, Salvador, 'Reign of blood: devotion to the wounds of Christ in late medieval Ireland' in J. Augusteijn & M.A. Lyons (eds), *Irish history: a research yearbook* (Dublin, 2002), pp 137–49.

Ryan, Salvador, 'Fixing the eschatological scales: judgement of the soul in late medieval and early modern Irish tradition' in P. Clarke & T. Clayton (eds), *The church, the afterlife and the fate of the soul*, Studies in Church History, 45 (Woodbridge, 2009), pp 184–95.

Ryan, Salvador, '"Reaping a rich harvest of humanity": images of redemption in Irish bardic religious poetry' in B. Leahy & S. O'Connell (eds), *Having life in His name* (Dublin, 2011), pp 239–51.

Ryan, Salvador, & Anthony Shanahan, 'How to communicate Lateran IV in 13th-century Ireland: lessons from the *Liber Exemplorum* (*c.*1275)', *Religions*, 9:75 (2018), 1–14 (www. mdpi.com/2077-1444/9/3/75).

Sadlier, T.U., 'Metal cross from Killeigh', *JKAS*, 9 (1918–21), 85–6.

Scott, A.B., 'Latin learning and literature in Ireland, 1169–1500' in D. Ó Cróinín (ed.), *NHI*, i: *prehistoric and early Ireland* (Oxford, 2005), pp 934–95.

Shee-Twohig, Elizabeth, 'Context and chronology of the carved stone at Clonfinlough, County Offaly', *JRSAI*, 132 (2002), 99–113.

Shepherd, S.H.A., 'The Middle English Pseudo-Turpin Chronicle', *Medium Aevum*, 65:1 (1996), 19–34.

Simms, Katharine, 'The medieval kingdom of Lough Erne', *Clogher Record*, 9:2 (1977), 126–41.

Simms, Katharine, 'Medieval Fermanagh' in E.M. Murphy & W.J. Roulston (eds), *Fermanagh history and society* (Dublin, 2004), pp 77–103.

Sims-Williams, Patrick, *Irish influence on medieval Welsh literature* (Oxford, 2011).

Smith, Brendan, *Crisis and survival in late medieval Ireland* (Oxford, 2003).

Smith, Brendan, 'Late medieval Ireland and the English connection: Waterford and Bristol, *ca.* 1360–1460', *Journal of British Studies*, 50:3 (2011), 546–65.

Smith, Charles, *The ancient and present state of the county of Kerry* (Dublin, 1756; reprint Cork, 1979).

Smith, Colin, 'The geography and history of Iberia in the *Liber Sancti Jacobi*' in M. Dunn & L.K. Davidson (eds), *The pilgrimage to Compostela in the Middle Ages: a book of essays* (New York, 1996), pp 23–41.

Spears, Arthur, *The cult of Saint Catherine of Alexandria in Ireland* (Rathmullan, 2006).

Stalley, Roger, 'Sailing to Santiago: medieval pilgrimage to Santiago de Compostela and its artistic influence in Ireland' in Bradley (ed.), *Settlement and society*, pp 397–430.

Stalley, Roger, 'Maritime pilgrimage from Ireland and its artistic repercussions' in Almazán (ed.), *Actas del II Congreso Internacional de Estudios Jacobeos*, i, pp 255–75.

Stalley, Roger, 'The end of the Middle Ages: Gothic survival in sixteenth-century Connacht', *JRSAI*, 133 (2003), 5–23.

Stalley, Roger, 'Reconstructions of the Gothic past: the lost cathedral of Waterford', *Irish Architectural and Decorative Studies*, 16 (2013), 94–131.

Starkie, Walter, *Spanish raggle-taggle: adventures with a fiddle in north Spain* (London, 1934).

Starkie, Walter, *The road to Santiago: pilgrims of St James* (London, 1957).

Stokes, Margaret, *Three months in the forests of France* (London, 1895).

Stones, Alison, '*Codex Calixtinus*' in Xunta de Galicia (ed.), *Compostela and Europe.*

Stones, Alison, 'Medieval pilgrimage writing and its manuscript sources' in L.J. Taylor, et al. (eds), *Encyclopedia of medieval pilgrimage* (Leiden, 2010).

Stopford, J. (ed.), *Pilgrimage explored* (York, 1999).

Storrs, C.M., *Jacobean pilgrims from England to St James of Compostela from the early twelfth to the late fifteenth century* (Santiago de Compostela, 1994).

Stradling, R.A., *The Spanish monarchy and Irish mercenaries: the Wild Geese in Spain, 1618–68* (Dublin, 1994).

Strijbosch, Clara, *The seafaring saint: sources and analogues of the twelfth-century Voyage of Saint Brendan* (Dublin, 2000).

Stringer, K.D., 'Nobility and identity in medieval Britain and Ireland: the de Vescy family' in B. Smith (ed.), *Britain and Ireland, 900–1300: insular responses to medieval European change* (Cambridge, 1999), pp 199–239.

Sumption, Jonathan, *Pilgrimage: an image of medieval religion* (London, 1975).

Swanson, R.N., *Indulgences in late medieval England: passports to paradise?* (Cambridge, 2007).

Tait, Clodagh, 'Namesakes and nicknames: naming practices in early modern Ireland, 1540–1700', *Continuity and Change*, 21:2 (2006), 313–40.

Talbot, Lynn, 'Revival of the medieval past: Francisco Franco and the Camino de Santiago' in S. Sánchez y Sánchez & A. Hesh (eds), *The Camino de Santiago in the 21st century* (London, 2016), pp 36–56.

Tate, R.B., *Pilgrimages to St James of Compostella from the British Isles during the Middle Ages*, CSJ Occasional Paper 5 (London, 2003).

Taylor, L.J., et al. (eds), *Encyclopedia of medieval pilgrimage* (Leiden, 2010).

Tomasi, Luigi, '"Homo viator": from pilgrimage to religious tourism via the journey' in W.H. Swatos Jnr & L. Tomasi (eds), *From medieval pilgrimage to religious tourism* (Westport, CT, 2002), pp 1–24.

Turner, Edith, 'Pilgrimage an overview' in Eliade (ed.), *Encyclopedia of religion.*

Turner, Victor, & Edith Turner, *Image and pilgrimage in Christian culture* (New York, 1978).

Tyerman, Christopher, *God's war: a new history of the Crusades* (London, 2006).

Tyerman, Christopher, *How to plan a Crusade* (London, 2015).

Unger, R.W., *The ship in the medieval economy, 600–1600* (London, 1980).

Van Herwaarden, Jan, *Between Saint James and Erasmus: studies in late-medieval religious life: devotion and pilgrimage in the Netherlands* (Leiden, 2003).

Van Liere, K.E., 'Renaissance chroniclers and the apostolic origins of Spanish Christianity' in K. Van Liere, S. Ditchfield & H. Louthan (eds), *Sacred history: uses of the Christian past in the Renaissance world* (Oxford, 2012), pp 121–44.

Vazquez de Parga, Luis, J.M. Lacarra & Juan Uría Ríu, *Las Peregrinaciones a Santiago de Compostela* (3 vols, Madrid, 1948–9; revised ed. Pamplona, 1992).

Verstraten Veach, Freya, 'Men's names among the Uí Mhórdha of Laoighis, *c.*1000–*c.*1500', *Ossory, Laois and Leinster*, 5 (2012), 187–211.

Verstraten, Freya, 'Naming practices among the Irish secular nobility in the high Middle Ages', *Journal of Medieval History*, 32:1 (2006), 43–53.

Waller, Gary, *Walsingham and the English imagination* (Farnham, 2011).

Walsh, Katherine, *A fourteenth-century scholar and primate: Richard FitzRalph in Oxford, Avignon and Armagh* (Oxford, 1981).

Walsh, Paul, 'The foundation of the Augustinian Friary at Galway: a review of the sources', *JGAHS*, 40 (1985–6), 72–80.

Walsh, Paul, 'The chapel of St James at Newcastle, Galway', *JGAHS*, 42 (1989–90), 150–5.

Walsh, Paul, 'An account of the town of Galway', *JGAHS*, 44 (1992), 47–118.

Walsh, Paul, 'The medieval merchant's mark and its survival in Galway', *JGAHS*, 45 (1993), 1–28.

Walsh, Paul, 'The topography of the town of Galway in the medieval and early modern periods' in G. Moran (ed.), *Galway, history and society* (Dublin, 2006), pp 27–96.

Watt, J.A., J.B. Morrall & F.X. Martin (eds), *Medieval studies presented to Aubrey Gwynn, SJ* (Dublin, 1961).

Webb, Diana, *Pilgrims and pilgrimage in the medieval West* (London, 1999).

Webb, Diana, *Pilgrimage in medieval England* (London, 2000).

Webb, Diana, *Medieval European pilgrimage* (Basingstoke, 2002).

Webb, Diana, 'Freedom of movement? Women travellers in the Middle Ages' in C. Meek & C. Lawless (eds), *Pawns or players? Studies on medieval and early modern women* (Dublin, 2003), pp 75–89.

Westropp, T.J., 'St Mary's cathedral, Limerick: its plan and growth [part 1]', *JRSAI*, 28 (1898), 35–48.

White Marshall, Jenny, & Claire Walsh, *Illaunloughan island: an early medieval monastery in Co. Kerry* (Bray, 2005).

Wilkinson, J., *Jerusalem pilgrimage*, Hakluyt Society, 2nd ser., 167 (London, 1988).

Williams, Glanmor, 'Poets and pilgrims in fifteenth- and sixteenth-century Wales', *Transactions of the Honourable Society of Cymmrodorion* (1991), 69–98.

Williams, John, 'The basilica in Compostela and the way of pilgrimage' in Xunta de Galicia (ed.), *Compostela and Europe*, pp 110–21.

Wooding, J.M. (ed.), *The Otherworld voyage in early Irish literature* (Dublin, 2000).

Wooding, J.M., 'St Brendan's boat: dead hides and the living sea in Columban and related hagiography' in J. Carey, M. Herbert & P. Ó Riain (eds), *Studies in Irish hagiography: saints and scholars* (Dublin, 2001), pp 77–92.

Woodruff, Eveleigh, 'The financial aspects of the cult of St Thomas of Canterbury', *Archaeologia Cantiana*, 44 (1932), 13–32

Xunta de Galicia (ed.), *Compostela and Europe: the story of Diego Gelmírez* (Milan, 2010).

Xunta de Galicia, *Directorio de asociacións de amigos do Camino de Santiago, confrarías e centros de estudos xacobeos* (Santiago de Compostela, 2015).

Yeoman, Peter, *Pilgrimage in medieval Scotland* (London, 1999).

Youngs, S.M., J. Clark & T.B. Barry, 'Medieval Britain and Ireland in 1982', *Medieval Archaeology*, 27 (1983), 218–19.

Youngs, S.M., J. Clark & T.B. Barry, 'Medieval Britain and Ireland in 1983', *Medieval Archaeology*, 28 (1984), 256.

NEWSPAPERS

Cork Examiner
Irish Independent
Irish Times
Ulster Herald
Westmeath Examiner

WEBSITES

Bardic Poetry Database – bardic.celt.dias.ie

Bibliography of Irish Linguistics and Literature – bill.celt.dias.ie

Camino Society Ireland – caminosociety.com

Camino Ways – caminoways.com

CELT: Corpus of Electronic Texts – ucc.ie/celt

CIRCLE – chancery.tcd.ie

Confraternity of St James – csj.org.uk

Dictionary of Irish Biography – dib.cambridge.org

Dresden, Sachsische Landesbibliothek – slub-dresden.de

EPPI: Enhanced British Parliamentary Papers on Ireland – dippam.ac.uk/eppi

Excavations – excavations.ie

Gothic Past: Visual Archive of Gothic Architecture and Sulpture in Ireland – gothicpast.com

Heritage Council – heritagecouncil.ie/unpublished_excavations

Irish History Online – irishhistoryonline.ie

Irish Newspaper Archive – archive.irishnewsarchive.com

Irish Script on Screen – isos.dias.ie

JSTOR – jstor.org

Loreto, Italy – santuarioloreto.it

The *Matthew*, Bristol – matthew.co.uk

MEMSO: Medieval and Early Modern Sources Online – sources.tannerritchie.com

Multiple Sclerosis Society – ms-society.ie

National Monuments Service – archaeology.ie

National Monuments Service: Historic Environment database–webgis.archaeology.ie/
    historicenvironment

NLI: Sources for the History of Irish Civilization – sources.nli.ie

Rubicon Heritage – rubiconheritage.com

Santiago Cathedral Pilgrim Office – officinadelperegrino.com

The National Archives (Kew) – discovery.nationalarchives.gov.uk

UNESCO – whc.unesco.org

Index